Strange Will Requests & Bequests

Exploring the Vaults of Somerset House

AJ Griffiths-Jones

Pen & Sword

FAMILY HISTORY

First published in Great Britain in 2026 by
Pen & Sword Family History
An imprint of
Pen & Sword Books Ltd
Yorkshire – Philadelphia

ISBN 978 1 03619 496 3

Typeset in INDIA by IMPEC eSolutions
Printed and bound in England by CPI Group (UK) Ltd, Croydon, CRO 4YY

The Publisher's authorised representative in the EU for product safety is Authorised Rep Compliance Ltd., Ground Floor, 71 Lower Baggot Street, Dublin D02 P593, Ireland.
www.arccompliance.com

For a complete list of Pen & Sword titles please contact:

PEN & SWORD BOOKS LIMITED
George House, Units 12 & 13, Beevor Street, Off Pontefract Road,
Barnsley, S71 1HN, UK
E-mail: enquiries@pen-and-sword.co.uk
Website: www.pen-and-sword.co.uk

or

PEN AND SWORD BOOKS
1950 Lawrence Rd, Havertown, PA 19083, USA
E-mail: uspen-and-sword@casematepublishers.com
Website: www.penandswordbooks.com

FOR UNCLE MARTYN

(Who Wishes To Be Buried Upright On His Motorcycle In Full Leathers)

Contents

Foreword

Writing a Last Will and Testament is an opportunity to pass on your fortune and treasures to family, right any wrongs, get even, make a charitable gesture or perhaps bequeath something to a complete stranger. For some it is an opportunity to avenge oneself by adding a codicil or condition in the last coherent pages of one's life. There is a great archive of cynical humour hidden away in Somerset House in the form of Last Wills and Testaments. Many men and women have yielded to the temptation to perpetrate a final joke or settle an old score, knowing that they would not be alive to contemplate the reactions of those who bore the brunt of their mocking bequests. This seems to have been a bone of contention which has gripped will-writers and their families from the earliest times. An interesting book on the subject of weird wills was actually published in 1912, the author being Virgil M. Harris, lecturer on wills at St. Louis University of Law in the United States. Harris notes that the first will humourist on record was Eudamidas of Corinth, whose joke was recorded by Lucian. It reads:

> I bequeath to Arethreus my mother to support, and I pray him to have tender care for her declining years. I bequeath to Charixenes my daughter to marry, and to give her to that end the best portion he can afford. Should either happen to die, I beg the other to undertake both charges.

Of course, it leaves us to ponder on the reaction of Eudamidas' next of kin, for they had no say in the matter of these unusual arrangements!

The oldest existing will was discovered by Professor Flinders Petrie at the ancient Egyptian town of Kahun. It is that of Sekhenren, and was made 4,500 years ago, and is so modern in form that it is said it might almost be granted probate today. In the document, Sekhenren left all his property and goods to his brother, Uah, a priest of Osiris. It included an attestation clause, was witnessed by two scribes and outlined specific conditions, one of which was the restriction of property demolition.

'To the worst of women, Claude Charlotte de Grammont,' wrote Henry, Earl of Strafford, who followed James II to France, 'unfortunately, my wife, guilty as she is of all crimes. I leave five-and-forty brass halfpence, which will buy her a poulet for supper.'

The last wills or testaments of historical figures are always of public interest, and some are quite remarkable, quite often reflecting the character of the person making them. Although the form of document as we now recognise it originated in Roman law, those who went before dispersed of their belongings in much the same way. Sennacherib, who lived around 700 B.C., bequeathed bracelets, coronets, trinkets, gold, ivory, and precious stones kept in the Temple of Nebo to his friends. Plato, Aristotle and Petrarch also left wills of great length and ornamentation, and Julius Caesar left his jewels, swords and military trophies to those acquaintances whom he thought would appreciate them most.

One of the curiosities in Somerset House is a plague will which was placed inside a bottle of spirit for disinfection purposes, another was written in a secret shorthand. During the war many wills, executed in moments of danger, had peculiarities of this kind. One instance is the photograph of a young girl with the words 'All to her' written on it, which was proven as authentic by the handwriting of its owner, and another will which was carefully engraved in tiny letters onto the back of an identification disc belonging to a sailor who was killed in the Battle of Jutland.

One case heard in Probate Court was that of a man who attempted to dispose of his £5,000 estate by writing a few words on an eggshell with an indelible pencil. Lord Merrivale held that the will was nothing more than an unexplained freak and refused to accept it as legal.

There is also a copy of a will in Somerset House which became something of a curiosity. Originally it was a parchment document of over two feet in length, but now only measures a few inches. The story goes that it was on its way abroad when the ship in which it was dispatched was sunk. It remained in a box at the bottom of the sea for many months before being recovered, and once opened it was discovered that as a result of the effects of the sea water the paper had shrunk to a tenth of its original size. The writing, which dwindled to microscopical proportions, is actually still legible.

Occasionally, there can be a need to hunt down the last will of a relative, they having secreted it away in some unknown location. One of the Earls of

Scarborough left his hidden in the hollow leg of his bed. Another example is a wealthy book-collector whose will consisted of three words, 'Will in Till.' After a prolonged search, relatives were about to abandon their quest when a close friend remembered the deceased's fondness for Tillotson's Sermons. The volumes had recently been sold to a dealer but were soon recovered, and on opening the first volume the missing will was found together with a £500 banknote.

In 1895, a statement from Somerset House claimed that:

> any person, not incapacitated from making a will, may sign, seal, and deliver, on payment of a fee of 12s 6d, his (or her) last will and testament, to be kept securely until death makes it operative. All such wills are safeguarded in a fire-proof room, and can never again be seen by the testator, although their provisions may be annulled, either wholly or in part, by the making of a fresh will or codicil, which may either be deposited at Somerset House or preserved in the testator's own safe-keeping. There, too, searches may be made for wills. The work of searching, indeed, is going on daily, both by experienced searchers and likewise by the inexperienced – the latter, too often the hollow-eyed and sunken-cheeked 'next-of-kin' crank. For a fee of 1 shilling any will may be seen; but it is forbidden to make copies: that has to be done by proper copiers, and a fee must be paid.

At the turn of the twentieth century, the will department at Somerset House was supposed to be the safest of all repositories, whether public or private, for testamentary documents. It was reasonably assumed that the State adopted every possible precaution to ensure the permanent safety of these invaluable deposits; after all, their destruction would have been nothing short of a national calamity. However, in 1900, one gentleman, having occasion to inspect the will of an ancestor filed around 150 years previously, paid a visit to the archives. After waiting for some considerable time, the required document was at last produced but in a sadly tattered condition. He was informed that the delay had been caused owing to the papers being partly rotted through damp. It had apparently been torn whilst being opened and clerks had dried it by a fire before attempting to mend the document with gummed paper. Only then could it be safely submitted for inspection.

In 1931, a new system was introduced at Somerset House, whereby every will registered was to be photographed before being filed away, and its negative prints made available to the public. By doing away with the laborious business of making manuscript copies, it claimed to save both public and private money. The prints were remarkably clear and whereas a copy of a will would have cost around half-a-crown, the reproduction was just eighteen pence per full page. For a search the fee remained at a shilling, but the negative of a will could be viewed free of charge. At that time, almost 45,000 wills were deposited in London alone, therefore searches, inspections and copying were a heavy and ever-increasing burden. The new technology was ground-breaking, and three cameras were employed in undertaking the work as quickly and smoothly as possible.

An article printed in September 1931 declared that the vaults of Somerset House in London were getting too full of documents, claiming that volumes and indexes of births, marriages and deaths dating from the year 1837 were piled 7 feet high, with over 150 million names in the registers.

Of course, special dispensation is made in the case of deceased royals, and the contents of their wills are rarely open to those outside the immediate circle. The terms of King George V's will, for example, is never to be made public. His will falls outside all jurisdiction and only members of the Royal Family were aware of its contents. The actual document was not examined by officials of Somerset House and was not deposited in the vaults there, being exempt from probate or death duties. A statement made to a *Yorkshire Observer* reporter in 1936, upon the King's death read:

> It is on Statute that there is no jurisdiction to make a grant against the deceased Sovereign, which means that the King's estate is immune from all taxation. Indeed, no Court has any right whatever to grant probate to a king's will. In Somerset House there are, to my knowledge, no wills of kings. In the circumstances, there is no necessity for their being kept as records, and certainly the wills of King Edward VII and Queen Victoria are not here.

In the following chapters, we shall explore the weird and the wonderful testators who left a lasting impression upon their family and friends in the form of their Last Will & Testament, citing stipulations, conditions and clauses that caused more than a ruffle of feathers amongst expectant heirs, such as the Bournemouth man who left £175,000 to his widow and nieces but placed marriage penalties upon their shares. As too a Leeds man, who left £130,000 to his wife but only £500 a year should she venture to remarry.

One of the strangest clauses in a will was that written by Charles Augustin Treverlyn Prideaux, who insisted that his beneficiaries should forfeit their legacies if they ate shellfish or certain other kinds of food without proof that the creature was painlessly put to death. Crab, crayfish, lobsters, shrimps, eels and other seafood were included in the protective clause.

Then there was John Silver of Addiscombe, who, in bequeathing his estate to his grandson, stipulated that he should not be vaccinated, drink alcoholic liquor, or contract 'the pernicious and injurious habit of smoking tobacco.'

Perhaps the most humorous clause in a will was that written by a man who lived in a South-West suburb of London. He directed that his wife should be given 'one pair of my trousers free of duty and carriage paid as a symbol of what she wanted to wear in my lifetime but did not.'

The most eloquently written, with tongue in cheek, was that of a man who asked for his wife to be paid 5 shillings to buy a rope to hang herself, and £5 to his son, his fare 'to go to the devil, if he has not already reached that destination.'

And finally, an Antrim man who left his brother the residue of his property on condition that he was kept out of a lunatic asylum. If the sibling was put away in an asylum, the £700 would go to the British Home and Foreign Bible Society.

Chapter One

Eccentric Testators

Every Christmas for many years about a dozen of the poorer inhabitants of Shotts, a Lanarkshire mining village, receive a sum of money as a Yuletide gift from an unusual source. Early in the eighteenth century a native of the area, James Mitchell, emigrated to the West Indies, where he engaged in the slave trade and amassed a large fortune. But his conscience became troubled over the origin of his wealth, and when he died in 1736, Mitchell left £500 in trust for the poorest residents of his native village. The fund was first administered by the kirk session, and afterwards by the parish council. The Lanark County Council afterwards undertook distribution of the money. It seems quite ironic that local legend has the village as being named after the giant highwayman Bertram de Shotts.

Many strange and curious customs have long been connected with the observance of Twelfth Night, the evening before Epiphany on 6 January. In England the principal rite of the evening used to be the cutting of the 'bean cake' – a cake in which a bean was cooked, the finder of which was made the king of the night and the following day. It was in commemoration of this custom that Robert Baddely, an eighteenth century English comedian, who was a long time favourite at the Drury Lane Theatre, made one of the strangest bequests on record. Baddely died in 1794 and in his will he bequeathed his cottage to a theatrical fund, requesting that a sum of £3 be spent annually on a cake, to be cut on Twelfth Night in the Green Room of the Drury Lane Theatre, and shared among the actors and actresses.

In 1806 a barrister working at Gray's Inn, London, bequeathed a rent-charge of £10 per annum to the Mayor of St. Ives in Cornwall, with the request that it be spent on a festival around his grave on every fifth anniversary. The barrister was buried in the local parish churchyard at St. Ives, but a memorial was built in his honour on a small hill within the grounds of the Tregenna Castle Hotel. The first festival attracted 2,000 visitors with a procession leading from the town which included a fiddler, 10 girls dressed in white and 2 old women. Everyone ascended the hill, together with the mayor, and a dance took place around the memorial. Each participant was given a prize, including one monetary gift to a couple over 60 years of age who had brought up ten children. A dinner costing £10 was then laid out in honour of the deceased barrister who had originally been a land-agent in St. Ives before being elected treasurer of Gray's Inn.

One of the most curious wills ever admitted to probate in England was left by Alfred Henry Frend of Richmond Road, Twickenham. He directed his trustees never to employ a solicitor or Public Trustee, and added in his will, 'Beyond taxation, none of my property shall ever go to the British State, whose oppression, intensified by officials, falls so terribly heavy on my class as to be slowly exterminating.'

After the death of his sisters, Frend's trustees were to assist persons of insufficient means 'to contest and embarrass any unlawful exactions and doubtful claims by the British Inland Revenue.' If steps were taken to set aside his will and the trustees could not remove the trust funds to another country, 'All the funds are to be put into a sinkable box and taken to sea and sunk in the mid-Atlantic, the captain of the ship to certify that such has been done, and to receive therefore a fee of three guineas.' The gross value of the estate belonging to Frend was £1,019.

Cordelia Angelina Read was known as the 'Old Lady of Stamford Street' after her death in a dilapidated house caused some sensation. Sometime after the eccentric woman's demise, it was discovered that she had accumulated a considerable fortune and was the owner of not only the property in which she resided, but also of houses in Snow Hill, Stoke Newington, and other parts of London, which she had all let run to ruin. Miss Read died worth around £100,000 and left her home full of curiosities, including one room full of caps and bonnets, and bags of small coins in the form of sixpenny, fourpenny and threepenny pieces. Many years before her death, Cordelia Read had quarrelled with her family and bequeathed all her household goods, including furniture, pictures, trinkets and jewellery to the treasurer of the Hospital for the Cure of Consumption at Brompton. The generous donation also included money in the bank and the will was signed on 10 December 1858. However, the property itself became a case for litigation, and solicitor Robert Johnson of Bedford Row was tasked with tracking down the surviving nearest relations.

When German poet Heinrich Heine died in 1856, he left his entire estate to his wife, Eugenie Mirat, with the stipulation that she could only inherit if she became a Protestant after his death. The couple had married in 1841, despite Heine disapproving of Eugenie being a devout Catholic and her refusal to convert. However, after her husband's death, the widow duly complied thus resolving their differences at the graveside.

One of the most eccentric wills of the nineteenth century was executed in May 1868 by Anne Burdett of Gilmorton, in Leicestershire. Her main testament was made in a codicil which directed the appointed trustees to brick up all the doors and windows of her house immediately after the funeral, ensuring that everything from the fixtures and fittings to the clock on the mantlepiece be immured for a period of twenty years. The only room to be left unsealed was the kitchen, where a respectable married couple were to be installed at a peppercorn rent of one halfpenny per week, their duty being to care for the premises and see that no attempt be made to unbrick the other doors and windows. In order for her wishes to be carried out in full Mrs Burdett gave certain benefits to the trustees of the will, which they would have to forfeit should the house cease to be completely boarded up. The will was disputed in Probate Court and eventually granted. The dissatisfied parties then took the case to the Chancery, arguing that the old lady was perfectly within her rights to dispose of her property and effects as she wished. Eventually, in 1882, some fourteen years after the old woman's death, Vice-Chancellor Sir James Bacon ordered the trustees to unseal and release 'this hitherto useless property and distribute it as the undisposed residue of real and personal estate.'

A wealthy tradesman, Thomas Heviant, died at the village of Croane-sur-Marne in France in the summer of 1875. In his will he made a number of singular bequests, among which was one to be carried out at the annual village fete. Heviant asked that one of the amusements should include a pig race, the animals to be ridden by men or boys. A sum of 2,000 Francs (around £80) had been set aside as the prize for the lucky rider of the winning pig. However, the prize was only to be handed over on the condition that the winner wore deep mourning clothes for the deceased Monsieur Heviant for a period of two years after the competition. The local Municipality accepted the eccentric bequest, and the race was held in accordance with the terms of the will.

A well-known American citizen renowned for both his wealth and eccentricity died in Brooklyn, New York, in February 1880, leaving a will that caused a great deal of anguish to the relatives with whom he had fought bitterly during his lifetime. It contained the following bequest:

I own seventy-one pairs of trousers. It is my desire that they be sold by public auction after my death, and that the product of their sale be distributed among the poor of my parish. They must, however, be disposed of severally to different bidders, no single individual being permitted to purchase more than one pair.

The executors dutifully carried out these directions, with the seventy-one pairs of trousers being duly purchased by seventy-one different bidders and the proceeds handed over to the parochial authorities. A few days later, one of the buyers decided to make a careful examination of his new trousers and to his great surprise found a small canvas sack sewn neatly into the waistband. Inside the pouch were ten $100 bills. Needless to say, it wasn't long before news of the discovery spread like wildfire throughout the city, with each purchaser taking it upon themselves to search their recently acquired purchase. Every single pair of trousers contained the same amount of money. A great deal of publicity followed, with the relatives of the testator instituting proceedings to recover the sums secreted in the garments, citing grounds of insanity when the will was made. Fortunately for the auction bidders the original will stood up to scrutiny and every purchaser was able to keep their unexpected windfall.

In October of the same year, it was reported in the *Daily Telegraph* that a wealthy burgess of Vienna had died, leaving his whole estate not to his rightful heirs but to the son of a retired Austrian General whom he had never met. It appears to be that this decision was made on the sole grounds of coincidence, with the young gentleman in question sharing the same Christian name as the testator. Having been informed of his rather unexpected inheritance, the legatee visited the residence which had been left to him with a legal representative. Their attention was firstly drawn to a fire-proof safe, the most likely place for important documents and money to be stored, but nothing was found inside apart from old envelopes and scraps of paper which had been cut up into tiny strips. A search of the rooms, however, revealed 40,000 florins crumpled up into a ball and hidden behind a curtain. More money was found stashed inside photograph albums containing forty portraits of pretty women in fancy costumes. Behind each photo was a sum of money corresponding to the deceased gentleman's appreciation of each ladies' respective charms, with a pale beauty being merited 2,000 florins and a brunette 3,000. A note pasted into the margins of the albums gave the newfound heir clues as to what he might find behind the images, but it also indicated the deceased's intention to bequeath each woman the sum hidden away behind her photo. Fortunately for the younger man this was never entered into the will and both the grand house and its hidden coffers fell into the hands of the rather delighted infantry lieutenant.

A third case, from the same year, although far more peculiar in its content, was that of John P. Bowman of Vermont, who made his fortune in the tannery business and moved to the Stony Point region of New York. At the age of 40, Bowman married a much younger woman, Jennie, and became a devoted husband and father. Tragedy came into their lives in 1854 when a 4-month-old daughter died, again in 1879 when the couple lost their daughter Ella, aged 23, and then the following year Jennie passed away. Left grief-stricken, John sold his New York tannery and moved to Cuttingsville, Vermont, where he employed an architect to build a mansion, mausoleum and greenhouse in order for the vaults to have continuous supplies of fresh flowers. Before his death, Bowman established a trust fund of $47,500 for the 'perpetual care of my properties in Cuttingsville,' and just before his death told the nurse, 'I'll soon be leaving for a little while, but I'll be coming back.'

By 1945, Bowman's mansion had seen three custodians, the most recent being George Jones who resided there for thirty-five years. In accordance with the testator's wishes, it was the caretaker's responsibility to keep the twelve-room home spotless and the pantry stocked with food in anticipation of Bowman's return. However, prices went up and interest from the trust fund decreased, causing the house to be closed.

In 1888 the death notice of a lady by the surname of Buckland was recorded in Winona, Minnesota. It was noted at the time that she was in some way related to a doctor of the same name who died ten years earlier in Connecticut. The *New Haven Daily Morning Journal & Courier* reported the following story on 28 January 1888:

It seems that the doctor, who was paralysed, after having been given up by the physician in attendance, succeeded in maturing a formula of his own, with which he cured himself of paralysis. The use and fame of this nervine spread slowly throughout the country, and a bottle of it came into the hands of the late Mrs Buckland, of Winona, who, having a grandchild that had been paralysed from birth, conceived the idea of trying it upon her, being impressed as much, perhaps, by the similarity of names between herself and that of the inventor of the remedy as from any other cause.

The surprising feature of the matter is that the girl, who was then a baby of fifteen months, was completely cured of her paralysis, and is today the healthy and blooming wife of a prominent merchant in Duluth, Minnesota. So monstrous became the faith of the old lady in the virtues of this nervine that, calling her lawyer, she made a will by which she left the sum of nearly half a million dollars to the proprietors of this remedy, with the proviso that every penny of it should be spent for the purpose of acquainting the people of the United States with its virtues.

The numerous and brilliant advertisements that have recently been appearing through the large newspapers of this country are all the result, from a pecuniary point of view, of the magnanimity of this lady. There can be no question but that this remedy, Dr. Buckland's Scotch Oats Essence, is the greatest known general tonic and special nerve and brain invigorant. The names of those whom it has cured of both grave and simple nervous troubles is legion, and it has the special advantage of being wholly and absolutely free from narcotics and purely vegetable.

The munificent sum placed at the disposal of the Scotch Oats Essence company by the late Mrs Buckland has enabled them to secure the services of some of the finest chemists Germany has ever produced, distilling and extracting apparatus of peculiar intricacy and value, and to thus make an extract or essence of oats that contains every particle of active medicina virtue in the grain.

It is a curious fact in this connection that experiments recently conducted in the School of Physiology in Paris, France, have demonstrated beyond peradventure that the kernel of the oat contains three medicinal principles, the first of which acts to calm, soothe and tone up the brain and nerves; the second yielding phosphorus to weakened and hungry nerve tissues, and the third residing in the husk of the oat or oatmeal, to act as a laxative and anti-congestive on the stomach, liver and bowels.

In January 1897, the death of Mrs Elijah Carson was announced. She was the wealthy widow of the late Samuel Carson, of Belfast, who during the latter days of her life spent a great deal of time travelling between England and New York, chiefly on board the RMS *Lucania*. When her will was filed in Belfast, it was found that Mrs Carson had bequeathed her entire fortune to the officers of the *Lucania*, including £10,000 to Captain McKay, and £5,000 each to her bankers in Belfast and New York. Her daughter, with whom the deceased had quarrelled after an attempt to cure the older woman's sea-faring mania, was left a paltry sum of just £200.

Doctor Bourne, a resident of France, left all his property to the University of Lausanne, on the condition that the revenue be accumulated for a period of 100 years. After that time, it was to be used to publish a manuscript entitled 'Maxims and Aphorisms' written by the doctor himself. The medic's last will and testament specified that the book be translated into all known languages and a copy sent to every library in the world.

In January 1883, a Parisian newspaper told the story of an eccentric old citizen who put a clause in his will that the funeral should take place at 6 o'clock in the morning, and that his belongings should be left to whomever followed the hearse to the graveyard. As there was nothing more than an old mattress left to attract mourners to the funeral procession, it was limited to the driver and a young neighbour of the deceased. Having laid the elderly gentleman to rest, the younger man retrieved the mattress as was his friend's wish and found 40,000 Francs stowed away inside!

The Irish Lord Chancellor at Dublin gave permission to a minor to proceed with a suit contesting the will of his father in June 1884. The testator left all his money to the Anti-Vivisection Society and directed that his body be cut open for surgical examination. The man was deemed to be of a somewhat eccentric character, having the habits of collecting pieces of scrap iron and preserving the hair cut from his own head after every trip to the barber shop!

Another will under litigation in the same year was brought before the court in Paris, with heirs pleading that the testator was undoubtedly of unsound mind. It ran as follows:

I possess a fortune of 70,000 Francs. How many tears, lies, and acts of treachery could I have purchased with such a sum? I first of all thought of bequeathing these 70,000 to the Assistance Publique, but 'What for?' The real benefactors of humanity are War and the Cholera. Besides,

I have a debt of gratitude to pay my dear wife, Celestine Melanie, who did me the greatest service I could have expected from her, that of leaving me one fine morning and never turning up again. Out of remembrance for that good action I appoint her my universal legatee. However, I attach a special clause to the legacy, and that is, that she gets married again directly the legal period has expired. In this manner I am sure my death will be regretted by at least one man.

Immediately after his signature, 'Doctor Vincent L…..', comes the postscript, 'Who cannot reproach himself with ever having saved the life of a single patient.'

An article published in the *Tavistock Gazette* on 4 September 1885, pointed out that 'there are so many uses to which a man can apply any money he leaves behind him at his death that it is difficult to understand why some people appear to go out of their way to dispose of their fortunes in such a manner as to justify the term eccentric in speaking of them.' The writer goes on to ask why, for instance, should a worthy wine merchant, a native of Hamburg, Germany, having neither kith nor kin, have taken the strange fancy of offering an annual prize of a thousand or more thalers to the baldest man in the place in which he, the testator, was born and in which he died. He points out, 'There is no merit in baldness: the state of society would not be improved were baldness to be on the increase; and as it is said the testator was not a lunatic, one is at a loss to understand why he should apparently have wished to encourage particularly bald men.'

According to the terms of the will, this prize of a thousand and odd thalers was to be awarded every year to the fellow townsman who had the fewest hairs on his head, the question of who had the fewest being decided by a given number of experts, who were to carefully examine the skulls of competitors. It goes without saying that no artificial means could be resorted to in order to produce baldness, nor shaving of the follicles permitted, and in the event of two or more competitors having an equal number of hairs on their heads, the prize was to be bestowed upon the youngest of them. Lastly, it was stated in the will, supposing it chances that one day a man came forward without a single hair left, the capital, of which the interest constituted the annual prize, would be his.

Miss Bridgita Molloy was the possessor of a large fortune in her own right, the estate having been left to her by her father. She had two sisters, Lucis and Judith, who had incurred the old gentleman's displeasure by running off and marrying men that he disapproved of and were not remembered in his will. One of the sisters had a son, Ferentz Steldi, and the other a daughter, Lucis Bridgita O'Birn. When Bridgita Molloy died in 1887, unmarried and without children, a will was found underneath her pillow and turned out to be a complete conundrum. It read plainly enough so far as minor bequests were concerned, including £1,000 each to the nephew and niece, and a shilling each to the brothers-in-law 'to buy mourning rings', but when it came to the bulk of the fortune here is what it read: '....... *And all the residue of my property, whether real or personal, I give, bequeath, and devise to GPXDNWMDYBDOVJWDMIHTIDZXZ.*'

That was all and, of course, it was simply nonsense as it stood. But while the relatives were examining the will a note dropped out in which they were told to lift up the carpet in a certain corner of the room. This was done and another note was found there, telling them to consult a certain page of a particular book. They also did that and found a third note saying, 'Key behind wainscot, three inches toward cupboard from dressing-room window.'

It took just a few minutes to remove a loose floorboard at the place indicated, but there they found a few half-eaten scraps of paper and nothing more. The parents of Bridgita's nephew felt certain that the code could be made to spell his name, but the parents of the niece were equally sure that the will meant her. As a result, each party brought in an expert to decipher the clue. As it happened, both men were able to create a fairly believable case for the cipher spelling out the names of the nephew and niece respectively, which in no part helped to decide who was the rightful heir. The only thing left to do, according to solicitors, was to take the case to Chancery Court and let the judge decide. However, it never got there. The cousins, Ferentz and Lucis, met for the first time, fell in love and married. Thus, after all, the will of Miss Molloy was finally carried to fruition exactly as she had planned and desired.

The *London Daily News* reported that a Polish landed proprietor, named Zalesky, played a cruel trick upon his relatives when he died in the province of Taurida in March 1889. Having left a will inside a sealed packet marked 'To be opened after my death', Zalesky foiled eager testators by making them wait to view the contents, as when the envelope was torn open another was found underneath with the words 'To be opened six weeks after the first envelope has been opened.' At the end of the second period, it was found that there was yet a third envelope, with the inscription 'To be opened in a year.' Yet again, after the year, there was another envelope which read 'To be opened in two years.' After patiently waiting for another period of time the will was finally opened. It was found that Zalesky had bequeathed 100,000 roubles, which amounted to half of his fortune, to the relative who had the largest number of children. The second half was to be invested for 100 years, at the end of which time was to be divided, together with the interest, among his descendants. The will became subject of a lawsuit soon afterwards, the family declaring Zalesky to have been of unsound mind at the time of settling his affairs.

In November 1891, a French lady by the name of Cabouret left a fortune of $1,600,000 to any Frenchman 'who may succeed in organising a caravan of 500 of his compatriots and penetrating farther than anyone has ever done before into the wilds of Africa.' The will stated that the caravan may contain a larger number of persons, but at least half of the entire number was to return to France safe and sound. The will was naturally disputed by the woman's relatives. A correspondent from Toulouse reported that the testator was a fervent admirer of Cardinal Lavigerie, the founder of French Catholic missions across Africa, and believed that the best way to abolish the slave trade was to make Africa well-known to the world.

This is an exact copy of a will sent to Somerset House for filing in 1894:

Charlie and Harry have each 400, if there's enough; 5 to Ellen, 4 to Mary; 4 to Sam; 400 to youngest sister during life, then all Harry, pay 50 for coal; 5 to Mr. Moore, St. Felix Street: 10 to Mr. Barber; 17 gas bill. I wanted my oldest sister to have something if she outlived her husband. Oldest brother to have 400 to buy a piece of land, 2-3rds of it to go to Mary. This is my last will and testament. H.W.T_____

The will was rejected as being vague, incoherent and incomprehensible.

One gentleman who seemed to be very clear on his wishes was the late Marquis of Queensberry who, when his will was lodged in Edinburgh in 1900, wrote:

At my death I wish to be cremated, and my ashes put into the earth enclosed in nothing – earth to earth, ashes to ashes – in any spot most convenient I have loved. Will mention places to my son – Harleyford for choice. I particularly request that no Christian mummeries or tomfooleries be performed over my grave, but that I be buried as a Secularist and an Agnostic. If it will comfort anyone, there are plenty of those of my friends who would come to say a few words of common sense over the spot where my ashes may lie. Places to lay ashes: the summit of Criffle or Queensberry in Dumfriesshire, the end of the terrace overlooking New Loch, Harleyford, Bucks. No monument or stone necessary or required, or procession, as ashes can be carried in one person's hand. Failing these places, any place where the stars shall ever shed their light, and the sun shall gild each rising morn.

A very curious will was upheld by the court at Bethel, Belgium, in 1905, its having been scratched on to a piece of iron by a man named Devie, who hanged himself some time before. Devie left everything to the village of Adon 'on the condition that £12 be given to the fire brigade to have such a carousal as was never seen before.'

Before daybreak on 6 February 1906, a cab drew up outside a house in a fashionable quarter of Sheffield. A plain coffin was placed inside, containing the body of Mr Horatio Bright, a man of eccentric habits, who had left strict instructions in his will as to the form of his funeral. The coffin was driven to the mausoleum which Mr Bright had built several miles away from the city, in which were the remains of his first wife and son. Bright, whilst still alive, used to visit the mausoleum frequently and would sit there in contemplation for many hours. He had established a world-wide reputation as a maker of dyes for Royal Mints. On retiring, Bright declined to sell the business, destroyed all the hundreds of books he had accumulated and allowed the firm to die out.

A very queer will and method of execution was that of Edith Marion Moore, of London, who died in 1907. A month prior to her death Mrs Moore suffered a stroke which rendered her paralysed, thus resulting in her being unable to express herself in words. In order to obtain her wishes with respect, her solicitor hit upon the ingenious idea of having two sets of cards printed, one with her various properties listed on them, the other with the names of her relatives. The solicitor then dealt out the cards and Edith signalled which property she wanted left to which person until her estate had been disposed of. The cards were then reshuffled to choose an executor, which was chosen as her brother. When the will was filed for probate two relatives contested the document on the ground that it was not properly executed, but the judge claimed that whilst the mode of arriving at Mrs Moore's wishes was novel, it was well-intentioned and completely satisfactory.

In November 1911, a jury in the New York Supreme Court found that a man who danced around with a cut-glass bowl on his head had not been in a mentally fit state to make a will, despite him having been worth a fortune. The eccentric testator was Alexander Miller of Brooklyn, a self-made millionaire and owner of the Vulcan Iron Works. The document cut off Miller's widow, Mary Ella, with just a token bequest of $12,500, leaving the greater bulk of the estate to his brother and sister.

Before his death in 1909, Miller showed a distaste for convention by hosting barefoot dinner parties at home and presiding at the festive board of his company in nothing more than his undershirt. If guests ever appeared to be bored whilst attending one of the millionaire's soirees, Miller was known to get up and perform for them, his favourite stunt being to place the salad bowl on his head as though it were a helmet and dance a Spanish saraband around the table. The iron manufacturer also had some very original ideas on how best to serve oysters. Miller would have a basket of the shellfish taken into the library, where he would proceed to open them on top of a polished mahogany table. As each oyster was opened, Miller hurled the shells at portraits of his ancestors which decorated the library walls. Whenever he scored a direct hit, the eccentric businessman would pause in his bombardment in order to carve the initials of said ancestor in the top of the table, encouraging his guests to follow suit. Apparently, much of the costly furniture in the Miller household was defaced in this way.

In the same year, the last testament of gambler and notorious horse-racing enthusiast George Brown Jr. was filed in probate court in Kansas City. It read:

'It is my desire, as far as possible, to repay every person, man, woman or child, any money that I may have won from them by gambling during my lifetime, and I direct my executors to make effort to learn their names and reimburse them to the full amount with interest from the day the money was won.'

Another unusual clause in the will instructed that a tombstone was to be erected above George and his wife bearing only their given names, omitting the surname 'Brown.'

French astronomer and author Nicolas Camille Flammarion (1842–1925) apparently received a most amazing legacy, skin taken from the shoulders of an Italian countess who was in love with him. The woman ordered that he bind the first copy of his book with it!

A strong dislike of the Irish inspired the will of an English gentleman who had inherited a property in Tipperary, on the strict condition that he should live there. When he died in 1915 the following provision was found in his will:

> I give and bequeath the annual sum of ten pounds, to be paid in perpetuity out of my estate, to the following purpose. It is my will and pleasure that this sum shall be spent in the purchase of a certain quantity of the liquor vulgarly called whisky, and it shall be publicly given out that a certain number of persons, Irish only, not to exceed twenty, who may choose to assemble in the cemetery in which I shall be interred, on the anniversary of my death, shall have the same distributed to them. Further, it is my desire that each shall receive it by half a pint at a time till the whole is consumed, each being likewise provided with a stout oaken stick and a knife, and that they shall drink it all on the spot. Knowing what I know of the Irish character, my conviction is, they will not fail to destroy each other, and when in the course of time the race comes to be exterminated this neighbourhood at least may, perhaps, be colonised by civilised and respectable Englishmen.

When an Irishwoman passed away in County Meath in 1917, it was thought that she had died intestate as no will had been deposited with her solicitor. Legal representatives of the next of kin embarked on a forty-day search, going through the huge accumulation of papers, documents and valuables that filled every room and hallway of the deceased woman's cluttered house. The whole place was piled high with loose papers, books and parcels of all sizes and descriptions, and litter on the staircase was almost knee-deep. Various sums of money were found in very unlikely places, amongst rubbish, in boxes, and even two bank notes glued to the floor. The solicitors recovered over £7,000 in cash and eventually recovered the old lady's will which left the bulk of her estate to various charities.

Despite Wellington R. Burt ranking as one of the wealthiest men in the United States at the turn of the twentieth century, he is probably best known for the controversial will that he left behind on his death in 1919. Aged 87 upon his demise, Burt's estate was estimated at almost $90 million (equating to around $1.58 billion today), yet most of his family saw none of this wealth. Having built up an empire of lumber mills, timber holdings, railroads, mining and financing, towards the end of his life Burt had become estranged from both friends and family, preferring to live alone in his Michigan mansion. It is not known why Wellington Burt created such a strange clause in his last will and testament, but the most likely reason was to avenge an ongoing family feud.

Although his children did receive small annuities of between $1,000 and $5,000 each, with a favourite son bequeathed $30,000 annually and one daughter being completely disinherited, the bulk of Burt's estate was to be held in trust until twenty-one years after the death of his last surviving grandchild. This condition was met when Marion Lansill, the last of Wellington Burt's blood relatives, died in 2010. Legal negotiations followed, with $110 million finally being shared between twelve very lucky and equally surprised descendants.

It was reported from Paris in 1921 that the King of Spain may have to appear in the Toulouse Court or risk losing a legacy of three million francs, left to him by a French royalist whose family had decided to contest the will. The legacy dated back to 1908 when Sapene de Cazarilh decided to disinherit his sister, Gabrielle, in a moment of 'spiteful madness', according to her attorneys, and left everything instead to the King of Spain. The will also transferred 'all noble titles to which I am entitled', although there never was any proven record of De Cazarilh's possession of any such titles. 'Chateau de Montauban de Luchen' where the will was purported to have been signed was merely a humble cottage where the testator lived a fairly miserable life.

Gabrielle de Cazarilh contended that her brother had twice been interred in an asylum as mentally unbalanced. On one occasion he road on horseback into a dry goods store shouting, 'At last a true knight', and terrified the salesgirls by brandishing a rusty sword. In turn, the King of Spain was loath to give up the bequest and engaged Paris lawyers to represent him. De Cazarilh's family responded by declaring that they would not accept testimony by deposition, insisting that the King must testify personally in court. The outcome is unclear.

In 1925, American authorities became flummoxed over the legal status of a will written on the hem of a woman's petticoat. The last will and testament of wealthy recluse George Hazeltine, who died in Los Angeles Hospital, left $2,000 each to the hospital proprietor and a nurse who had cared for him, with the remainder of the $100,000 estate going to a grand-niece. After the petticoat was filed for probate the Young Women's Christian Association and Pomona College sued to have the will set aside, both organisations believing that they were intended beneficiaries of Hazeltine. They argued that the old man was not in full possession of his faculties when he drew up the will on the cotton garment and attorneys found that, in a previous will written some years before, Hazeltine had indeed left most of the fortune to those charities.

Another similarly unusual probate case occurred at the Parisian courts in 1930, when the will of Auguste Pasquier was presented to be read. It had been engraved on the leg of one of the gentleman's dining room chairs!

When Canadian financier and lawyer Charles Millar died in 1926 his will sparked a legal battle that lasted for over a decade. Under provision of his will, Millar left $500,000 to the Toronto woman who could give birth to the most babies within the ten-year period following his death, ending on 31 October 1936. The frantic competition that followed was known as 'The Great Stork Derby' and ended with four women each giving birth to nine children within the specified period. After a litigation battle the prize money was eventually shared between the four winners in 1938, with Justice Middleton announcing the decision at Toronto Supreme Court. They were Annie Smith, wife of a city fireman, Kathleen Nagle, wife of a carpenter and mother of twelve children, Alice Timleck whose husband was employed by the city parks department and had fourteen children, and Isabel MacLean, wife of a civil servant in the Ontario legislative buildings. Two other claimants to the estate were ruled out as one had several illegitimate children and the other gave birth to some stillborn babies.

In 1928, several unusual will bequests were reported in American newspaper *The New Britain Daily Herald*, and included a testator in Toronto who left a large brewery to a group of Methodist ministers, knowing fair well that they were staunch prohibitionists. The same man bequeathed shares in the Ontario Jockey Club to three opponents of Canadian horseracing, requesting that they use the rights in full by drawing on dividends and exercising membership privileges.

Perhaps it was his inherent dislike of females or an unrequited love that caused businessman T.M. Zink to leave a very strange bequest in his will in 1930. A sum of $50,000 was set aside in order for a library to be established in his hometown of Le Mars, Iowa, on the proviso that it should not contain any literature written by or about women! The will also directed that the library should be used only by men. Eventually as social attitudes changed and legal challenges were presented, the money was put to use for other purposes, with no women-free library ever being established.

Beatrice Cecil Allfrey of Temple Hill, East Budleigh, Devon, died on 18 March 1947, leaving her fortune of £76,307 not in a lump sum nor divided between her heirs, but instead left in trust with each of her six nieces and nephews taking a turn to live off the income for a year. The will read:

> The income from the residue I leave for one year's duration to go in turn to Dennis Biddle, Honora Drummond, Margorie McKean, Daphne Spiller, Auriol Butler and Hermione Spiller. After the six have had their one year's income, to start again with the eldest and go down in ages, and so on. If any of them die, they drop out of their share and the one that survives the longest gets it all.

Mrs. Allfrey was described by her relatives as a loveable old lady with a sense of humour and not in the least eccentric. Perhaps the idea was to let each heir experience a year of stress-free spending courtesy of their old aunt.

In 1950 a man in Bologna, Italy, wanted to ensure that his love for playing the clarinet would endure beyond his lifetime, and instructed his executors to arrange for his bones to be made into clarinet mouthpieces!

Occasionally, there are the testator's personal effects to be distributed amongst their heirs, and in the case of pianist and Hollywood entertainer Liberace his $10 million estate included a four-foot-long ceramic zebra, thirteen pianos, a Venetian mirror and a black mink bedspread. The flamboyant entertainer made his final will on 22 January 1987, less than a month before his death caused by complications from AIDS. According to the *Los Angeles Times*, the bulk of the estate went to the Liberace Foundation for the Creative and Performing Acts, which was founded in 1976. However, on discovering that they had been omitted from the will, Liberace's nephews and nieces began a very public legal battle the following March, claiming that they had been close to their uncle. A representative lawyer for the estate claimed that this was untrue, stating, 'I understand they embarrassed him at his mother's funeral in 1980. I think he wrote them off at that time.'

One of the most recent unique legacies was that of wealthy Portuguese aristocrat Luis Carlos de Noronha Cabral da Camara, who picked up the Lisbon phone directory and picked seventy people at random to become beneficiaries in his will in 1987. The illegitimate son of an aristocratic woman, he was rich but had few friends, never married and had no children of his own, having been brought up by a nanny and inherited a great deal of real-estate from his grandmother, which Luis gradually sold off to fund his three great passions in life: motorbikes, shooting and drinking. When he died aged 42, from excessive drinking, there were no living relatives.

With a twelve-room apartment in Lisbon city, a house close to the northern town of Guimaraes, two brimming bank accounts, a luxury car and two motorbikes to his name, it was estimated that each of the seventy heirs would inherit several thousand euros each. Luis Carlos was also a renowned cat lover and left provision for his twelve felines to be cared for in his mansion for the rest of their lives. Anibal Castro, a friend who witnessed the will said,

He was determined that nothing should go to the state, which he thought had been robbing him of money all his life. He probably wanted to create confusion by leaving his things to strangers. I remember the notary asking him several questions to make sure that he wasn't mad after he asked her to hand him the Lisbon regional phone book.

Finally, to complete this chapter of eccentricity, let us remember the humour of one Edward Molyneaux of Mayfair, London, who dared to raise the hopes of his heirs by this clause in his will: 'I am sometimes accustomed to carry banknotes in the fob of my breeches. Please search the said breeches to see if there are any!'

Chapter Two

Bequests to Pets

Of bequests to animals, a few may be mentioned in brief. In 1781, a peasant from Toulouse made his horse universal heir of his belongings. Doctor Cristiano, of Venice, left 6,000 florins for the maintenance of his three dogs, with the condition that at death the sum should be added to the funds of the University of Vienna. A Mrs Elizabeth Hunter in 1813 left $1,000 a year to her parrot, and the Count de Mirandola bequeathed a considerable legacy to a pet carp. Lord Chesterfield left a sum for the support of his favourite cat, so also did Frederick Harper, who settled $500 on his 'young black cat', the interest to be paid to his housekeeper, Mrs Hodges, as long as the cat should remain alive.

The most singular of these wills, however, was that of a Mr Berkeley, of Knightsbridge, who died in 1805. He left £125 to four of his dogs. During a journey through France and Italy this gentleman, being attacked by brigands, had been protected and saved by his dog. The four animals he pensioned by his will were the descendants of this faithful friend. Feeling his end near, Berkeley asked that two armchairs be brought to his bedside and the four dogs seated on them, where they received their last caresses, which their master returned with failing strength and died in their paws. By an article in his will, Berkeley ordered that the busts of his four dogs be carved in stone and placed at the four corners of his tomb.

Every once in a while, we hear of some cat lover leaving a request for their pet to be cared for after their demise, but it was most likely among the feline-loving Egyptians that bequests for the maintenance solely for cats originated. The first known example was that of the will of Sultan Ed-Daher-Deybars, the reigning sovereign of Egypt around 1260 A.D. Although reputed to have been a very wicked and uncompassionate ruler, the sultan evidently had a soft spot in his heart for felines and on his death left a garden, later known as 'The Cat's Orchard', which was to be devoted to the care of Cairo street cats. As the years passed, the area became badly run down, with a resulting lack of funds, but it soon became a tradition amongst cat-lovers that bequests would be left to cover the costs of feeding strays. Officials charged with the disbursement of these charitable bequests ruled that the food provided was to consist of leftover meat purchased from butcher's stalls and chopped into fine pieces. Century after century the tradition continued, feeding time corresponding to the afternoon call to prayer, at which time cats in the area would immediately respond and race to the garden to eat their fill.

Numerous bequests to animals, birds, and even fish, have been cited over the centuries. The following clause from a will was in the English papers for March 1828:

> I leave my monkey, my dear, amusing Jackoo, the sum of £10 sterling to be enjoyed by him during his life; it is to be expended solely in his keep. I leave to my faithful dog, Shock, and to my beloved cat, Tib, £5 sterling a piece, as yearly pension. In the event of the death of one of the aforementioned legatees, the sum due to him shall pass to the two survivors, and on the death of one of these two, to the last, be he who he may. After the decease of all parties, the sum left shall belong to my daughter G———, to whom I show this preference above all my children because she has a large family and finds difficulty in filling their mouths and educating them.

One woman left £70 for the maintenance of three goldfish and even made provision for flowers to be placed on their graves after death. Another lady left an annuity of £100 to her parrot. Lord Eldon, in 1838, left £8 a year to his dog Pincher, whose portrait was afterwards painted by Landseer.

In fact, among the many curious and embarrassing bequests to the late Queen Victoria were several of pet animals whose owners wished to provide them with a distinguished asylum. Thus, one testator left to Her Majesty three goldfish, accompanied by his entire fortune, and, that there might be no mistake as to the identity of the fish, they were described in the will as follows: 'One is bigger than the other two, and these latter could be easily recognised, one being fat, the other thin. If the fish on quarter-day when visited by my solicitor at Osborne, which I suggest as a suitable residence for them, are found to answer this description, the money is to be paid forthwith.'

Even less desirable than the goldfish were sixty snakes which another too-loyal subject bequeathed to the Queen. 'I have always loved snakes,' ran the will of this eccentric gentleman, 'and my only grief is that I cannot train them to recognise me. Perhaps Your Majesty may be more fortunate.' Still another testator left £100 a year to Queen Victoria on condition that she took under her charge a favourite parrot and poodle, and sent them, under escort of a member of the Royal Household, to Margate for a fortnight's holiday every year. A tradesman not only left his cats to the Queen but also designed a house for their reception. 'I am aware,' he wrote, 'that such a building if erected close to Your Majesty's residence would result in an increase of nocturnal noises, so I would suggest that it be placed in Windsor Park, but not more than one mile from the Castle.'

A Doctor Joseph Fischer died at Korneuburg, in Austria, in 1863, leaving 1,000 florins to a favourite cat and canary bird, and another to his dog. The interest on the whole amount was to be received by an old servant charged with keeping the animals. As soon as all three pets died, the money reverted to the doctor's rightful heir.

An amusing will case was brought before judges in the St. Petersburg law courts in June 1886, when a very rich lady, and enthusiastic dog-lover, bequeathed a legacy of 400 roubles for the support and comfort of her dear dog, Million, until the day of his death. Anna Wassilevna was appointed guardian of the canine and, in the event of Million surviving her, the care and charge of the dog was to pass to Ludmilla Ivanoffva. Anna conscientiously fulfilled her duty for several years until Million passed away. The remainder of the money became Anna's property, as she had managed to keep the pet comfortable on a percentage of the capital. However, no sooner had the dog been buried, when Ludmilla appeared, demanding half the money as she was in possession of one of Million's puppies. The will had stated that 'descendants' of the dog were to share in the benefits of the legacy, although Anna was adamant that Million had not given birth to any offspring. It was left to the court to decide, but as no proof could be brought forward to support Ludmilla's claim, it was dismissed.

An extraordinary will was probated in 1889 at Nashville, Tennessee. Mary Ann Schaub, an aged German lady, died at her home where she had lived for almost half a century, and having no family had surrounded herself with a number of cats and dogs. The property was a handsome house valued at around $6,000, which she left in trust for two of her favourite canines. Ms. Schaub provided that a sufficient sum should be reserved to maintain the dogs in comfort for as long as they lived and ordered a bed and clothing for their occupancy. A young lady whom she adopted some years before was made second beneficiary upon the condition that she lived in the house and cared for the animals for a period of eight years.

When a very wealthy woman died in Lisbon in 1902, the reading of her will caused disgust amongst her relatives, as Madam Silva had left her entire property to a cock. The lady in question was a keen spiritualist and firmly believed in the theory of the transgression of the soul, imagining that the soul of her dead husband had entered the body of a rooster. A special fowl house was built close to the house and servants were ordered to pay particular attention to the 'master's' needs. However, Madam Silva was extremely jealous of the hens who shared Pedro's coup, and whenever one of them was found coquetting with the rooster its neck was wrung. The case was not required to enter probate court after the old woman's demise, as the heir next in succession to the fortune had the foresight to have the cock killed.

Henrietta Carlisle-Kent was one of the strongest and most unique female characters of Wyoming at the turn of the twentieth century. For many years she ran a ranch near the Devil's Tower and died in March 1904 of blood poisoning, resulting from the bite of a pet dog. Henrietta's estate was valued at just under $50,000, with her principal heir being a niece who was summoned from Ireland. Ms Carlisle-Kent owned several hundred horses and cattle and for years had kept dozens of dogs of all breeds around the house. Several weeks before her death, one of the animals playfully bit Henrietta in the face, removing the end of her nose. Blood poisoning followed and resulted in her death. The funeral was held at Sundance, the seat of Crook County, Wyoming. Ms Carlisle-Kent's eccentricities were betrayed in her will whereby she directed that all her pet dogs and several of her horses be chloroformed, to prevent their falling into the hands of strangers.

An old lady who lived in the Quartier Batignolles, Paris, who died in 1905, left a will, the preamble of which read: 'In the name of the Father, of the Son, and of the Holy Ghost. Amen. This is my will.' The testatrix went on to say that she bequeathed her little fortune, equating to £800, to the Society for the Protection of Animals and the Jardin des Plantes in remembrance of the love she had borne towards the dumb creation and the wonders of nature, which had been a ceaseless source of joy to her in life. And she added, with an unmistakable dig at the sorrowing relatives, 'All these mute beings have but to join their silence with mine when I shall be no more.' In a codicil she directed that her stuffed cat and canaries should be buried with her. This, says the *Morning Leader*, was too much for the mourning relatives. That they should be disinherited in favour of an elephant, a white bear, a hyena, and other estimable inhabitants of the Jardin des Plantes was bitter enough, but to bury the dear departed alongside her cat and canaries, 'never, so long as there are judges in Paris!' They applied to have the will set aside on the ground that the old woman was non compos mentis at the time of drawing up the document.

A remarkable will was admitted for probate in September 1910, made by a Spanish lady who resided in Paris. It was dated 3 June, 1908, and read: 'This day (Wednesday), at eight o'clock in the morning, I am alone as usual, so there is no one who could influence me, and although I am in bed with a swollen leg, my head is sound of judgment, so that what I write here is done with my full knowledge.'

She then goes on to state that she is about to inherit between 120,000 and 150,000 francs from her mother's estate. She left 'ten thousand francs to the Society for the Protection of Animals – in particular dogs – on condition of placing in the meeting hall a picture with my name and title of 'Protecting Friend of Dogs', and that all the three dogs – that is to say, Mirza and her two little ones – the cat and her little kittens, shall be received and well cared for by the society until they die of old age.'

It further states 25,000 Francs (then the equivalent of £1,000) upon trust, for her husband but he could not touch the bulk or do anything whatsoever with it. Instead, he was to live off the interest from that sum and if he remarried the income and capital would no longer be his.

The final clause read: 'As to my sisters, nieces, nephew, brother-in-law, and cousin, nothing, nothing shall come to them from me, but a bag of sand to rub themselves with. None deserve even a goodbye. I do not recognise a single one of them. It is useless even to communicate my death to them; they have too much abused and lied against me. This is my will.'

Twelve carriage horses were the sole beneficiaries under the will of wealthy bachelor Emil von Bizony, who died at Budapest in 1911. Bizony was the brother of a prominent Hungarian politician, was a confirmed woman-hater and was on bad terms with all his relatives. Upon his death, Emil's personal and real estate was valued at $200,000 and all of this he bequeathed to his beloved horses, naming the Society for the Protection of Animals as executors. The will stipulated that the interest accruing from Bizony's property should be devoted to the maintenance and care of the horses and that, in the instance of one of them dying from old age, another old horse should be taken in and cared for in its place so that the round dozen might always be maintained. Naturally Emil's relatives fought the will with his brother, Deputy Alusius von Bizony, starting the proceedings. It was recorded that an attempt was made to agree terms with the Society for the Protection of Animals by offering them $20,000 but this was refused and the original will was given precedence.

In the same year, the late Marie Douglas of Keithgrove, Uxbridge Road, West London, left an estate of £18,000, from which she bequeathed £250 to her coachman, Henry Bosher. Mrs Douglas also left Bosher her horses, ponies, dogs and parrots, all still alive at the time of her death, directing her trustees to pay him £4 a week so long as any of the animals may be living, 'and he shall humanely and efficiently feed, maintain, and care for such animals as from time to time shall be alive.'

Another case from the same period was a bequest of $2,000 to care for an old horse, with further directions that it never be sold or worked, contained in the will of Ellen Mulvell. Richard W. Clifford, former judge of the Circuit Court, who was named as executor of the estate, said that it was the first time to his knowledge that provision had been made for a horse in a will filed in Chicago. The clause referring to the care of the animal read: 'I give and bequeath the sum of two thousand dollars to my executor to be used and expended in the care of my old horse for the period of twenty years. I direct that the horse be never sold or worked, and whatever remains out of the $2,000 shall be divided among my sisters and brother.'

Mrs Mulvell had owned the horse for nearly seventeen years and was much attached to it. She left an estate valued at $170,000.

In September 1912, a group of women crowded into a strange little apothecary shop in St. Louis to discuss the death of its proprietor Doctor Sarah Wells. For years, the medic had kept locals in fear through the mystic powers that she was reputed to possess. A graduate of Oberlin University, Dr Wells was the founder of a medical college, author, lecturer and keen traveller. Despite having a large fortune invested in tenement houses in Dayton and Kansas City, as well as real estate in Florida and government bonds, Sarah Wells spent her last days sitting in a broken chair suffering from burns received after falling into a bathtub of hot water. Eventually she was persuaded to call a doctor, but knew she was dying and waited painfully for the end surrounded by wonderfully rich possessions from the Orient and trunks full of exquisite silk gowns. Doctor Wells' last act was to send for her upstairs tenants, Della Huddy and Madame Bee, a local fortune teller, to whom she gave her fifteen beloved cats. It was said that the cats held a superstitious terror amongst the neighbourhood, and when the old woman's husband had been alive he was known to have sat creating poems with one feline on his shoulder and another on his knee.

Former chairman of the Royal Society for the Prevention of Cruelty to Animals, Lieutenant Colonel Alexander Keith Wyllie, left an unsettled estate when he died in 1928. However, after probate was finally administered, the society inherited almost £200,000. Sir Robert Gower, MP, stated rather ambiguously, 'Colonel Wyllie's legacy will enable the council to pursue the more progressive policy upon which we recently decided.'

Mr. Rockwell Sayre hated cats. When alive he offered £100 to the person who brought him the greatest number of dead cats. When he died, he provided in his will for a packet of sweets to be sent to any famous person who also disliked cats. On the other hand, in 1937, the will was published of a lady who so loved her cats that she made bequests of £26 a year for the care of each of them. She was Miss Mitcheson, of London Road, Forest Hill, London.

There have been cases where testators appear to have thought a lot more about animals than they did about human beings. The will of a woman who died in Rome in 1935 was being disputed in the courts. She left no less than £5,000 to cats, the money being left in the interests of those creatures to the Roman Society for the Protection of Animals.

After more than twenty years of faithful service, Daisy, a thirty-one-year old mare, was willed stocks and bonds worth $100,000 by its late mistress. Susan Monroe, of Fall River, Massachusetts, declared in her will that she had left the money so that the horse might not want for anything in its old age and that it might enjoy the remainder of its life feeding on the best pastures. For twenty years, Daisy had drawn Mrs. Monroe on her business and pleasure trips through the cities and towns of Bristol County. The mare inherited a savings account and shares of stock in two of the richest mills in Fall River, all of which was to be held for the animal's benefit by a trustee and the income used for her comfortable maintenance and support. Provision was also made for the attendance of a veterinary surgeon, and the bequest stipulated that when Daisy passed away to equine heaven, she was to be given a fitting burial.

In September 1918 a retired soap manufacturer left the sum of $1,100 dollars, 'to found a home for homeless cats and dogs' but stipulated that the money was not to be touched until the year 2163, by when the donor estimated it will have increased to $200 million.

'Screechings' of the boys' choir of the exclusive Fifth Avenue Episcopal Church of St. Thomas caused the transfer of a society woman's bequest in 1923.

On 1 May, Mrs. Sidmon McHie, a wealthy broker's wife, visited police to complain about the dreadful noise coming from the Gothic place of worship that faced her home across the street. An investigation was promised. Mrs McHie had recently surprised her society friends with the announcement that her entire fortune was to be left for an animal memorial hospital, with the inscription over the door: 'The more I saw of humans, the more I thought of dogs.'

The prominent lady had previously announced that her will bequeathed the estate to a hospital for incurable children and did not explain her reasons for changing her mind and her will. However, after the complaint to the police, Mrs McHie admitted that the 'screechings' of the choir boys, followed by a feud which she carried on with church officials, caused her to change her will. She also confessed to trying to combat the choir's Sunday efforts by playing records on her phonograph, sending the music into the church by means of a powerful amplifying device.

Remarkable provisions were contained in the will of Sarah Martha Grove Grady, a lonely widow who died at Crowborough, East Sussex, in November 1925. The 84-year old's sole interest was in the care of animals. She abhorred unnecessary suffering and killing for sport, and in her final testament the pursuit of deer, stags, foxes, rabbits, hares and fishing, were denounced as cruel practices. Her will left almost £600,000 to societies and institutions devoted to the care of animals. She specifically left £10,000 to the Royal Society for the Prevention of Cruelty to Animals on condition that the chairman and members of the committee be anti-vivisectionists and oppose hunting. In a statement issued in January 1926, the secretary of the RSPCA said that the legacy had to be refused owing to the conditions. The residue of Mrs Grove Grady's fortune was bequeathed to the foundation of an institute to be called the Beaumont Animals Benevolent Society and to purchase land which was to be a sanctuary for wild animals and birds.

Two fortunes, one consisting of a £40,000 estate, were bequeathed for the care of animals in wills proven in 1926. Lucy Gordon Roberts, of Avenue Road, Brockenhurst, Hampshire, left, amongst other legacies:

£1,500 to the People's Dispensary for Sick Animals of the Poor
£800 to the Cricklewood Home of Rest for Horses
£500 to the Canine Defence League
£500 to Our Dumb Friends' League branches
The residue of her £40,000 property was to go to the RSPCA.

The will read:

> I am leaving a good large portion of my money to try and make the lot of poor dumb animals less hard, because so few people seem to think of them at all. Even the agony suffered by animals by vivisection on man's behalf and their cruel deaths in the slaughterhouse fail to move the average man to pity or to see that God's dumb creatures never have rights as well as human beings.

The other fortune intended for animals was that of William Thomas, of Brynheulog, Merthyr Tydfil, who left £12,095, the greater part of which was to go to the Our Dumb Friends' League. This bequest included Russian bonds which were valued at £494, but with overdue interest would be worth £11,944, if the Russian Government decided to meet their liabilities to bondholders, more than doubling the bequest to the league.

Mitzi, an eighteen-year-old cat became the owner of a $15,000 legacy and a beautiful estate at San Gabriel, Los Angeles, in 1930. Dr Maude Cain, just before her death, stipulated that Mitzi should receive the money and house and 'upon said premises proper care for cat Mitzi must be provided so long as she shall live.' Pauline Agnes Goetze received $25 per month while she lived in the house and cared for the cat.

When Alice Hunter of Chicago died in 1932, she left half her property to her adopted daughter and half to her dog. This 'Red', the Irish Setter, became half-owner of an apartment building, a property held in trust for him and another pet, a cat, for the rest of their lives. The value totalled $27,500. On their deaths the money was to be divided between animal shelter activities and charity.

Four pedigree pets, three cats and a dog, inherited the estate of Harriet Draper, spinster daughter of the late Dr Daniel Draper, former New York City meteorologist. Miss Draper, who was 42, was killed in a car accident near her home at Hastings-on-Hudson in October 1932. In her will, filed the following month, she left bequests to five relatives and then provided that all her 'stocks and bonds and other property shall become a trust fund for the pets.' Her attorney said that Harriet Draper had personal property worth $5,000 in addition to securities in a safety deposit box which could not be opened until a court order was obtained. He had no idea of the worth of the securities at the time of his comment to news reporters.

Animals and birds benefitted from the bulk of a £109,083 fortune left by widow Maria Isabella Slimon of Clacton-on-Sea, Essex, in 1939. Immediate bequests included £3,000 to the Home for Lost Dogs, Battersea, and similar sums to the Home of Rest for Horses and the Royal Society for the Protection of Birds. Another dogs' home and a pit pony society were also included amongst a number of other institutions receiving money, with the residue of Mrs. Slimon's property being left to her niece and a companion. On their deaths it was directed that any remaining funds to be divided between Our Dumb Friends' League and the previously mentioned societies.

The Reverend Charles Cunliffe Brookes, who died at Middle Aston House, Oxfordshire, in March 1941, inherited a fortune of £10,000 from his wife and then gave it away to be spent on the benefit of animals. Son of a former rector, Brookes was Rural Dean of Leamington from 1916 to 1922, and vicar of Duns Tew from 1922 to 1932. The money was inherited by Mrs. Brookes from a rich relative, but the couple continued to live together on £400 a year in a country vicarage. The bequest was distributed among animal societies in Great Britain.

New York socialite Ida Evelina Bliss died, aged 81, on 31 July 1942. For many years her physician had been the only man to have entered her eighteen-room house on the exclusive Kings Point, Long Island. Miss Bliss left almost half of her two-million-dollar estate to humane societies to be used to make the trapping of animals painless. Her will, filed for probate on 18 September of the same year, showed that the remainder of the fortune was to be split among those who worked for her and a few friends, with two second cousins, described as wealthy, receiving just $5,000 each.

The probate court at Waupaca, Wisconsin, was swamped with advice on the disposal of a will in October 1942, in which Nina Joy Beglinger bequeathed her $100,000 estate to her Boston bulldog 'Lady Pooh.' Least mercenary of the offers to care for the dog came in a letter from a 12-year-old girl. It read: 'I love dogs, so if you will let me take Lady Pooh I'll give her as nice a home as any one can give her and you don't need to pay any money if you don't want to.'

An old lady living in a Kansas village offered to take care of Lady Pooh for one-third of the estate. She added: 'Be sure to send me a check and be sure it's certified.'

Mrs. Beglinger, a former Detroit schoolteacher, died on 25 May at an Iola hospital. A will penned on her death bed left her Detroit home and estate to the dog with the provision that her servant, Tatiana Rhune, be given the income to pay expenses. The late Mrs Beglinger's daughter, Mrs Engebretson, contested the will in a Detroit court without success.

Lily, a coal-black kitten who received $5,000 in the will of her mistress, Annie Hansche, in 1938, was claimed as being down to her last $2,686 by 1942. C.H.S. Bidwell, trustee of the fund, who appointed his own wife to the $50 a month job as Lily's custodian, died earlier in the year. Mrs. Bidwell told the court that she had been unable to collect her ward's board bill because a new trustee had not been named after her husband's untimely death. She reported that Lily's appetite for liver, grade A milk and catnip had consumed all but the remaining couple of thousand dollars of inheritance money.

Margaret Myers, a well-to-do Detroit woman, who died on 24 October 1944, left her dog more than $20,000 and cut off her son without a cent. The will was revealed in probate court by Judge Joseph Murphy in January 1945. The handwritten will which left the money to Jack, an eight-year-old fox terrier, said simply: 'I bequeath everything to my dog, Jack. Whoever shall care for him in my home, 3771 Northwestern, shall have the place rent free.'

The will, which was made the previous July, set no specific sum, merely mentioning a value of $20,000 or more. The son, Joseph White, of Abiline, Texas, was not mentioned. Mrs Myers was the widow of a real-estate agent and Joseph was her son by a previous marriage. Since the time of Mrs Myers death, the newly rich dog had been cared for in small animal hospitals and by friends.

In 1951, a 79-year-old blind man from Perth, Australia, whose dog had led him about for the greater part of its life, left his whole estate for the upkeep of the animal until it died. 'For many years I have been totally blind and Toby has been a faithful companion to me,' Howard Hope Hills wrote in his will. Ten-year-old Toby was provided with enough money per week for his expensive tastes, which included rump steak, crayfish, pies and cakes.

Richard Beresford Burrows' great love was the protection of wild birds and as a result he founded the Dungeness bird sanctuary in Kent. Leaving an estate of £15,232 on his death in 1956, the bachelor bequeathed money to various bird and wildlife institutions, with the residue shared between the Wild Life Protection Society of South Africa and the Fauna Protection Society. Mr Beresford Burrows hoped to benefit the cause for large rare antelope and zebra.

Maltese-born underworld figure Joseph Borg once said that there was not one human he could trust. This piece of rhetoric was proven when Borg's will was opened, after his murder in Sydney in 1970, when he left his estate of

25,000 Australian dollars to the Royal Society for the Prevention of Cruelty to Animals.

More recently, Lady Cassie Madeleine De Lacy Neville, of Mill Road in Worthing, Sussex, left an estate valued at over half a million pounds. Having passed away on 16 November 1993, Lady Neville left just £200 each to the Battersea Dogs Home, Whitebreads Social and Sports Club, and the Donkey Sanctuary near Plymouth, with the residue of her estate going to a niece.

In 1992, Esme Berni spent £170,000 to buy former dog kennels at the village of Barrow Gurney on the outskirts of Bristol. The wife of Aldo Berni, the wealthy Bristol restaurateur who founded the Berni Inn chain, said that animals were the love of her life and when she died four years later they were not forgotten, with most of the widow's fortune being left to animal charities. The main beneficiary was the Bristol and District branch of Animal Concern – a charity which saves unwanted or abandoned animals and rehomes them, receiving between £3.5 and £4 million.

Chapter Three

Curious Bequests

In his will of 13 June 1626, Thomas Hole left 13s. 4 pence annually from land at Hoden, near Sandwich. Ten shillings of this was for the poor of Herne, while three shillings and fourpence was to go to those who rang the bells of Herne Church every Saint Thomas's Day, 21 December. The story goes that one day Thomas Hole was lost in Blean Woods. He heard the bells of Saint Martin's Church and was able, by listening to the sound, to find his way out. To repay the bell ringers for their unintentional good deed, he left the money, which was of course worth much more in those days.

In years gone by it was not unusual for testators to write up their wills in poetic verse or with a literary flourish. A curious rhyming will was proven in an English court in 1737 and was uncontested. It was that of John Hedges of Finchley, Middlesex, and in part runs as follows:

This fifth of May,
Being airy and gay,
To trip not inclined,
But of vigorous mind,
And my body in health,
I'll dispose of my wealth;
And of all I'm to leave
On this side of the grave,
To some one or other,
I think to my brother.
But because I presaw
That my brother-in-law
(If) I did not take care
Would come in for a share
Which I no ways intended
Till their manners were mended –

And of that there's no sign,
I do therefore enjoin,
And strictly command,
As witness my hand,
That nought I have got
Be brought to hotch pot
And I give and devise
Much as in me lies
To the son of my mother
My own dear brother,
To have and to hold
All my silver and gold,
As the affectionate pledges
Of his brother, JOHN HEDGES.

From another example in the year 1804, the will of Joshua West was probated, it read:

Maybe I am not worth a groat,
But, should I die with something more,
I leave it all, with my old coat,
And all my manuscript in store.
To those who will the goodness have
To cause my poor remains to rest
Within a fitting shell and grave;
This is the will of Joshua West.

One of the most curious bequests was that of Madame Juliette Recamier, the beautiful French socialite, prominent in both literary and political circles during the early part of the nineteenth century. Born Jeanne Francoise Julie Adelaide Recamier in 1777, she left 20,000 francs as an annual prize for the best treatise on the influence of grief as the cause of illness and death. Juliette was buried in Montmatre Cemetery, Paris, in May 1849.

Many persons who wish to bestow charity have strange ways of carrying out their wishes. For example, Englishman James Moss left $500 to be invested in land, the rent of which was to provide fine gowns, according to the will, 'of a sad blue colour' for as many aged and poor men living in the town.

Even stranger than these odd bequests is the arrangement for suicide made by Lord Southey, as reported in the *St. James Gazette* dated 22 August 1895:

Lord Southey once, in a fit of disgust with life, had a magnificent guillotine erected in the drawing-room of his splendidly appointed house in the Rue de Luxembourg, at Paris. The machine was an elaborate affair, with ebony uprights inlaid with gold and silver. The framework was carved with great artistic skill, and the knife, of immense weight, and falling at the touch of a spring, was of ornamental steel, polished and as sharp as a razor.

The spring which liberated the knife was placed within easy reach of anyone kneeling upon the scaffold; in fact, every detail was arranged with a view to the convenience of the would-be suicide. The day that the engine of death was quite finished, Lord Southey completed his testamentary dispositions, shaved, had his hair cut and clothed in a robe of white silk, knelt upon the platform under the knife. The guillotine was placed before a large mirror, wherein the person committing suicide could see his own image until the last. Murmuring a short prayer, Lord Southey placed his head in the semi-circle and pressed the spring.

The next morning he was found calmly sleeping in his bed. The spring had failed to work, and, after several fruitless efforts, Lord Southey was compelled to relinquish his attempt upon his life. Thoroughly cured of his spleen, he presented the guillotine to the Glasgow Museum, where he made an annual pilgrimage to see it until the end of his life.

In the pocket of a ragged coat belonging to one of the inmates of the Chicago poorhouse there was found, after his death, a will. The man had been a lawyer. The document was so unusual that it was sent to an attorney and the story goes that he was so impressed by the contents that he read it before the Chicago Bar Association. This is what it contained:

I, Charles Lounsberry, being of sound and disposing mind and memory, do herby make and publish this my last will and testament to distribute my interest in the world among succeeding men. That part of my interest which is known in law as my property, being inconsiderable and of no account, I make no disposition of. My right to live, being but a life estate, is not at my disposal, but these things excepted, all else in the world I now proceed to devise and bequeath.

Item: I give to good fathers and mothers, all good little words of praise and encouragement, and all quaint pet names and endearments; and I charge said parents to use them justly, but generously, as the deeds of their children shall require.

Item: I leave to children inclusively, but only for the term of their childhood, all and every flower of the field and the blossoms of the woods, with the right to play among them freely according to the custom of children, warning them at the same time against thistles and thorns. And I devise to children the banks of the brooks and the golden sands beneath the waters thereof, and the odours of the willows that dip therein, and the white clouds that float high over giant trees. And I leave the children the long, long days to be merry in, in a thousand ways, and the night and the train of the Milky Way to wonder at, but subject, nevertheless, to the rights herein-after given to lovers.

Item: I devise to boys, jointly, all the useful idle fields and commons where ball may be played, all pleasant waters where one may swim, all snowclad hills where one may coast, and all streams and ponds where one may fish, or where, when grim winter comes, one may skate, to hold the same for the period of their boyhood. And all meadows, with the clover blossoms and butterflies thereof; the woods with their beauty; the squirrels and the birds and the echoes and strange noises, and all distant places, which may be visited together with the adventures there found. And I give to said boys each his own place at the fireside at night, with all pictures that may be seen in the burning wood, to enjoy without let or hindrance or without any encumbrance or care.

Item: To lovers, I devise their imaginary world, with whatever they may need, as the stars of the sky, the red roses by the wall, the bloom of the hawthorn, the sweet strains of music, and aught else they may desire to figure to each other the lastingness and beauty of their love.

Item: To young men jointly I bequeath all the boisterous, inspiring sports of rivalry, and I give to them the disdain of weakness, and undaunted confidence in their own strength. I leave to them the power to make lasting friendships and of possessing companions, and to them, exclusively, I give all merry songs and choruses to sing with lusty voices.

Item: And to those who are no longer children or youths, or lovers, I leave memory; and bequeath to them the volumes of poems of Burns and Shakespeare and other poets, if there be others, to the end that they may live the old days over again, freely and fully without tithe or diminution.

Item: To the loved ones with snowy crowns, I bequeath the happiness of old age, the love and gratitude of their children until they fall asleep.

The following instance of a peculiar will is taken from a magazine published in 1854:

Mr Railing, of New Hampshire, was among the victims of the last railroad accident between London and Brighton. His heirs, after having paid him the customary funeral honours, did what all heirs do in similar cases – opened the will of the deceased to ascertain what share each was to have in his posthumous liberality. As he had never given a penny to any of his relatives during his lifetime, they expected to be richer now that Railing was no more. One may imagine the surprise caused by the first line of the will:

'This is my testament. I give and bequeath all my goods, moveable and immoveable, in England or on the Continent, to that railroad company on whose road I have had the happiness to meet with death, that blessed deliverance from my terrestrial prison.'

Further on Railing gives the reasons for his bequest. The idea had taken firm possession of his mind that he was destined to die a violent death, and the most desirable one in his view was that caused by the explosion of a locomotive. He travelled, therefore, constantly on the railroads of England, Belgium and France. There was not a station where he was not known. All the conductors were familiar with Railings peculiar costume, and he narrowly escaped death several times. Once he was shut up in a carriage under water, another time he was in the next carriage to one that was shattered, and he described with the greatest enthusiasm those terrible accidents, when he saw death so near without being able to obtain it. Disappointed in Europe, he went to the United States, making frequent excursions to Ohio, Mississippi, Ontario and Niagara, but notwithstanding the frequent explosions, he returned with a whole skin. Railing was destined to be crushed under a carriage of his mother country. It is sad that his relatives attempted to set aside the will on the ground of insanity, but the railroad company won the suit, in spite of the proverb that 'the murderer never inherits from his victim!

The *Popolo Italiano*, of Genoa, dated January 1865, related that

Dr. Tagliaferro, a physician, died lately at Pammatone, leaving in his will a sum of 1,500 Francs to the families of the two poorest men that might happen to die at the hospital of Pammatone on the same day as himself. It so happened that on the day in question there was but one death at the hospital, that of a woman; and on the day following six women died, and not a single man. The legacy, consequently, reverts to the heirs–at–law.

In the same year, a 78-year old man died in Buenos Aires, leaving a will which contained a clause leaving 10,000 cigars for those who might attend his funeral. This eccentric testator also expressed his desire that his friends should not leave the house of mourning without drinking to his memory all the wine left in his cellar.

The German ferry SS *Schiller* was one of the largest vessels of her day, making transatlantic passage from New York to Hamburg via Southampton. On the evening of 7 May 1875, she was sailing off the coast of the Scilly Isles with 118 crew members, 254 passengers, a cargo of sewing machines and a large quantity of gold coins, when she encountered thick fog. The ship slowed to four knots in search of the Bishops Rock Lighthouse but it could not be seen and the hull hit the Retarrier Ledges reef. After managing to reverse off, two large waves hit the Schiller broadside, and the hull started to break up. Many of the lifeboats had been damaged and as some were cut loose many passengers were crushed between the ship and the rocks. Boats were deployed to the rescue but sadly only thirty–seven people survived, none of them children.

Among the victims were John Suppiger and his family, of the United States. Just prior to their departure on the SS *Schiller*, Mr Suppiger added a strange codicil to his will, leaving relatives wondering whether he had experienced a premonition concerning the trip. The last sentence of the codicil read: 'The above codicil shall have full force and validity in case myself, my wife Catherine, my daughter Adeline, and my son John should have the misfortune, all and every one of us named, of being lost and meet with death on the ocean, on our trip to Europe, now about to be undertaken.'

The will, in which Suppiger left his estate to his brothers and sisters, together with the codicil attached, was filed for probate. No other conclusion could be drawn from the language of the document than that John Suppiger, before his departure, had a foreboding that the voyage would prove fatal to himself and his family. Many strange instances are on record of persons in perfect health having vivid premonitions of death but this has to stand out as one of the most startling ever related.

In October 1878 Alex McGill, a wealthy and well-known citizen of Pittsburgh, became fearful that he might die and that his fortune would fall into the hands of the wife that he had divorced some years before. In order to set out his wishes legally, McGill bequeathed a small sum to the former wife and everything else to his sister. On the death of his sibling, the money was to be divided between three aunts, all sisters of his father whom he believed to be living in County Tyrone, Ireland. Should they happen to die in the meantime, their children were to inherit and, God forbid, should the children also be deceased, the whole estate was bequeathed to the President of the United States, only on the proviso that he be a Democrat, holding the money in trust for the interest and success of the Democratic Party. The will was proven before County Registrar Gray on 19 October 1878, and the inventory showed personal effects to the value of $21,924 with the property worth considerably more. Two Democratic politicians examined the records and forwarded their findings to President Cleveland.

A curious bequest was made to the poor of London in 1882 by Neapolitan gentleman Pasquale Farale, 'in memory of his wife, who was born in London, and with whom he lived there many happy years.' The bequest consisted of an unpublished opera in three acts, which was to be presented to Queen Victoria and performed 'for the benefit of the London poor.' Also contained in the will was the sum of 18,000 Francs, to be used for the purpose of granting three marriage dowries per year of 300 Francs to three poor girls residing in London, chosen by lot, between the ages of 16 and 25.

A most unusual bequest was the subject of proceedings before the Irish Master of the Rolls in Dublin. It was made in the will of the late Elizabeth Haughton of Eccles Street, Dublin, who died on 25May 1884, last possessed of personal estate amounting to £7,000. An action was brought by Samuel Haughton, her brother and executor, for the direction of the court as to certain trusts in the will, which was dated 9 September 1883.

The testatrix provided as follows:

I give and bequeath, after my death, the sum of £1,000 sterling to the national cause for the independence of Ireland – liberty for my country to rule herself. Being a Repealer in my youth, I am unable to understand the political phase of the present day, and I prefer the interest of the £1,000, which I hope will be £50 per annum, to be given yearly by my executor. I appoint my brother, Samuel Haughton, my executor, and I leave the power in his hands to dispose of my bequest towards the highest and purest form of obtaining a national Parliament for my beloved country. I thank God for His mercies and for permitting me the power of thus testifying to my country the approval of every effort she makes to rise to freedom.

By provision of his will in September 1884, Charles Reade's notebooks and scrapbooks were to be open for inspection to professional writers, especially of dramatic or narrative fiction, for a period of two years. They were only permitted to be viewed at the home of the novelist's godson and executor, Charles Liston, who was requested to advertise the bequest publicly.

One of the oddest bequests on record was that made by author Robert Louis Stevenson, as it was witnessed and gifted while he was still alive. In 1891, at the age of 41, Stevenson transferred his birthday to American girl Annie Ide, on account of her having been born on 25 December and missing out on a separate celebration as people were too wrapped up with festivities. Here is the very unusual document: I, Robert Louis Stevenson, advocate of the Scot's bar, author of 'Master of Ballantree' and 'Moral Emblems,' a civil engineer, sole owner and patentee of the palace and plantation known as Vailima, in the Island of Upolu, Samoa, a British subject, being sound in mind and pretty well I thank you, in body.

In consideration that Miss A.H. Ide, in the town of Johnsbury, in the County of Caledonia, in the State of Vermont, the United States of

America, was born out of reason on Christmas Day, and is therefore, out of all justice denied the consolation of a proper birthday. And considering that I, the said Robert Louis Stevenson, having attained to an age – on, never mention it, and that I have no further use of a birthday of any description. And in consideration that I have met H.C. father of the said A.H. Ide, and found him about as white a land commissioner as I require.

Have transferred and do hereby transfer to the said A.H. Ide all and whole my rights and privileges in the thirteenth day of November, formerly my birthday, now hereby and henceforth the birthday of the said A.H. Ide to have, hold, exercise and enjoy same in the customary manner, by sporting of fine raiment, eating of rich meats and receipt of gifts, compliments, and copies of verses, according to the manner of our ancestors.

And I direct the said A.H. Ide to add to her name of Annie H. Ide, the name Louise – at least in private – and I charge her to use my said birthday with moderation and humility, '*et bone tamquam filia familiae*' the birthday being not so young as I once was and having carried me in a very satisfactory manner since I can remember. And in case the said A.H. Ide shall neglect or contravene either of the above conditions I hereby revoke the donation and transfer my rights in the said birthday to the President of the United States for the time being. In witness whereof I hereto set my hand and seal this nineteenth day of June in the year of grace, 1891.

Witnesses: Lloyd Osborne & Harold Watts.

Naturally the little schoolgirl who received the new birthday was delighted and acknowledged it in a grateful letter. Three years later Robert Louis Stevenson died.

Occasionally, disputes regarding the bequests of land can cause surprising turmoil, with one testator causing a political ruckus. A Frenchman died in July of 1887, leaving the whole of his estate to the German Government for the purpose of founding a solely German settlement. The story of how this strange bequest came to be made is interesting.

Monsieur Bareiller, ex-Mayor of Boissise-Le-Roi, a country town situated in the Seine-Et-Marne district, not far from Paris, was sentenced to a year's imprisonment in 1886 for having fired at and wounded a workman who pressed him for payment of a ten Franc debt. M. Bareiller, who was naturally of an ungovernable temper, was driven mad with anger by this sentence. During his detention this sense of bitterness grew deeper on account of his inability to give vent to it, added to the hardships of prison life. His constitution became shattered and the disappointment of not receiving a pardon on 14 July, Bastille Day, wrought an alarming change in his condition. From that day forth, Monsieur Bareiller could eat no food and on 20 July 1887, he died at the Melun Hospital, where he had been taken some hours previously. The ill-fated man was a landowner of fortunate means, being worth the equivalent of £24,000. He was a cultured and gifted scholar and, it was claimed, would have been an instructive conversationalist but for his many crochets and oddities.

Shortly before his trial, Monsieur Bareiller had offered as a free gift to the Department of Seine-Et-Marne his property at Boisisse, on condition that it was made a farming settlement but, as he stipulated that he should manage the estate during his lifetime, the offer was rejected for fear that his terrible temper might eventually bring trouble upon the department. However, the landowner still clung to his original idea and made a will in 1885 which was opened after his death, whereby he bequeathed the land to the State for the same objective. During his imprisonment, Bareiller conceived an abhorrence of his country on account of his countrymen and he declared that he would spare no opportunity of revenging himself for all the infamy cast upon him by the French judges. He drew up two wills at different periods by which he left his property of Boissise to Germany, represented by the Crown Prince, with the purpose of establishing there a settlement of young Germans.

In November 1889, a steamer arrived at Bardsey Island, off the Caernarvonshire coast, bearing a coffin containing the remains of the late Lord Newborough of Glynllifon. Sixteen months previously, reported by the *Daily Telegraph*, the body of the nobleman was interred in the family vault in Landwrog churchyard. Here it remained, as per instructions in the will, until the specified time when it was to be taken from the vault and conveyed to its final resting place on Bardsey Island. The late Lord Newborough was deeply attached to the area on account of its historical associations, the island having been given by Edward VI to a member of the Glynllifon family, a standard bearer, for conspicuous bravery displayed at the battle of Norwich. The late

Lord took a lively interest in the welfare of the islanders, built them cottages and a chapel to accommodate eighty worshippers, and also erected a monument with an inscription to commemorate the deaths of 20,000 saints who, according to Welsh custom, were buried on Bardsey Island. A handsome mausoleum was constructed and in this the coffin of Lord Newborough was safely deposited.

Robert C. Greiner made a very unusual bequest to the University of Michigan. Greiner was a native of Jackson and was killed, together with his wife, in a boiler explosion at the Gumry Hotel in August 1885. The will was written by Greiner himself and the last clause directed that after his death his right foot should be amputated above the ankle and presented to the Ann Arbor medical school. It was then to be mounted as a skeleton preparation and labelled 'Bob's Game Foot.' Apparently, Mr. Greiner had a peculiarly deformed ankle and dislocated toe, which had been a great source of trouble to him. It was such a puzzle to physicians that he came to take great pride in it, hence the desire to restore the abnormality for posterity. According to university authorities they knew nothing of the bequest until the letter was opened and were unable to confirm whether Robert Greiner was ever treated at the medical facility.

When Annie Guldstone died in 1890, she left in her will a bequest big enough to rattle the nerves of reformers and Prohibitionists. In a London bank was to be deposited a sum of £3,000, its interest to be used for the purchase of several bottles of the best champagne for the use of actors and actresses on every occasion when a play called for wine drinking on the stage. Henry Irving was appointed trustee of the fund by the testatrix.

In most cases, the task of making a will is anything but a humorous occupation, although one New York resident, who died in 1891, could not have concocted a more bitter joke on his friend. After reciting the obligations he was under to this particular legatee, the man bequeathed to him, at the bottom of the first page of the will, 10,000.... Of course, the delighted friend presumed that the amount was dollars as he turned over the sheaf of paper, but the bequest turned out to be 10,000 thanks!

Just as odd was the codicil of the death-stricken humourist who left some of his dear relatives 'as many acres of land as shall be found equal to the area enclosed by the track of the centre of the oscillation of the earth in a revolution round the sun, supposing the mean distance to be twenty-one thousand six hundred semi-diameters of the earth from it.' This was over two hundred years ago and, as the problem could not be satisfactorily worked out, the legatees were kept at a *mean distance* from the property for their entire lives.

Monsieur Xavier Marmier, of Paris, who was a passionate collector of old books, added an unusual codicil to his will on the occasion of his 80th birthday:

In memory, of the happy moments which I have spent in the midst of the second-hand booksellers of the quays on the left side of the river, and I count among the most agreeably animated of my existence, I bequeath to those good stall keepers a sum of 1,000 Francs. I desire that that sum may be employed by those kind and honest tradespeople, who number about fifty, in providing themselves with a joyous dinner, and in passing an hour full of merriment in thinking of me.

The most unique bequest ever received by Yale College was recorded in June 1893, when eccentric Monroe citizen Minot Booth left them several quarries to be used for geological purposes. The areas had good practical value, being composed of common granite used for building purposes, although Booth concluded that the quarries would be invaluable for scientific research. The bequest, however, may have left a bitter taste in the mouths of his heirs, who were cut off without a cent. The remainder of Booth's estate was left to the town for the maintenance of local bridges.

The following bequest to the Corporation of Bath appears to indicate that the testator was not particularly happy in his domestic arrangements:

I do hereby give and bequeath to the Mayor, Senior Alderman, and Town Clerk of Bath for the time being the sum of £50 per annum in trust, for the use, benefit, and enjoyment of the set of ringers belonging to Abbey Church, Bath, on condition of their ringing on the whole peal of bells, with clappers muffled, various solemn and doleful changes, allowing proper intervals for rest and refreshment, from eight o'clock in the morning until eight o'clock in the evening of the 14th day of May in every year, being the anniversary of my wedding day; and also on every anniversary of the day of my decease to ring a merry, mirthful peal, unmuffled, during the same space of time, and allowing the same intervals as before mentioned, in joyful commemoration of my happy release from domestic tyranny and wretchedness. And for the full, strict, and due performance of such conditions, they (the said ringers) are to receive the said £50 per annum, in two payments of £25 each, on those respective days of my marriage and decease.

Rossi Arturo, who lived at Pellagrino, near Parma, in Italy, left 30,000 Francs to any person who could fulfil the conditions of his will in 1894, which were as follows:

I leave all my substance and possessions to him among my fellow countrymen who, in the space of three years after the date of my death shall write a book to cast light on the following facts which have remained hidden, and have tormented my mind during these last months, in order that the lovers of impostures and cliques may be unmasked if they be found to merit the name.

1. If Adriano Lemmi, the head of the Masons, be really the man that was condemned for theft at Marseilles before '48. If it be true that he has made millions out of the government tobacco affair. How is it that he is so powerful in Italy?
2. If it be true that the Italian Government has subtracted money for the Banca Romana under Signor Tanlongo, for the purpose of carrying on the elections?
3. Who was it told King Humbert to make Signor Tanlongo a senator?
4. If Rignor Mieli has restored to the creditors of the Banca Romana the 5,000 lire taken for his journal or for the Liberal cause, and what became of the other 5,000 which went to his journal and the same cause?
5. If it be true that so many other men in high positions have taken money from the Banca Romana without ever restoring it, and are still Deputies and Ministers sent to the Chamber by the electors, and if among such men be the Ministers of Finance and of Grace and Justice?

I wish my burial to be religious and decent, but without discourses, that a stone be erected over my grave bearing the date of my birth, January 6, 1820, the date of my death, and these other words: 'He lived and died without being made a knight.'

Over the centuries, odd will bequests have often become subject to litigation as disgruntled relatives of the testator wrangle with the deceased's unusual decisions. One such case was that of a certain Mr. Russel from Aberdeen, who left the sum of £13,000 to a local policeman and a group of scavengers, giving each a total of one shilling per week out of the pot until it was all gone!

At the turn of the twentieth century a Frenchwoman died at the age of 90 and left a will containing the following: 'I leave to my physician, whose enlightened care and wise prescriptions have made me live so long, all that is contained in the old oaken chest in my boudoir. The key to the chest will be found under the mattress of my bed.'

Naturally, the old lady's relatives were disturbed by the bequest, imagining their own shares of her fortune rapidly diminishing. However, the physician arrived and a notary passed him the key to the chest. It was opened and found to contain all the drugs and potions, still intact and unopened, which the doctor had given to his patient for the past twenty years of her life!

The most enthusiastic art collector of the nineteenth century was undoubtedly Monsieur Borniche, who on his death bequeathed no fewer than 24,000 paintings to his only daughter. However, as he purchased only paintings which had been rejected at various salons and galleries, they were of no commercial value. The daughter, on inheriting his property and finding that the pictures could not be sold, ordered them to be locked up in the upper rooms so that she might never be troubled by the sight of them.

It turned out that Mademoiselle Borniche was as eccentric as her father and spent much of her time dressing the numerous statues in the grounds of the house, clothing them in foliage in summer, and specially made woollen dresses in winter. Every morning her gardeners were summoned to give an exact account of every apple, pear and nut growing on the estate, and each day she would make a trip through the adjoining village in a wheelbarrow propelled by a female servant. In May 1897, the eccentric dame died at the age of 73 and left everything to a complete stranger picked from a directory. The relatives of Mme Borniche immediately endeavoured to get the will revoked but there was no evidence to corroborate the allegation of the old woman being of unsound mind and judgment was found in favour of the will. As for the paintings, which had originally cost Monsieur Borniche in the region of 2,000 Francs, they were valued at one shilling and sixpence each, including the frames!

One of the most curious bequests on record at the end of the nineteenth century was that of wealthy businessman Anthony Bowling of Tennessee. He left his entire fortune to whichever young girl under the age of 16, residing in the city of Memphis, who had hair closest matching a lock that had belonged to his dead wife. The executors had a difficult task in selecting the heir but eventually decided that little Eunice Cleves had the shade closest resembling the sample lock and she was awarded $1,200 a year for life.

Another odd bequest of the same era was that of an American banker named Bruce, who left $10,000 to a girl he had never met in order for her to break a record for the most windfalls. At the time, the girl in question, Dulcie Farr, and a Mrs Grant, had each come into four separate and successive fortunes one after the other in the United States. Bruce left the money to Dulcie Farr so that she could break the record with five fortunes in succession.

A remarkable codicil was incorporated in the will of the late Henry G. Moore, an American who died in London in 1900. By this strange provision $105 was set aside for any person who was willing to cut his throat after death. This precaution was taken to preclude the possibility of Moore being buried alive. It is not known whether the testator's last wishes were carried out.

When Dr. Von Jirusch, a professor of pharmacology in the University of Prague, died in 1902, it was found that he had bequeathed $15,000 to the National Museum of Prague on one condition. All of the doctor's belongings, furniture, clothes, pictures, manuscripts, letters, books, plates and linen were to be packed in airtight cases and sealed up. The cases were then to be deposited in secure vaults and not opened for 200 years. Von Jurisch's objective was to enlighten the people of the twenty-second century about the manners and customs of their predecessors.

According to a special despatch from Madrid, the will of the late Cardinal Sebastian Herrero y Espinosa de los Monteros, Archbishop of Valencia, contained an extraordinary bequest. $10,000 was to be given to the 'First Spanish General landing in United States territory with an army sufficiently strong to avenge the defeats of Cuba and the Philippines.' Pending the happenings of this event the legacy was to remain deposited in the Bank of Spain.

A curious codicil was discovered in the will of Charlotte Vansittart, of 162 Castle Street, Reading, who, dying at the age of 83 in July 1903, left £41,453. She had a nephew, once a well-known radical member of Parliament for a Cornish constituency, and to him the codicil referred: 'I dislike Augustus' politics so much,' it read, 'that I would not willingly leave him anything, but I leave him £50 as a present.'

Miss Vansittart was an ardent Conservative and was one of the most constant subscribers to the Reading Conservative Association.

The following month, a suit went before Sir Francis Jeune in the Probate Division of the High Court in respect of the testamentary dispositions of the late Henry D. Spencer Kingdom. The question was whether or not a codicil in the will should be admitted to probate. In his will of April 1901, the testator had left all of his money to his grandson, but in a subsequent codicil had provided for the maintenance of a mausoleum for himself, his wife and mother. Kingdom had also made provisions against any of his descendants becoming Roman Catholics or Ritualists, and wished part of his estate to go towards forming an agnostic institution. It was alleged that at the time of writing the codicil the old man was not of sound mind and the family doctor gave evidence to show that this was indeed the case. There being no contest on the matter, his Lordship found for the will and against the codicil.

Sir Francis Jeune had another strange case brought before him the following year, when the story of the disappearance of the codicil to a will was told in connection with an application made in London's Probate Court. It referred to the will of Edmund Brook. The judge heard that Oswald Ballard, in whose possession the codicil had been placed, was travelling from Royston to London on his motorcycle when it caught fire. Ballard claimed to have put out the flames with his coat, and the codicil, which was in the pocket, was destroyed. 'That is a somewhat novel way of accounting for a document,' said Sir Francis, and expressed his doubt as to the 'cock-and-bull story' told by Mr. Ballard, as he was solely responsible for the trouble and the judge ordered Ballard to pay the costs of the application.

'The first person who shuts him or herself up in a tomb at Pere Lachaise for exactly twelve months will get an income of $1,250 a year,' wrote the Paris correspondent of a London newspaper. Apparently, an eccentric Russian lady had died at Paris, in 1904, bequeathing her fortune to anyone who could bear the conditions. She wrote: 'You are offered lodging in a stone cell built over the vault in which my remains repose, must never leave the abode night or day for one whole year, must communicate with no one in the outside world save the person who will bring your food morning and evening, and never must have a light in your lonely lodge among the dead.' A Parisian journal stated that only one man attempted to earn the money and that after eight month's residence in the cell he lost his reason and ended up in a lunatic asylum!

In olden times, when rushes were strewn on the floor in lieu of carpets, many people left bequests of money and land for providing rushes for the floors of churches. The usage, of course, has long been discontinued, but in certain places the church wardens attend to the preservation of the rights by cutting a little grass each year and strewing it on the church. But perhaps one of the most eccentric bequests was that of a certain John Ridge, of Trysull, Staffordshire, England, who in March 1906 left £1 a year for a poor man to walk round the parish church while the sermon was being preached, awakening those who were slumbering and ejecting any stray dogs that might invade the premises.

The will of Martha Burns Thomas, great granddaughter of Scotland's national bard, Robert Burns, was read in 1906 and contained the following:

I give the Poet's, Robert Burns, my great-grandfather's, original seal, chained in bog oak casket, as exhibited in the Burns Exhibition, to the Museum of the Burns Monument at Ayr on condition that the sum of £100 be paid yearly for ten years to my cousin, Robert Burns Hutchinson, of British Colombia, great grandson of the Poet Burns, as I value the Poet's seat at one thousand pounds, and I wish to secure it for Scotland.

Mr. Justice Joyce, presiding over the Chancery Division in December 1907, was faced with an unusual clause in a will. Arthur James Kenward devised half of his property to the Zion Congress for the resettlement of Israelites in Palestine. He named certain lands and said the people were to be selected by casting lots. The gift, which was worth between £2,000 and £3,000 was duly claimed by the Zionist Congress. However, his Lordship decided that the bequest could not stand, as it was too vague and indefinite. It was not a charitable gift, he said, as a scheme for settling Jews in Palestine was political. The property, therefore, went to the heir-at-law and next of kin.

In a queer and physically heavy will, opened in 1911, with fifteen codicils, Frank Work, father of Mrs James Burke-Roche, disposed of an estate valued at $4 million. The will was made in 1901 and altered whenever his daughter or her household did anything that pleased or displeased Mr. Work. The result was a bundle of documents weighing two pounds. To benefit from the will, Mrs. Burke-Roche's sons were directed that they must drop their father's names in favour of that of Work, become American citizens and always live in the United States. Frank Work's granddaughter, Cynthia, then married to Scott Burden, was to forfeit her share if she did not marry an American or failed to stay away from Great Britan during her father's lifetime. Mrs Burke-Roche herself was ordered to stay away from her first and second husbands, about whom Mr. Work was very uncomplimentary, or suffer the same penalty!

Property bequests featured in the will of the late Mrs Fanny Salmon, a London lady, who left estate of the gross value of £10,655 in 1914. Amongst her legacy were three cottages in Whitehawk Road, Brighton, each of which was adorned with a scriptural text painted in black letters on white stone inset over the doorway. Number 28, left to Mrs. Salmon's former servant, Kate Smith, bore the words, 'Remember the Sabbath Day to keep it holy.' Number 29, left to James Ezra James in token of appreciation for his work at Jamaica Road Congregational Church, had the text, 'How shall we escape if we neglect so great salvation' and Number 32, left to her faithful servant Mary Emma Hardwick, was inscribed, 'Prepare to meet thy God.' Other cottages in the row of ten bore the texts, 'God is love', 'Be merciful to me a sinner', 'Seek ye first the Kingdom of God', and 'God is our refuge and strength.' In her will Fanny Salmon expressed the desire that the persons to whom these premises were left should retain the scriptures over the doors and, if the cottages were sold, should make conditions with the purchasers that the texts may always be retained. At the time of Mrs. Salmon's death, the cottages, which were built in the late 1880s, were let at eight shillings and sixpence a week to respectable and hardworking tenants.

A curious bequest for the benefit of Christmas Day babies was left by a man who died in 1915. By the terms of his will each child born in the testator's native town on 25 December was to receive £5 as a birthday gift.

George Millar Bowman, of Logie in Scotland, who died in February 1916, left a personal estate valued at £4,050, and was the proprietor of a library which women and children were not allowed to access. Bowman was the tenant of the Logie estate and ancestor to Andrew Bowman who bought the property in 1750. The library consisted of valuable editions of the ancient classics and a valuable collection of engravings. According to the conditions of George Millar Bowman's will, his heir was prohibited from lending out books and was bound to always keep a suitable library room in the house. He was to allow free access to the neighbouring gentlemen there to read and study. The terms were exactly as those of Bowman's predecessors, directing that a basin of water and towel must also be provided, so that the books may not be soiled by unclean hands. The final stipulation was that women and children were expressly prohibited from having access to the library.

A curious will was settled in a Scandinavian town in 1917 when a supposedly poor gentleman died. It came as a great surprise to his friends and family that he had left 34,000 Florins. The 30,000 was signed and sealed in a package and marked to be given to the testator's native town. One thousand each was bequeathed to the man's three brothers and the final 1,000 to a friend with whom he had quarrelled. It was stipulated that none of the four should follow the body to the grave, a suggestion that the three brothers gladly accepted.

The fourth man, the quarrelsome friend, walked alone behind the coffin and forfeited his 1,000 florins for the sake of paying his final respects to an old friend. When the town package was opened a few months later, it disclosed another will, giving the 30,000 to any one of the four men who had dared to disregard the first stipulation and had attended the funeral.

Shocked by the news that Chief Manamba Kavula of the Buluba tribe was planning to hand over fifty of his wives to his young son, an American missionary named Miller headed off to the Belgian Congo from New York to dissuade the chief from his intention. Mr Miller, speaking in September 1926, said that he had learned that Manamba had decided to abdicate and to transfer half of his harem to his heir.

A bequest of his fortune to people bearing the surnames of Sharples and Hesmondhalgh, was contained in the will of Thomas Sharples of Cheadle Hulme, Cheshire, a chartered accountant whose estate was sworn at £120,727. Subject to certain provisions, he left all his property upon a trust for a 'Thomas and Richard Sharples Charity Trust', directing that the income from his estate should accumulate for three years, and the whole handed over to six trustees, 'all of whom must be legally entitled to the surnames of Sharples or Hesmondhalgh.' The net income from the trust in each year was to be divided amongst persons 'legally entitled' to the above surnames, born in England, Wales, Scotland, or Ireland, who shall be over 60 years of age, and whose total other income (including any of the wife in the case of married couples) did not exceed £40 per annum. The payments to the qualified beneficiaries were to be made monthly by cheque.

John Cusack, a grazier who died at Shean's Creek, near Euroa, Australia, in April 1925, left a curiously worded will, the last phrase of which runs:

'One hundred pounds shall be invested and the interest arising therefrom shall be paid to the parish priest at Euroa at Christmas and Easter of each year while grass shall grow and water run for Masses, for the repose of the souls of myself and my late wife and family.' The deceased left around £6,000.

The longest will on record was proven in 1925, when Frederica Evelyn Sitwell Cook left four large gilt-edged books containing 95,940 words. Mrs Cook and her secretary had spent several hours every day to will-writing, recording in minute detail all of her belongings valued at £20,000, with the bequests going to three different people. In stark contrast to this was the will of John Andrew Beck, an American financier, who left $300,000 in eight words: 'All my belongings I leave to my family.'

A will written on a twenty-four-inch square handkerchief was brought to light in 1926 by Mitchell Robin, a probate clerk in Chicago. Don Big Yee, a native Chinese who died in 1925, had written his will on the cloth in Chinese script and left an estate worth $25,000 to his American wife in Hong Kong.

A fund of £10,000 to enable young men and women, between the ages of 20 and 30, to go abroad to study industrial, social or educational conditions of interest to the co-operative or Labour party movements was provided by the will of Sir Arthur Dyke Acland, the former Liberal Minister for Education, in 1927.

In the same year, a curious clause in the will of the late William Joseph Murells, a leather manufacturer of Richmond, Victoria, in Australia, who died in June 1927, asked that any money that his friends otherwise would have spent on flowers for his grave be given to the poor as an offering for the eternal repose of Murell's soul. He left £1,000 to charity and £7,000 to his wife.

A member of a London law firm recalled many unusual cases of curious bequests when he spoke to a *Belfast Telegraph* reporter in 1929, saying: 'One man left his spouse the sum of one farthing, to be sent to her by post, in an unstamped envelope. The wife had to pay two-pence for excess postage, and a registration fee of eightpence because the letter contained coin and was not registered.'

Of course, freak wills do go before the law courts from time to time, but one curious document engaged the attention of the Supreme Court in April 1929. Peter E. Radcliffe was a retired officer of the United States Army, who died in 1928 in Victoria, Australia, leaving real estate in San Francisco valued at $47,000 and personal property in Victoria worth $600. As a preliminary, Radcliffe, who was 67, stated that he was of sound mind and not acting under duress or fraud. He then declared: 'I have no children, but in the event that any should claim to be such I hereby give and devise them the sum of one dollar each and no more.' Probate was granted by the court on the terms set out in the will.

In the will of Sir Francis Bernard Dicksee, artist, illustrator, and late President of the Royal Academy, appears a direction empowering the executors: 'In their absolute discretion to withhold from sale or destroy, if advisable, any sketches, unfinished works, or other of his productions which they may have reason to think he would not have desired sold or disposed of, as being calculated to injure or affect his professional reputation.' Dicksee died on 17 October 1928, aged 74, leaving estate valued for probate at £37,905. He was best known for his dramatic literary, historical and legendary scenes, and was also a noted painter of fashionable women which helped to bring about success in his own lifetime.

A will in which a man bequeathed his wife five shillings to buy 'a book in which to write down all the lies that she had told me', went before Justice Mann in the Victoria Practice Court, Australia, in June 1932. The testator was Edwin William Halse, a fishmonger from Dana Street, Ballarat. Halse's widow, Marion, lodged a caveat against the granting of probate and a compromise was reached, with one-third of the estate, valued at a gross of £2,600, be allocated to the widow, and the remainder to their three children when the youngest of which reached 25 years of age.

When Juan Boedo-Yanez, a naturalised British subject, died in Cheshire in the early 1930s, his will concluded:

> And finally my solemn and dying recommendation to my beneficiaries is to make work and knowledge their principal hobbies (following Francis Bacon, the great scientist's motto 'to take all knowledge to be my province') to control their purse, health, passions and temptations, to help to be kind to mankind, particularly the genuine poor, to cultivate love, to abhor intoxication, never to speculate, bet or gamble, but to be proud of the fact that whatever they possess, apart from legacies, are the fruits of their own labour – to protect our dumb friends, the animals, especially the much-abused cart-horse and costermonger's donkey – to lead a straight, clean, and honourable life throughout and to prepare themselves to meet a religious death.

A remarkable document, in which a man allegedly bequeathed to his wife one shilling and 'a pencil and a notebook to keep a record of all the misery she had caused him', was mentioned in a strange will suit before Justice Harvey in the Probate Courts, Sydney, Australia, in 1933. The document purported to be the last will of George Reekie, a farmer of Rose Hill, who died on 18 October 1928. Aubrey Seymour Kilduff, the defendant in the suit, was appointed executor. The document was admitted to probate and later Kilduff was bound over on a charge of forging the will. Reekie's wife, Lillian, asked for probate to be revoked and the will declared null and void.

Kilduff, a sawyer, of Granville, said that he had known George Reekie for twenty years. He said that at the end of July 1928, Reekie told him that his life had been threatened, and that certain people were trying to get him. At that time Reekie had not lived with his wife for ten months and had said he was going to divorce her. He told Kilduff that he wanted to make out a will but thought 'all lawyers were burglars.' Later, Kilduff bought a form for Reekie to fill in and told his friend that he intended to 'cut his wife right out.'

Aubrey Kilduff said he kept a record of the will, which he had since mislaid, and in August 1928 made out an exact copy on a form similar to the original. He then signed Reekie's name. Later, Kilduff's wife found the original will and sent it to the solicitors for probate. Kilduff said he saw it but did not look at the signature and was surprised when he was charged with forgery.

One of the most protracted pieces of litigation relating to a will was recalled by the death of Lady Houston in 1936. After the death of her husband, Sir Robert Houston, an issue was raised in the Jersey Royal Court as to whether Lady Houston had the ability to properly administer her estate. The court held a public enquiry into the state of the widow's mind and it was contended by relatives that she was under the delusion that she was being cruelly persecuted and was about to be murdered. Eventually the court appointed a curator to conduct her affairs. On 22 June 1926, a statement was issued declaring 'Lady Houston is mentally and physically normal', with the statement being signed by a judge and a doctor. Still a sick woman, having been attended constantly by specialists since her husband's death, Lady Houston promptly proceeded to petition the court to annul the curatorship. On 5 July in the same year, the court granted her petition, expressing the opinion that it would be unjust to keep her under restraint for any longer. Relatives of Sir Robert, who had been granted letters of administration, were generously treated by Lady Houston, despite the fact that the court decided against their claims. They were reported to have received a sum of £50,000 each. Attention was brought upon Lady Houston once again concerning the engraving upon her husband's tombstone, which read 'who died most mysteriously.' The widow refused to explain her reason for this action.

'Should _____ be alive, will someone shoot him in an instant and bury him for me please.' This was the strange codicil in the will of the late Jane Saunders of Nelson, near Riverstone, New South Wales, Australia.

Miss Saunders, who died in 1938, left an estate worth £200 and also left special directions for the future welfare of her cow, Daisy. It was to be given extra food in times of drought.

A year before his death, in 1936, Isaac Cooke from Surrey created a most unusual will in the form of a seven-verse poem entitled 'My Will & Testimony'. It read:

This is my one, and only Will,
Without a legal flaw
Which makes it easy to fulfil
Without going to law.

For I am leaving everything
Including all I've got
And all the future yet may bring
Unto my lawful lot.

To Alice Cooke my loving wife
For her to keep or use
Without reserve throughout her life
However she may choose.

My body also shall be hers
I definitely state
With which to do as she prefers
To bury or cremate.

And if my wife dies intestate
My two sons shall prepare
And so divide the whole estate
To each an equal share.

Now G.O.C and C.H.C
My sons I do declare
My two executors shall be
To see that all is fair.

I think this covers all I need
As far as I'm concerned
So I will this, my act and deed
By signature confirmed.

The document was signed and witnessed on 11 May 1935.

In 1939, a veteran of the South African war and member of the 11th Battalion in the First World War, Mr. E. Coleman, formerly of the Lands Department in Australia, put a clause in his will which affected those who attended his funeral. After the burial service, Captain W. Kruger, President of the 11th Battalion A.I.F. Association, of which Coleman was an executive member, announced to the sixty mourners at the graveside that the will requested that all who attended the funeral should have two pints of beer at the expense of the deceased's estate. On behalf of the executor, he invited all present to go to the nearest hotel so that the executor's liability under the will in this respect might be discharged. Thirty men went to the hotel and consumed 30 shillings worth of beer.

When he died in June 1944, Conrad Cantzen, an actor whose career had been liberally sprinkled with layoffs, was given a pauper's funeral. Then followed a will in which Cantzen disposed of more than $226,000 left to establish the 'Conrad Cantzen Shoe Fund for the Purpose of Supplying Footwear to All Needy Actors, Even if They Aren't Members of Equity.' An explanation for the strange bequest was found in a will clause which read: 'Many times I have been on my uppers, and the thinner the soles of my shoes were, the less courage I had to face the manager in looking for a job.'

When Justice Kingsmill Moore described John Rutter Carden as 'a picturesque character' in 1949, it was the two codicils in the deceased man's will that came as a shock to the High Court in Dublin. Carden, known locally in his hometown of Barnane, County Tipperary, as 'Woodcock' actually died in 1866, but it wasn't until much later that an application for an order for the distribution of £32,000, the dead man's remaining estate, was made by Garrett Gill on behalf of the Public Trustee which held the proceeds of the sale of Carden's freehold lands to the Irish Land Commission.

Mr Gill explained to the judge that Carden had served two years in prison for the attempted abduction of an English lady, Miss Arbuthnot, but had never married. He was believed to have suffered a broken heart to the end of his life, having never married or had children. Gill also explained that Carden had made two codicils after his release from prison, one of them containing an unusual provision. It was to the effect that if he died by assassination, his heir was to eject every Catholic tenant on his estate. In default, the heir was to forfeit everything. Justice Kingsmill Moore said that from what he had read, Carden's tenants had considerable objections to paying rent and he proceeded to wholesome evictions. 'He had turned his place into a kind of fortress and mounted a gun on the roof.' As a consequence, Carden had become a well-known target for local marksmen. On one occasion, it appeared that two men shot at him. Carden then knocked one of them senseless, followed and caught the other. He tied the two of them up with his stirrup-leathers and marched them to the police station. Both men were hanged for attempted murder.

The question of John Rutter Carden's rightful heirs was a complex one. The brother, Andrew, died in 1876, five of his six sons were dead and the sixth, Lionel Berkeley Carden, went to the United States where he worked on the railroads. Lionel married in 1889, had one son, James Hamilton Carden, and divorced his wife in 1896. Lionel married again in 1898 and had another son, Lionel Gillette Carden, who lived in San Leandro, California. A photograph from the family archives noted that the younger son, Lionel Berkeley had died in December 1920. A search for the eldest son was unfruitful and despite heirs to the estate being advertised for in twenty-one American newspapers, no satisfactory claim was forthcoming. Justice Kingsmill Moore said that in the circumstances he would make an order declaring Andrew Carden's two sons dead and found in favour of the great-nephew, Lionel Gillette Carden as entitled to the property.

Under the provision of a will made by Los Angeles real estate speculator Percy Martin, two women were bequeathed $300 a month for life and rent-free homes. However, they were directed to meet these conditions; never drink or smoke, remain unmarried and unengaged, and refrain from immorality. The two ladies named in the will were 48-year-old spinster Frances Miller and 50-year-old widow Helen Dill. Martin died in 1952, at the age of 76, and left an estate estimated at over half a million dollars. The will, dated 30 June 1950, named two trustees to make 'reasonable investigations' into the conduct of Miss Miller and Mrs Dill. In connection with each woman the will stated:

> Any and all payments herein provided shall immediately cease, and are never to be paid again, in the event that subsequent to my death she becomes engaged to marry, marries, or at any times lives with any man out of wedlock, or in any manner whatsoever engages in or pursues an immoral or otherwise socially not acceptable life, or makes any use of tobacco or alcoholic beverages.

Martin became a widower more than twenty years before his death when his first wife died. A second marriage ended in divorce.

In 1959, a Manchester surgeon left the bulk of his fortune to found scholarships at Aberdeen University but stipulated that the benefitting students 'must not undertake to use tobacco in any form.' However, there were many much stranger incidences during this period, such as the man who walked into a tattoo parlour requesting that his will be inked onto his back. The request was carried out in two sessions of over two hours each. It is believed that the legalities of depositing such a will were solved by the filing of a photograph. One long-term American prisoner wrote his will on the wall of his cell. In the ensuing lawsuit, relatives paid for the wall to be torn down and taken into court as an exhibit!

Throughout his married life a rich American's wife never allowed her husband to smoke cigars inside the home. Winter or summer the man had to step outside to smoke in the garden. However, getting revenge in his will, the businessman left his spouse $357,000 'so long as she smoked to the end five cigars daily.'

When Reverend Atherley Hill-Jones died in October 1961, it was evident that the heating situation at his former place of preaching was still very much on his mind. The rector left £4,000 and his house at Broughty Ferry to St. Catherine's Episcopal Church in Blairgowrie, Scotland, where he was situated from 1946 to 1956. A clause in the will dictated that the bequest, totalling £15,174, be used to remove the church's electric radiators from the ends of the pews and fix them unobtrusively to the walls within a year of his death. Reverend Hill-Jones also left £100 to meet the costs of the alterations, a task which was accepted by the Parish Council.

American actor George Raft became the unlikely owner of a small shoe repair shop in Brooklyn, New York, in 1936, when it was bequeathed to him in the will of an old Italian childhood friend. Raft, best known for his roles in crime films, was very fond of his old pal and, rather than selling the business, employed someone to take it on as a going concern.

James Callan unexpectedly became the owner of an Iron Cross, one of Germany's highest decorations, when a former Luftwaffe pilot died in 1969. Mr. Callan, who lived in Glasgow, was in the Royal Air Force in 1942, and pulled a German pilot from a Stuka bomber when it crashed. The men exchanged names and addresses but had no further contact until Callan received a letter informing him that the German had died and left him his war medal.

In 1975, the last instructions of Edward Horley to his solicitor were to buy a lemon with what was left of his estate after tax. The lemon was to be cut in half, with one piece sent to the Inland Revenue and the other to the tax collector with the message 'now squeeze this!'

The lift in The Woodlands old people's home in Penn Road, Wolverhampton, was always breaking down, prompting resident Lydia Beckett to leave £500 in her will to have it fixed. Deputy warden William Turner told the *Express and Star*, 'It was a most unusual bequest and a very kind thought. Miss Beckett's room was very near the lift, which did frequently break down. We have spent the £500 on repairs and now it works perfectly.' Lydia Beckett, who died in March 1976, left £68,000.

In August 1987, the bodies of Diane Shirley, aged 43, and her two children, Paul and Kathryn, were discovered at their home in Hampton Magna, Warwickshire. All three had been bludgeoned to death three days earlier. The following day, husband Ivor Shirley was found drowned in the River Avon, naked and weighed down with tractor weights. A coroner's inquest heard that Mr Shirley had been dismissed from his job as a senior field test engineer for Massey Ferguson two days before the killings. In a strange twist, it was found that Ivor Shirley had made out a will some years before leaving the whole of his estate to the Warwickshire Nature Conservation Trust and the Quorn British Butterfly Conservation Society in Leicestershire. There was a great deal of discussion over the bequest, with the society's chairpersons believing that the donation should not be accepted under the circumstances, and it was left to the solicitor to decide whether or not Shirley's will was valid.

In 1990, Scottish-born doctor William Gray died in Toronto, Canada, and left an estate worth $769,000 to the people of West Germany. It remains a complete mystery as to why the 93-year-old city-centre resident left his fortune 'to the German people through the German consul in Toronto.' The handwritten unwitnessed will did not specify whether Gray intended the money to benefit East or West Germany, but a fifteen-page written judgment released by Judge Robert Sutherland ordered that the funds be delivered to West Germany through a plan created by the government body in Bonn. Whilst there was much speculation about the medic's motives for favouring Germany over his country of residence, where he became a Canadian citizen in 1952, lawyers commented that it was possible Gray had studied there for a time and had perhaps become close friends with an unknown German. Several distant relatives of Doctor Gray's were left nothing in the will.

Former casino owner and property developer John Redhead, of Gate Helmsley, near York, had always been a bit of a joker but also maintained a strong work ethic. Apparently, John's dying wish was to have his ashes made into a pair of egg timers with one each given to the tax man and his bank manager as a final gesture that he was 'still working for them.' However, Ann Redman, the widow, refuted the request and instead had her husband's remains scattered in York Crematorium's Garden of Rest. She added that if she should happen to find a couple of egg timers that resembled ashes inside, she would buy them as a gift for the tax man and bank manager and have them suitably inscribed!

Chapter Four

A Family Affair

One of the most famous and unusual bequests of all time was made by playwright William Shakespeare, who didn't exactly compliment his wife by leaving her 'his second-best bedstead.' This also brings to mind the will of a man living just outside Birmingham who left the sum of threepence in order for the named person to buy his 'dear wife' a halter, which the testator hoped she would make good use of without delay. In a contrary will, Napoleon I made bequests of thousands of francs to his friends, regardless of the fact that there were no adequate funds from which they could be paid.

It is not unusual for a husband to leave all his property to his spouse with the proviso that if she remarries, she would forfeit the legacy. However, Governor Morris, the celebrated American statesman had no such plan in mind for his wife. Morris had married Ann Randolph very late in life, a woman who was much younger than himself, and lived very happily with her. He bequeathed a very handsome income to her and then provided that in case she married again the income should be doubled.

The longest lawsuit which ever took place in England regarding bequests arose in a litigated question respecting certain possessions near Wootton-under-Edge, in the county of Gloucestershire, between the heirs of Thomas Talbot, Viscount Lisle, on the one part, and the heirs of Lord Berkley on the other. The suit was instituted towards the end of the reign of Edward IV and was still pending in the reign of James I, at which time a compromise took place between the parties – thus embracing a period of 120 years!

A curious story was told relating to the will of a certain Peter Columbell, one of the old Derbyshire family, who for eleven generations occupied Nether Hall. In the will, all the testator's possessions went to his son, Roger, and was dated 20 October 1616. Some thirty years before, tobacco had been introduced into England and evidently Peter Columbell set his mind steadfastly against the habit, as the will contained a clause to the effect that his son must refrain smoking if he desired to retain the property. If caught by his brother or sister with a pipe in his mouth, Roger was liable to forfeit all claim to the estate. However, as Roger's wife was totally devoted to her husband, and the closest to his personal living space, he was probably afforded plenty of opportunities to indulge in the delights of smoking.

A will drawn up in 1664 became activated in 1915 after a family feud, when Prince Wolfert Webbert, of Holland, became disgruntled with his daughter, Princess Anneka, for marrying a non-royal. The Prince instead willed her share of his extensive overseas holdings to the seventh generation of her descendants. The Dutch government held the property in trust for the intervening years, waiting for Anneka's great-great-great-great-great-grandchildren to arrive. In the meantime, the princess moved to New Amsterdam, New York, where she told the story of the islands and her lineage to her family. From Anneka there were two lines of descent, children from her first husband who was lost at sea, and those from her marriage to Pastor Evaradus Bogardus of the New Amsterdam Church. In the centuries that followed, the lineage chart travelled back and forth between Holland and the United States dozens of times and was drafted in its final state at a cost of $4,000. Finally, Louise, Nona and Lillian, daughters of Augusta Gardner Keeline, the only child of the almost extinct line, learned that they were to be the heirs of property in Dutch Borneo.

In 1921, the Bismarck Tribune reported that one of the women, Louise Landrock from Omaha, was setting off to the Pacific where she intended to settle down as part owner of a $10 million dollar estate. For the previous five years Mrs Landrock had employed a representative in Dutch Borneo and the Fiji Islands who took care of her crops which included coffee, pineapples, coconuts and rubber plantations. In a letter to his employer, the overseer told of a man in his employ who had been killed by cannibals, but unperturbed Louise Landrock set off with a Malay dictionary under her arm and landed in Fiji as the seventh descendant of Princess Anneka.

One of the most unusual wills ever written was that of Joseph Cappur, a wholesale grocer in London, who had amassed a fortune worth a quarter of a million pounds by speculating in securities. Cappur had very eccentric habits, living in the same hotel for over twenty-five years but only ever booking his room and board one full day in advance. Joseph was renowned for always insisting upon sitting at one particular table, drinking out of only one cup and always using the same cutlery for meals. His habits of eating, sleeping and walking never varied, with his sole amusement seeming to be killing flies in the summertime. At seventy-seven, Joseph Cappur suddenly died and his will was found at the bottom of a chest of clothes, curiously worded and scribbled on dozens of old bank checks. It appears that the old man had detested his poor relations during his lifetime for one reason or another yet distributed every last penny amongst them in his will, save for £8,000 which he left to two nephews.

There is nothing quite like frankness when preparing a Last Will & Testament, which is exactly what Doctor Dunlop, one time member of the Legislature for Upper Canada, did in 1869, stating:

In the name of God. Amen. I, William Dunlop, of Gairbread, in the township of Colborne, county of Huron, Western Canada, Esquire, being in sound health of body and mind, which my friends who do not flatter me say is no great shakes at the best of times, do make my last will and testament as follows, revoking, of course, all former wills. I leave the property of Gairbread and all other property I may be possessed of to my sisters, Helen Boyle Story and Elizabeth Boyle Dunlop, the former because she is married to a minister who (may God help him) she henpecks; the latter because she is married to nobody, nor is she likely to be, for she is an old maid and not market rife. And also, I leave to them and their heirs my share of the stock and implements on the farm, providing always that the enclosure round my brother's grave be reserved, and if either of them should die without issue the other is to inherit the whole. I leave to my sister-in-law, Louisa Dunlop, all my share of the household furniture and such traps, with the exceptions hereafter mentioned. I leave my silver tankard to the oldest son of old John, as the representative of the family. I would have left it to old John himself, but he would have melted it town to make temperance medals, and that would have been a sacrilege. However, I leave him my big horn snuff box – he can only make temperance horn spoons out of that.

I leave my sister Jenny my Bible, the property formerly of my great-great-grandmother, Betsey Hamilton, of Woodhall, and when she knows as much of the spirit as she does of the letter she will be a much better Christian than she is. I leave my late brother's watch to my brother Sandy, exhorting him at the same time to give up Whiggery and Radicalism, and all other sins that do most easily beset him. I leave my brother-in-law, Allan, my punch-bowl, as he is a big gaudy man, and likely to do credit to it. I leave to Parson Chevassie my big silver snuff-box I got from Simcoe Militia, as a small token of my gratitude to him for taking my sister Maggie, whom no man of taste would have taken.

I leave to John Caddell, a silver tea-pot, to the end that he may drink tea therefrom to comfort him under the affliction of a slatternly wife. I leave my books to my brother Andrew because he has been jingling wally, that he may yet learn to read with them. I leave my silver cup, with the sovereign in the bottom of it, to my sister, Janet Graham Dunlop, because she is an old maid and pious, and therefore necessarily given to horning; and also my grandmother's snuff-box, as it looks decent to see an old maid taking snuff.

A sarcastic clause in the will of a Glasgow doctor who died at the turn of the nineteenth century read: 'To my wife, as recompense for deserting me and leaving me in peace, I expect the said sister Elizabeth to make her a gift of ten shillings to buy a pocket handkerchief to weep after my decease.'

The following English will is a far more polished and malicious jest by an unknown testator:

Since I have had the misfortune of having had as a wife Elizabeth M____, who since our marriage has tormented me in a thousand ways, and since, not content with showing her contempt for my advice, she has done everything in her power to render my life a burden to me, so that Heaven seems only to have sent her into the world for the purpose of getting me out of it sooner, and since the strength of Samson, the genius of Homer, the prudence of Augustus, the skill of Pyrrhus, the patience of Job, the subtlety of Hannibal, the vigilance of Hermogenes, would not suffice to tame the perversity of her character, and since nothing can change her, though we have lived separated for eight years without my having gained anything by it but the loss of my son, whom she has spoiled, and whom she has persuaded to abandon me altogether; weighing carefully and attentively all these considerations, I have bequeathed, and do bequeath, to the aforesaid Elizabeth M____, my wife, One Shilling.

A Mr Sergeant of Leicester made his bequests to his nephews, conditional on their rising at five in the summer months and at seven in winter, and occupying themselves for two or three hours in open air exercise, study or business. Illness alone was to excuse them, and in that case the missing days were to be made up in instalments adding hour upon hour each day after recovery. Another case with a strange clause was that of a Yorkshire clergyman whose will provided that his daughter should lose her inheritance in case she continued to display a 'depraved mind' by wearing dresses that left her arms bare up to the elbow!

A prejudice against moustaches was aired by Henry Budd in 1862. He left his estate, Pepper Park, to his son Edward, with a provision that if he wore 'moustaches' it would go to the other son, William. Budd then left his Twickenham Park estate to William with the proviso that if he wore moustaches it should go to Edward. How the sons arranged the matter is, however, not recorded!

Around 1875, a wealthy old lady bequeathed to her nephew, John Marsh, an old family Bible. However, being severely disappointed with the trifling gift, he never opened it. Some forty years later, in 1915, Marsh and his daughter were discussing the exact wording of a particular text and the girl opened the Bible to prove her point. She discovered £8,000 in bonds between the pages!

An old French cook named Durijot, who died in October 1884, left a most extraordinary clause in his will which threatened to give rise to a curious lawsuit. Durijot was a well-known Parisian cordon bleu chef, who was second in command in the royal kitchen in the reign of Louis Philippe and afterwards became head chef at the famous 'Les Freres Provenceaux', where he amassed a considerable fortune, which he increased by lucky speculations on the Bourse Stock Exchange. Dying at the age of 75, Durijot left a sum of almost £10,000 to his two nephews. However, the eccentric testator added the following clause to his will in his own hand:

> Wishing to be useful after my death to my fellow citizens and finding that epitaphs which celebrate the virtues of defunct persons serve no practical purpose, I hereby enjoin that instead of such an epitaph, a bronze frame covered with a grating shall be placed on a marble column over my tomb. On this column my name shall be inscribed, and every day my heirs shall see that a cooking recipe, legibly written, shall be placed in the bronze frame.

Monsieur Durijot added that he had left in his cash box 365 of these recipes, which he hoped would enable persons visiting the tombs of their relatives to carry away useful instructions in the culinary art from the cemetery. In the event of the heirs failing to carry out his instructions to the letter, the chef directed his solicitor to hand over his fortune to public charities. In consequence of this, the two nephews carried their case into the law courts, the solicitor refusing to put them in possession of funds owing to their refusal to comply with the peculiar clause insisted upon by their uncle. The nephews lost the case, and the judge ordered the money to be distributed as seen fit, as per Durijot's instructions.

One of the most controversial wills involving family was filed for probate in Jamaica by the executors of the estate of the late Horatio G. Onderdonk in 1886. The document covers sixty pages written by the testator himself but the value of the estate remained hidden, as Onderdonk forbade the filing of an inventory to prevent inquiring and curious eyes. It was believed to be worth several millions. Although Horatio Onderdonk was married twice, the will gave preference to the children by his first wife. Those from the second marriage were allowed to inherit under only the strictest of conditions. The eldest son from the second marriage, John, was entirely disinherited for 'insolent, defiant, calumnious and inhuman conduct.' Nor could any of the money left to others be used for John's benefit.

The second son, Francis, was bequeathed $30,000 on the condition that he remain practising law, but should he ever take up a different profession the money was to revert to his siblings. Francis would also forfeit his inheritance if he married before the age of 28, used liquor or tobacco, or dared to visit racetracks or gambling houses.

It was evident that Horatio Onderdonk deeply disapproved of the extravagant habits of his second wife and the unthrifty habits of their children. In his will, the gentleman said, 'A great deal of money was wasted on their education' and he feared that any money left to them would be squandered. He therefore made his bequests to them very small.

Andrew Onderdonk, the eldest son from the first wife, was made sole executor and received $100,000. Nevertheless, despite the generous amount, stipulations were attached to the sum. Andrew must marry an estimable lady of wealth, with any money passing only to blood relations, and he must be betrothed to wed before collecting the inheritance.

All the other children were given an equal share of their father's estate, with a penalty attached to any of the heirs who brought disgrace upon the Onderdonk family name. Finally, the will states that the deceased had intended to give a large sum to the town of New Hempstead, but that on reflection he had changed his mind as he didn't believe that the townspeople had justly appreciated his services to them.

The *Citizen* newspaper stated that probate had been granted on a will dated 18 June 1887, of a testator who died leaving all his residuary estate to two granddaughters. He appointed a daughter as sole executrix but bequeathed to her just £25, and to his wife one farthing which he directed the daughter to forward to her by post unpaid as an indication of his disgust at the treatment which he had received at her hands. The will read that this was especially in regard to the abusive language such as 'Old Pig!' and other names which she had used in circumstances which he explained, but did not think justified such opprobrious language. The will was evidently carefully drawn up, although not by a solicitor, and was duly executed by the daughter.

In July 1889, the Queen's County judge in New York denied a motion to open the will of John Sowden who died in Hicksville in 1875. The motion was made by the children of Sowden's first wife, whom he deserted in England where she died of a broken heart. At that time, he was known as John Ruttinger, but eloped with Charlotte Sowden, whose name he took. Under the will she and her children became the beneficiaries. John Sowden's estate was valued at $50,000 and the judge ordered that his will should stand, disinheriting his children with the first wife and making his unlawful wife and offspring the heirs.

A very neat reproach was conveyed in the will of an uncle who bequeathed eleven silver spoons to his nephew in 1891, with the remark: 'If I have not left him the dozen he knows the reason, the young scapegrace having stolen the twelfth spoon some time before.'

An eccentric old bachelor who died at Odessa, Russia, in December 1895, bequeathed around $2 million to his four nieces. However, the inheritance was on condition that they first enter into service as chambermaids, washerwomen or coal women for a period of no less than fifteen months. So legally binding were the instructions, that local police were charged with the duty of ensuring that the young women complied. It was reported that since news of the bequest broke out, the heiresses had received 863 offers of marriage!

A singular will made by a Belfast Presbyterian clergyman went before the Irish Vice Chancellor in July 1896. One of the provisions was as follows: 'As I abhor tobacco smoking, I have told my sons, John Richard and Samuel Marcus, that if they indulge in this habit they would forfeit £500 each to be divided amongst their sisters, and should they afterwards at any time begin this habit their sisters could sue each for £500.' The Vice Chancellor held the clause to be entirely void.

In July 1897, Phoebe McKay sailed for Scotland to claim a fortune left by her uncle who had died five months earlier. For the previous seven years, the young woman had worked as a cook in Flushing, New York. The uncle had been engaged in trade in South Africa, but Miss McKay had no idea that he had amassed a great fortune until she received notice of his death. Her information at that time was that her relative had left the bulk of his wealth to a Presbyterian church in Scotland, but soon afterwards learned that she had also been mentioned in the will. However, Phoebe continued working, giving the legacy little thought, until she received a letter from the solicitors who were settling the affairs of her uncle's estate. It directed her to leave for Scotland at once, saying that her fortune would be in excess of $1 million! Miss McKay told newspapers that her intention was to return to Flushing where she would take up residence.

William Olmsted from Cassopolis, Michigan, who died in April 1898, left $10,000 to Barnum's circus. It seems that he was an eccentric old man and did not live in harmony with his relatives. He decided to get even with them by leaving all his possessions, with the exception of a small farm to his wife, to the famous circus. There was no way to account for the strange bequest except the possibility that Mr. Olmsted may have received at one time free tickets for the show.

Requests by persons on the verge of death often put their children under great obligations. Often a wish is expressed that a relative must not marry or else he or she forfeits the fortune that is left, but occasionally a rather more shocking request is asked of those left behind. For instance, take the case of an Austrian tobacco king who, before he died, vowed that his son, who was to inherit a large fortune, should dress as a girl until he was 14 years of age!

Perhaps on the opposite side of the coin, John Maris Conrad Steinhelt of Folkestone, left £11,980 6s 11d and directed in his will: 'My portrait in oils representing me as a little boy in fancy costume be taken out of the frame and burnt.' One does wonder why, if Mr Steinhelt were really so concerned with the portrait being viewed in the public domain, he didn't set fire to the offending painting many years before!

In 1901 the *Philadelphia Record* reported on an eloping daughter's share in her rich father's property as follows:

Runaway marriages are becoming so common that it is interesting to recall a stern parent of this city who refuses to ever again see his only child, a daughter, who had offended him in this manner. Years passed, and the time came for his death without having brought to him any softening toward the girl. As he was a man of great wealth, considerable curiosity was felt to know whether she would be mentioned in his will or whether in death, as in life, she was disinherited. Bets were offered and taken whether her name would even be mentioned. After many and generous bequests to charity the following clause in the will was read:

'I give, bequeath and devise unto my daughter Jane the sum of five dollars, in order that she may purchase some strongly written tract on filial obedience.'

In the same year, a curious case brought before the court at Posen created intense interest amongst Polish nobility. Count and Countess Zbigniev Wesierski-Kwilecki were both of aristocratic descent but were only blessed with daughters, therefore another branch of the family presumed that they would inherit the Count's estates upon his death. However, in 1897, sixteen years after the birth of her youngest daughter, the Countess gave birth to a son. The disappointed family members refused to believe that a lady of 50 years old could give birth again and appealed to law courts to address the matter, citing false accouchement and the substitution of someone else's child in order to ensure the inheritance was kept to the Count's own children. A large crowd watched the court proceedings, which lasted eleven hours, as fifteen witnesses and a team of physicians gave evidence on behalf of the Countess. The child, then aged 4, was also presented in court for inspection. The presiding judge was satisfied that the Countess had indeed been enceinte and ruled that the plaintiffs accept the little boy as his father's rightful heir and that they pay all costs of the proceedings.

The indignant family of Juan Durand, a larger-than-life inhabitant of Colombes, near Paris, who died at the age of 60, contested his will in 1903 as it disinherited all of his relatives, leaving a fortune of $100,000 to a resident of Nanterre whom Durand had only known by sight. The businessman had amassed his wealth from the sale of vegetables and carefully invested speculations. After his death several flowerpots were discovered underneath straw in Durand's stables, each one containing pieces of gold, which it was rumoured that the elderly gent loved to rub between his fingers. Far from being a miser, 'Pere' Durand, as he was known, generously treated his companions to drink at his expense. On one occasion, a friend took up residence with Juan for fifteen days, during which time the pair consumed fifty-five gallons of wine! Residents of Colombes recalled one occasion when Durand was joyously drunk and had his friends carry him through the streets on top of a table. Counsel assisting the heirs insisted that the testator was of unsound mind when he made the will.

In December 1903, public attention was drawn to the singular provision contained in the will of the late David Jacobs, who was in the tailoring and clothing trade, and left property valued at £65,000. Mr Jacobs stated that he would disinherit his son, Julius, if he sought a seat in parliament, on the County Council, or continued to be a member of the Liverpool City Council. At the time of his father's death, Julius Jacobs was a strong member of the Conservative party and considered the will to be both capricious and detrimental to public welfare. David Jacobs left an annuity to his daughter and, after making other legacies, left the rest of his estate in trust for a period of twenty-one years in order for interest to accumulate, after which it was to be divided between his two sons and daughter, dependent upon Julius' conditions being met. It was reported shortly afterwards that Mr Julius Jacobs had tendered his resignation as a member of Liverpool City Council.

Mrs Martha J. Coston, widow of the well-known signal inventor, who died in 1904, made the following odd bequest in her will: 'To my niece I leave, in addition to the forementioned articles of jewellery, my rings stolen from me at my house on Staten Island. She will guess where they are.'

In August of the same year, Mademoiselle Dolores, as she was famously known to audiences in Honolulu, Hawaii, came into the possession of her mother's jewels after contesting the will which had disinherited her. The previous year, Mlle Dolores was billed to sing in Australia under the name Madame Trebelli, but due to everyone thinking it was her mother, with the same name, who would grace theatre-goers with her dulcet tones on stage, she changed it to Mademoiselle Dolores. Soon afterwards, the singer's mother died and many presumed that her only daughter would become rightful heir to the property. Sadly, however, the elder woman had become jealous of Dolores' success and left nothing of much value to her in the will. Madame Trebelli was a huge supporter of the Royal Academy of Music and bequeathed them a magnificent collection of French jewels. Disregarding the will, Dolores left

England and took the aforementioned jewels with her, causing a lawsuit to be instituted and a writ issued against her. Avoiding the British Isles entirely, Dolores continued to fulfil engagements in Europe and became increasingly popular. Managers vied against each other, some offering to pay the value of the jewels if Dolores would promise to hand them over to the academy, but for the slighted songstress it was more a matter of principle than money. Friends intervened on Dolores' behalf and a suitable agreement was reached with the Royal Academy of Music, allowing Mademoiselle Dolores to return to the London concert circuit with the retention of her mother's valuables intact.

Genevieve McLeod, of Chicago, was an artist, musician and short story writer, and felt perfectly content in her spinsterhood until a visit to Colorado Springs made her think twice about its implications. During the trip in November 1904, Miss McLeod was notified that she was the beneficiary of her late uncle Frederick Foss' will, but the sum of $15,000 cash was only to be made payable upon her marriage. A clause implied that should Genevieve insist upon remaining single, her legacy should be divided among other heirs. It was reported that the young woman was giving due consideration to the matter as she was desperately in need of the money.

A Frenchman who died in Constantinople, now modern-day Istanbul, left $45,000 to his nephew Monsieur D'Albi, from Paris, in October 1905. However, there was a condition that the young man cycled to Constantinople to fetch the legacy!

When Bloodgood Haviland Cutter passed away in 1906, his relatives were hopeful that the poet had died intestate, which would allow them to divide his $750,000 estate between them. Cutter was famous for being immortalised by Mark Twain as the 'poet lariat' in 'Innocent's Abroad' after the pair met on a five-month voyage aboard the *Quaker City*. Twain described him:

> He is fifty years old, and small of his age. He dresses in homespun, and is a simple-minded, honest, old-fashioned farmer, with a strange proclivity for writing rhymes. He writes them on all possible subjects, and gets them printed on slips of paper, with his portrait at the head. These he will give to any man that comes along, whether he has anything against him or not....

However, hope was lost when Cutter's will was found in a secret drawer of an antique cabinet by William Purchase, who had acted as the poet's valet for years.

According to the document twenty half-brothers and sisters were bequeathed a $5,000 life interest in the estate, the balance being left unconditionally to the American Bible Society. Also known as the 'farmer poet,' Cutter gave his vast collection of curios, enough to fill three large farmhouses and gathered on fourteen voyages around the globe, to the Metropolitan Museum of Art. In addition, a library of 5,000 volumes was left to the Long Island Historical Society.

In September 1906, Federal Judge Pollock rendered a decision in an unusual case brought before him in Kansas. It was the result of an alleged bigamous marriage by a man named James McLaughlin. McLaughlin was an old soldier who deserted his wife in Pennsylvania and, travelling to Kansas with a young woman called Annie Scott, married her and lived with her for thirty years, raising eight children together. Upon his death Annie Scott, who said she knew nothing of the previous marriage, applied for a pension and this in turn led to the discovery of the first wife. The court decided that the Pennsylvania wife was entitled to half of McLaughlin's estate, while his children from Annie Scott were awarded the other half, she in turn being entitled to nothing, even though it was largely through her efforts that the property had been accumulated.

It was reported in *The Topeka State Journal* in January 1907 that by the will of Doctor Broadbent, once controller of the treasury, the executors were directed to purchase an estate near South Newmarket, New Hampshire, and to alter the house to make two comfortable tenements for the occupancy of his cousin, Olive, and his niece, Cornelia, on the following terms: 'They are each to set apart a garden, sixty feet square, which they are to plant with currants, strawberries, thimbleberries, raspberries and other suitable fruit. Harriet, the child of Olive, is to post herself on the planting of fruits and to allow no weeds to grow up in this plantation, thus correcting carelessness on the part of her father.'

An Austrian army officer, who died around 1907, left the whole of his fortune to a nephew on the condition that he should never glance at a newspaper. The will stated that the heir, who held a government office, was far too fond of reading newspapers, a habit which the testator considered most pernicious. Three trustees were appointed to keep watch over the nephew and, in the event of a single infringement of the will clause, the fortune was to be distributed among other members of the family.

The late Charles Morgan, a wholesale stationer of London, left estate valued at £154,198 in 1909. He left the residue of his property to his wife and a quarter to his three daughters. However, the will directed that if any of the young women should marry a minister, of any religious denomination, half of that daughter's share should be retained in trust for her benefit for life, with the remainder going to her sisters.

In the same year, a wealthy New Jersey resident named William Grevell left fifteen pages of instructions regarding the disposal of his body. As a short, almost afterthought, in his will, the rather eccentric gentleman left the bulk of his money to his son and adopted daughter, on condition that they forever abstained from smoking cigarettes. Mr Grevell also left a large stable of horses to his wife Wilhelminia, on the proviso that no one but her coachman, her friend Adele, or herself took them out.

'If,' wrote Grevell, 'any reputable citizen sees anyone else driving the horses, and makes an affidavit to the effect, they are to revert to the estate and be sold by public or private sale, with the provision that they are not driven out of the county.' The money realised on the sale of the horses was to be turned over to the overseer of the poor, to be used for persons under his charge.

A third case in 1909 was that of the late Alderman Benjamin Minors Woollan, of Tunbridge Wells, and formerly of South Africa, who left the whole of his residuary estate amounting to almost £200,000 to his son. However, a condition put upon the bequest was that the son have a male child who attained the age of 3 years, and that the child was then certified by two physicians of good standing that it was of sound mind and body. Provision was made for the son and his family, but failing the fulfilment of the mentioned conditions, the residue of the money should be left to form a 'Woollan Trust' for the education and maintenance of waifs, for the provision of old people with relief income or shelter.

Finally in 1909, an extraordinary will suit involving the distribution of $10 million was decided in the United States against William Copeland Rhinelander, the eldest son of the late celebrated American millionaire. William was disinherited by his father for marrying one of the household's servant girls, Margaret McGinnis, in 1876. When his first wife died, he further estranged his family by a second wedding, which they also deemed inappropriate. William Copeland Rhinelander senior never forgave his son and, when he died in January 1907, bequeathed the bulk of his fortune to the two younger sons, Philip and Oakley Rhinelander. A codicil authorised the executors to pay William $100 yearly. The disinherited son immediately started a suit to have the will declared invalid, but after a hearing of less than an hour the jury rendered a verdict in favour of the executors.

An elderly spinster who died in Vienna in 1910 left a fortune of around £50,000 to be divided between her six nephews and nieces on the following conditions:

> The six nephews and nieces must all live in the house formerly inhabited by their aunt, with the executor, a lawyer, whose business it will be to see that the conditions of the will are strictly observed. None of the nephews is to marry before reaching his 40th year, nor the nieces before their thirtieth, under the penalty that the share of the one so marrying will be divided among the others.

> Further, the six legatees are admonished never to quarrel among themselves. If one should do so persistently, the executor is empowered to turn him or her out of the house and divide the share as in the case of marriage.

> The executor is himself forbidden to marry or to reside elsewhere than in the house with the legatees as long as he holds his office, to which a handsome remuneration is attached.

The old maid is said to have made this peculiar will because her nephews and nieces continually worried her during her life by asking her to give them money to enable them to marry, requests that she always refused. On the death of their aunt, the nephews were 24, 27 and 29, while the nieces were aged 19, 21 and 22.

In the same year, the will of a Spanish lady proven in London denounced the majority of her relatives and left them nothing but 'a bag of sand to rub themselves with.'

In November 1910 the will of an aged Cornishman came to light. It ran: 'I have not much to leave, but I bequeath my wife, Millie Marjorie, to my poor old brother Bob, together with the whole of my savings (about £500), on the condition that he (Bob) marries her (Millie) at the Cathedral of Truro within two weeks of my decease.'

If Robert refused, the money and other effects were to go to the first man who offered Millie a home. The testator added that he could thoroughly recommend her. 'She is twenty-four this 7th day of August, 1910.' The brother, Robert, agreed to marry Millie on 26 November and he asked her 'not to forget to bring the money.' By the date of the wedding, however, Millie was already on her way to America with the money and a more youthful husband!

That a wife is no relation to her husband was the gist of a decision made by Probate Judge Brown in Oakland, California, in September 1911. By the terms of this decision, the nine children of Jose de Gulart of Hayward inherited the entire estate valued at $21,000, while the children of his wife, who died some time before him, inherited nothing. California law at the time made the husband sole heir of the community property on his wife's death, and her heirs were excluded from sharing it. Both De Gulart and his wife had children from previous marriages, but as Jose did not adopt his wife's children their mother's share of the estate lapsed when she passed away. Had she legally been a blood relation of her husband, her children would have held inheritance rights on his estate. It was stated in court that only one similar decision had been given in the United States at that time.

An elderly waterman, falling ill on board his barge on the River Marne in France, called the two deckhands who formed his only crew, and told them he was dying. He also told the young men that he had disinherited his family and that they could share whatever money they found on the boat. When he finally expired two hours later, the men ripped up the old man's mattress and found a fortune amounting to £2,000 in notes, £280 in gold and almost £3,000 in securities. The family of the deceased were traced and found to be living in Belgium and were notified of their relatives last wishes.

The following paragraph was contained in the will of Mrs. Louise E. Warner, read in June 1912, and revealed that the once prominent Los Angeles woman was never reconciled to one of her daughters, who went abroad to live: 'To my daughter, Edith Alice Ogelby Titcombe Druse, living in the Champs Elysee, Paris, I bequeath $5 with which she must purchase the work of a reliable author on the wages of sin and ingratitude.' Her two other daughters, Elizabeth and Clarine Maude, received the bulk of the estate estimated at $250,000.

In July of 1912, the Denver (Colorado) Courts had to deal with an amusing case in which a millionaire spiritualist wished to disinherit his wife and family, in order to leave his money to spiritualistic societies and further the cause of psychic investigation. The plaintiff, a Mr. Thompson, formerly a prominent Missouri auditor, declared that he had become a millionaire by consulting the spirits and taking their advice on financial matters, and out of gratitude he wanted to leave his wealth to them when he died. Mrs. Thompson rather naturally objected and asked for a court order that the proper share of her husband's millions should be bequeathed to herself and the children. She contended that her husband's 'spiritual advisers' were evil spirits, but Mr. Thompson stoutly denied this and provoked roars of laughter by stating that the only bad advice he ever had from the spirits was when they advised him to marry. The court heard evidence as to the plaintiff's sanity and reserved judgment on this delicate matrimonial problem.

Fearing that the 'large sum of money' she bequeathed to her granddaughter 'might attract incompetent and designing persons to her,' Caroline Falconer Butterfield provided in her will that the granddaughter may never marry a 'McKeague', and that when she did marry the man that she chose, it must meet with the approval of at least four of the five trustees of the estate. Dorothy Bullard Smith was bound by this odd codicil in the Butterfield will which was filed in New York City in August 1912. She was, at the time, just blossoming into womanhood and had spent most of her life in London.

Six codicils in the will were devoted to the granddaughter and the problem of marriage. Dorothy was cautioned against a hasty marriage, advising that she consult her mother. She was warned never to marry a McKeague, although it appeared that the grandmother was a former friend of a Mrs McKeague. It was duly noted, however, that none of the three McKeague boys had ever been attentive to the young woman. A further stipulation was that if the codicil was broken, the money set aside for Dorothy was to go to six charitable institutions. Dorothy Bullard Smith was to enjoy the income from the Butterfield estate until she was thirty, when the full estate would come to her in her own right, unless she married not in accord with the directions in the will.

A bequest of £1 was all that was left to Mrs Alexander Peacock by her late husband, the eccentric millionaire partner of the late Andrew Carnegie. Mr. Peacock, who made a fortune of millions of dollars out of steel, merely said in his will, 'make only this provision for my wife for reasons well known to her, including the fact that I have amply provided for her during my lifetime.' Another curious feature of the will was that two sons and two daughters received the equivalent of only £20 each, while another daughter, Joan, was left most of the fortune. A secretary was given £2,000 and a valet £500. Two sisters of the dead millionaire received £10 a month for life. Friends said that they were not surprised at the freakish will of Alexander Peacock. His life was a succession of eccentricities, they asserted. He was a clerk in a Pittsburgh department store when Mrs. Carnegie became attracted to him by his courteous manner. She found out where he was born and the next day, he was summoned to

Carnegie senior's office where he was given a job because his father had been a fellow townsman of Mr. Carnegie. Years of wealth as a successful steel magnate followed.

On rare occasions, the act of disinheriting a family member can bring dire consequences, as was the case when Senor Galacia died in Spain, in December 1913. Leaving the equivalent of over £1 million, the elderly Senor bequeathed most of his estate to his youngest son. The eldest son, furious at losing what he considered to be his rightful inheritance, killed his mother and brothers, and then committed suicide by shooting himself with a revolver. The whole fortune reverted to the State.

William Rhinelander was disinherited for the third time in six years in 1914, because of his marriages, first to a family servant and then to a restaurant waitress. Serena Rhinelander, William's wealthy aunt, cut him off without a penny, as did his grandfather many years before, while his father, who passed away in 1908, left him the equivalent of £1,000 per year as long as he didn't return to New York. It was estimated that William Rhinelander's marriages had cost him over $1 million.

One of the most peculiar sufferers from the First World War was the Hindu servant of an American woman who lost both his father and brother in the Indian Army fighting in France. Apparently, the brother left what was considered to be a handsome fortune in India, but there were strings tied to his sibling's inheritance. The custom of their caste was that any surviving brother of a married man must marry the widow of the deceased, but in this case there were three wives. It is amusing to consider that when the man returned to his native country there must have been three pairs of arms greeting him in addition to those of his own wife who waved him goodbye!

A strange story was told by James Fay, a labourer, of Wallace Street, Woollahra, New South Wales, Australia, in his affidavit to Justice Simpson in the Equity Court in June 1917. The matter came before the Court as an application under the Testator's Family Maintenance Act, for an order that adequate provision be made for Fay out of his deceased wife's estate. James Fay stated that his wife died in the previous September, leaving a will under which her personal estate, valued at £400, was bequeathed to her brother, James Higgins, a farmer living in Tullamore, Ireland. Nothing at all was left to the husband.

The couple were married in 1911, and had no issues in their marriage, the judge heard. Fay had been constantly employed on the railways and had regularly handed his wife the whole of his fortnight's wages as he received them, being allowed by her three or four shillings as pocket money. James Fay trusted his wife with full control of their financial affairs, and she placed what money she could in the bank, as he believed, for their mutual benefit. However, Fay did not make any arrangements for protecting his own interests, as he fully believed the money that his wife was saving was to be used to purchase land for investment to provide them with stability in their old age. When Mrs Fay fell ill her husband nursed her and carried out all the domestic duties in the home up until the time of her death. James Fay said they had always lived on good terms. In January 1917, James Fay resigned his employment in order to enlist in the army but was rejected. His Honour made an order for the husband to receive £200 out of the estate, £50 to be paid at once and £150 when required.

One can never underestimate the importance a dying man might give to a seemingly trivial bequest, as was the case when United States resident Jacob Wile drew up his will in 1919. He left his daughter part of his estate and gave her permission to 'maintain the clothesline where it now hangs.'

Magnate Alfred Hayman caused a stir in theatrical circles when the terms of his will were published in 1921. Hayman's wife and family, whom he had amply provided for during his lifetime, were completely cut off in favour of actress Ann Murdoch, who was bequeathed over a million dollars.

On Christmas Day 1921, a young woman was disinherited by her grandfather in a codicil made just before he died. The well-known industrial magnate from the Midlands revoked provision for her in his will, stating:

As I have seen more of her, and especially on this visit, when she has shown herself without affection as regards her grandmother or without either affection or interest as regards myself. Although we have done a great deal for her, she has also avoided doing any of the little things I have asked her to do, and I am unable to see in her any of those sweet traits for which her mother, my beloved daughter, was noted above all in our family.

He therefore stated that he would leave her to be provided for by the family whose surname she now bore, in other words her husband's family.

It was reported in the *Evening Star*, Washington DC, in 1922, that a gentleman from the English town of Hastings left some $230,000 to be shared equally between his two children, a son and daughter. However, the son had left home some years earlier and hadn't been in contact since, therefore instructions left with the trustees of the will were told to presume that the heir was dead if he could not be found within seven years of the father's death. The man was found after a long search and was making a living as a taxi driver in London, living on the top floor of a Soho lodging house. His real name was William Rouse Upjohn, but had adopted the name of Sidney Upjohn.

As news of his inheritance was forthcoming, Mr. Upjohn said, 'I left home because it did not suit me to marry the wealthy girl whom my father had in mind for me, and I found it necessary to earn my own living without any assistance. I was then eighteen and my existence since has been a hard one, but I would not have changed it for the lazy life at Hastings.'

Sidney's brief record of jobs included cinema attendant, film actor, mail van driver, char-a-banc driver, omnibus driver and taxi driver, but by the time news arrived of his substantial inheritance, Upjohn was doing so well that he owned his own vehicle and was in the process of buying two more cabs.

Because they were disloyal to him during a divorce trial against his wife over a decade before, the late Augustus Hartje, millionaire paper manufacturer, disinherited his two children in his Last Will & Testament. Hartje took the document to court to file for probate in 1922, stating that Mary Louise and John Scott Hartje had spurned his efforts to gain their sympathy after the divorce ended in a victory for their mother. During the hearing of the case the son and daughter had clung to their mother and refused to acknowledge their father in any way. In the will, written in his own hand, Augustus Hartje wrote: 'In view of the disloyalty of my two children during the divorce trial, I do not want them to participate in my estate.'

When Anna Marie Bolchi Benjamin sailed for Europe in July 1923, it was under remarkably different circumstances from those which marked her arrival in America as a young Italian immigrant. At the age of 12 Anna took employment in the home of Park Benjamin, famous lawyer, editor and financier, and soon became a great favourite of his. When she reached maturity, Benjamin made Anna governess for his daughter Dorothy and the young woman travelled extensively with the family across the United States and Europe. It was in 1919 that Park Benjamin astonished his family by taking steps to adopt Anna Bolchi, causing them to try every means to stop the action but to no avail. In December 1919, the adoption went ahead, and Anna became a recognised member of the Benjamin family. A few years later, Dorothy caused great heartache to her father when she married the singer Enrico Caruso, of whom he heartily disapproved. With Anna being a native Italian, and the apple of Park's eye, the couple expected her to persuade Dorothy's father that the match was justified, but Anna failed to do anything of the kind. Despite Caruso proving himself to be the most devoted husband, Dorothy was unable to win the old man's forgiveness.

However, on Park Benjamin's death a few years later it was seen that he had done more than put Anna on a par with his natural children by disinheriting them and, with the exception of a few minor bequests, had left everything to his adopted daughter. The estate was valued at over half a million dollars. In his will, Benjamin was not satisfied with disinheriting his flesh and blood but also asked that instead of burying him alongside his family, Anna scatter his ashes mid-ocean between America and Europe. In a further twist, Arthur Louis Fullman, personal attorney to Park Benjamin and custodian of the estate's finances, became a close adviser to Anna and eventually the two formed a bond that led to marriage at the Catholic Church of Corpus Christi in London.

An interesting story from the royal household in Prague in 1923 shows that even those born into nobility are not necessarily safeguarded from losing their inheritance. According to the Central News Agency, Prince Edmund Karel Maria Schwarzenberg, a member of one of Bohemia's oldest nobility, gave up his fortune when he married Marie Pourova, a chorus girl employed at a local theatre. Their love dated a long way back. After the revolution, Edmund, second son of Prince Johann, began studying to become an engineer. It was while pursuing his studies that he made the acquaintance of beautiful Marie, who lived with her mother and sisters in a modest dwelling near Edmund's bachelor home. The Prince's family bitterly opposed the idea of a marriage and Edmund was sent to England in the hope that he would forget all about the young woman while studying at university. However, Edmund returned to Prague more in love than ever, causing his family to disinherit him. Sadly for the couple, a firm who had promised Edmund an engineering position failed to keep their promise, so the newlyweds moved to Eger, just outside Prague, where Edmund found work, enabling them to live very humbly in rooms.

Lucy Elizabeth Chaddock of Congleton, Cheshire, who had lived as a recluse for some years, left all her property valued at £17,295 to Margaret Taylor of Bath, as long as she did not allow any of her sisters or brothers or any other members of the Chaddock family to have one farthing. If this condition could not be complied with, everything was to be given to the Workhouse of St. Giles-in-the-Fields, London, for the entire use of the charity as long as it existed. The will was dated 23 July 1887, some thirty-seven years before her death in 1924.

Appearing in Probate Court in Paris in Augus 1925, Andre Fraysse flew into such a rage when his wife's will was read that he actually ate the document, destroying it in just a few swallows. Monsieur Fraysse was distraught at having discovered that his spouse had disinherited him but later faced prosecution for his rather extreme actions.

A testator's Last Will & Testament can often be subject to family feuds followed by rifts being healed, with a good example of a tumultuous relationship being that between one eccentric old gentleman and his children.

A dispute concerning the estate of Francis William Robbins Barham, valued between £60,000 and £70,000, was brought before Justice Hill in March 1928. Barham, formerly of Pembrokeshire, died on 8 December 1926 and left a will and a number of codicils covering the period from 1912 to 1922. The plaintiff in the case was the testator's only son, Cyril Hugh Sackville Barham, who claimed a life interest in the estate and stated that his father had not been of sound mind when drawing up the documents. King's Counsel, Roland Oliver, acting on behalf of the executors said that Francis Barham was 86-years-old at the time of his death and was undoubtedly an eccentric old man. It was alleged that his unsoundness of mind was a direct result of sunstroke when he was a soldier in India in 1870. There was no doubt that he was a most extraordinary man, the court heard. If anything happened to annoy him. Barham would write letters saying the most terrible things and could be awfully vindictive, although some said that he also forgave easily.

Among his family, Francis Barham was known as 'The Wolf', addressing his wife as 'Little Wolf', and his son as 'Wolf Cub.' Another member of the family was known as 'The Dog', his eldest daughter as 'The Cat' and the youngest daughter as 'Pullet.' The housekeeper went by the unfortunate name of 'The Hyena' and a companion was called 'The Panther.' Unfortunately for Barham senior, his married life was a failure, and from early on his wife taught the children to ignore and insult their father. In 1877, Mrs. Barham obtained a decree of judicial separation, causing Francis to resettle his property and cut her off. In 1895, he made a will in favour of his son, Cyril, on condition of him obtaining a degree at an agricultural college. Cyril failed to get the diploma and this resulted in the pair becoming at loggerheads once more.

Mr. Oliver, explaining the situation to Justice Hill and the attending jury, revealed that Francis Barham's letters displayed a continuous hatred for his son. One note telling him of an old-fashioned cure for toothache advising Cyril to kiss a donkey, and in order to rid himself of a cough, to embrace two donkeys. In the will of 1912, Barham said that his reason for disinheriting his children was that their conduct towards him had been abominable and unnatural. His son had wasted time with his mother after promising to have nothing to do with her. His daughter, Winifred, had entered a convent and became a nun against his will, although she left it two years later. After a reconciliation, Barham said that he was prepared to treat her as his child again as long as she did not correspond with her mother, a condition that Winifred refused to accept.

Occasionally, family ties become known only after the demise of a distant relative or forgotten link. Such was the case of pantry maid Leona Sigart in July 1921, when she received notice that not only was she the niece of the late Lord Aberdeen of England, but also heiress to a fortune of three million dollars!

Another will, taken to probate in 1921, was that of Emma Bogardus of Poughkeepsie, Dutchess County, New York, who died in 1915. According to the deceased's wishes, her $100,000 estate was to be divided between the American Tract Society, the American Bible Society and the American Seaman's Friend Society, but this was ruled invalid by Surrogate Gleason at Dutchess County Court after Miss Bogardus' sister challenged her sibling's last wishes. Mary Fisher, of Washington, made the charge that Emma had been unduly influenced by a letter written to her by their mother in 1883, seven years before the old woman's death. It was marked 'keep and read' and was given to Emma with instructions not to be read until after her mother's death. It read:

> Give whatever there is left when God calls you back to the Lord, either to the American Bible Society or to the American Tract Society, which is always doing the Lord's work. After Mary, you have no relatives to care for in that way. Try to keep track of her, and should she be needy it will be your duty to do something for her. These last words, my dear child, I speak to you from the grave and from the eternal world. I know the utter loneliness you will feel when you realize that your last earthly friend is gone from you forever. Therefore, I have written these lines both to direct and comfort you.

In court, Mary Fisher said that she had married Henry Fisher in 1864 and was disowned by her father when he learned that her husband had taken no part in the civil war. She never saw her parents again and did not see her sister until many years afterward. Justice Jaycox presiding over the trial concluded that Mary Fisher had not succeeded in establishing her contention that her sister had been unduly influenced and reversed the previous ruling, declaring that the charitable bequest was valid and Mrs Fisher would receive nothing.

A shilling and a cracked bowl left in an unusual bequest were believed to be an act of retaliation by gardener Isaac Lund, of Cowling, near Skipton, Yorkshire, when he died in 1928. Lund was described as very eccentric by locals and left £274 to the Cowling Parish Council, who planned to use it to create a children's playground. Having lived alone for several years, Lund married a widow with grown-up children who worked at Cowling Mill, the boys supporting the family and allowing Isaac to take his ease. The result of this attitude was that Mrs. Lund became fed up, removed most of the household goods and went to Keighley, leaving her husband with a cracked bowl, which obviously rankled him until death. In the same year a British sailor treated his wife somewhat disrespectfully when he requested his executors to pay her one shilling to buy hazel nuts 'as she has always preferred cracking nuts to mending my socks.' Perhaps the worst provision in that era was that of a London publican who, in some perverse kind of revenge, stipulated that in order to receive the property she must walk barefoot to market on each anniversary of her husband's death. She was also directed to read a confession that 'if her tongue had been shorter, her husband's life would have been longer.' The conditions were refused to be met and the wife received an alternative amount of just £100.

When the last will and testament of an Irishman named Doherty was submitted to Somerset House in 1930 it caused quite a stir. According to the document it named sixteen wives and fifty children as beneficiaries, all resident in Lagos, West Africa, where Mr. Doherty had spent most of his working life. Each wife was given a house from the £600,000 legacy and the children handsome monetary bequests. One of the lawyers handling the document apparently noted that each beneficiary was a native African, many with unpronounceable names running into fifteen letters. The will was written over several pages.

The search for the heir to Sir Thomas Brooke, who died over 500 years before, was still being pursued in 1931, although it was considered that the chances of tracing him or her were remote. One of his descendants, Francis Capper Brooke, who died in 1886 after having disinherited his son, left his estate in Suffolk to his daughter, Constance Lethbridge, who on her succession changed her surname back to Brooke. However, a strange development followed Constance's death. Her father left an extraordinary will, leaving out his eldest son, Colonel Reginald Brooke, who was still alive, and decreeing that as soon as his daughter died – provided she left no heir – the trustees of the estate at Ufford were to advertise for the rightful heir of Sir Thomas Brooke, a knight who lived in the fourteenth century. In the event of the failure to find the heir, the fortune was to go to Major Blois, brother of Sir Ralph Blois, apparently because 150 years before a Brooke heiress had married a member of the Blois family.

In the same year, a curious story was revealed as the result of an announcement of Montague Napier's will, which disclosed an estate of £1.2 million, on which the duties amounted to £500,000. The widow was disinherited and Napier's four children were left annuities of only £1,000, leaving approximately £700,000 in trust to Norah Mary Fryer, who was living in the south of France, with any remainder to be given to cancer research. In an interview with the *Sunday Express* a friend of the family explained that the widow was, at the time of her husband's death, returning from South Africa, and that the Napiers had agreed to separate twelve or fourteen years earlier. At that time Montague Napier told his children that they must not rely on his money but must learn to stand on their own legs and make their own way in life. Apparently, the siblings acted upon this advice, pursuing their various careers. One of the sons said, 'Dad is entitled to do as he pleases with his money. We do not care twopence.'

Norah Fryer, aged 50 when Napier died, was the widow of the doctor who attended the testator for many years and continued to act as Napier's nurse and secretary after her husband's death. She wrote all of his letters, including those to the children, to whom Montague Napier made occasional acts of generosity. Although a millionaire, the old man lived simply, as did Norah Fryer who had her own independent means. Mrs Fryer commented that she did not intend to change her style of living, despite the large bequest.

In July 1931 an American man appealed to the Lord Provost of Aberdeen to help him fulfil a strange condition attached to a bequest which involved a considerable amount of money and property. Edmond E. Lovekelly of Raleigh, North Carolina, in a pleading letter, explained that under his late mother's will he was left $90,000 and property in America, but with the proviso that he should marry and maintain a wife for a year. Edmond had been unemployed for some time and was penniless, and the only hope of his getting the money was to find his aunt, Martha Copenhager, whom he thought had left the States for Scotland. Lovekelly asked Lord Provost Rust to help to trace the relative so that she may come to his financial rescue.

A report from Belgrade tells of a man who was disinherited after a near fatal accident. Zhizoja Rankovitch, a 40-year-old peasant, had a row with his wife in March 1934, which ended in her throwing him down a well in their farmyard. The man was rescued, still alive but seriously injured. However, when Rankovitch's grandfather, a fairly wealthy landowner, heard about the incident, he immediately cut Zhizoja out of his will.

'Pah!' he explained, 'nobody who would let a woman push him down a well is going to inherit anything of mine!'

It was reported that a young man was left the equivalent of £30,000 by his uncle in Europe in 1935, but only on one condition. The legacy could only be retrieved in the form of firewood, which the nephew must chop with his own hands and sell by his own means. A second nephew was appointed to ensure that these conditions were fulfilled and should they be broken, the second nephew could lay claim to the bequest. Another will around the same time left a rather considerable sum to a relative on the condition that he never again picked up a newspaper to read.

An 82-year-old recluse found herself in a court battle over the $66,000 estate of her husband in 1937, for the simple reason that she refused to believe he was dead. Sophie Holtz was known as 'the last of the Israelites' to her neighbours and was a member of an English religious sect that declined to acknowledge death. Mrs Holtz was taken to court by her late husband's relatives because she refused to make a will. As a member of the sect, she deemed a will to be unnecessary because 'my husband is not dead. I am not a widow because my husband is only resting. He'll come back and see me. I'll never die,' she declared. For their entire married life the couple had lived in a barricaded house surrounded by barbed wire fencing, only leaving the property to buy groceries. Since her husband's death eleven months earlier, Sophie Holtz had only left the house once a week, a handkerchief held over her mouth to escape the air of the 'polluted world.' The old lady told Probate Judge Edward Command, 'I have spent thirty-five years in heaven already. When I joined the Israelite Church of England I was assured of eternal life.' A request was granted for the relatives to appeal on the will decision.

Doctor Daniel H. Sheehan, nephew of the wealthy Doctor Denis A. Sheehan, of Portsmouth, who died in February 1938 leaving £132,318, had twenty years in which to decide whether he would accept his uncle's legacy. Doctor Sheehan Senior, who was an Irishman and well-known practitioner in Portsmouth, after several family bequests, left the residue of his estate to nephews and nieces, and, in the case of Daniel, made the condition that to receive his share he must take up permanent residence in Ireland within twenty years of his uncle's death. In April of that year, after the will was read, Daniel Sheehan told a reporter, 'I do not know when I shall go. It will not be immediately.' Doctor Daniel Sheehan took over his uncle's practice in 1931 when the older man retired.

Because he married a waitress, Potter Dorsay Palmer, scion of a socialite family, was cut off from a $50 million fortune. Palmer made the announcement at the wedding breakfast in Sarasota, Florida, and then cheerfully toasted the bride, Pluma Abatiello, with a beer.

One of the most bitter family feuds brought to court was that of Isabel D. McHie's will, a millionairess who was once named America's most beautiful woman. After adopting Mme de Sevigny's famous sentiment, 'The more I see of men, the more I admire dogs,' as her own, Isabel McHie made The Seeing Eye, a foundation that provided guide dogs for the blind, her chief beneficiary. However, soon after the will was filed in 1939, a hoard of self-appointed heirs began a legal battle that was to last for five years. The first person to come forward was Isabel's own mother, Susan Mulhall, who was disgruntled over the small portion of money left to her and attempted to sue for fifty per cent of the total, citing a New York law which, at the time, held that a person with living relatives could not leave more than half of their estate to charity. Isabel's father, John, filed a similar suit, much to the annoyance of his wife who hadn't seen her husband for so long that she had presumed him dead.

Later a nephew, Robert Owen Beatty, a Northwestern University student, produced a will which left him the lion's share, but this was thrown out of court. Next came Isabel's ex-husband, Sidmon McHie, from whom she had been separated for many years. Sidmon told the Federal Court judge that he and his ex-wife had made a mirror will in each other's favour whilst they had been married, which was accepted, but the US Supreme Court reversed this decision and found in favour of The Seeing Eye charity. In the meantime, a series of different wills appeared from various parts of the United States, all naming Isabel's father as sole heir, which was hardly surprising as it was proven that he had written every single one! Finally, in August 1944, Murray Baron, trustee and attorney for the Fifth Avenue Bank of New York, Isabel McHie's executor, signalled the end of the legal wrangling by handing over a cheque for $123,205 to the dog's charity, just as the testatrix had wished.

Smoking, drinking and gambling were banned under the will of Rear Admiral John Weston, who was murdered on his farm in Natal Province, South

Africa, in 1950. The veteran left a total of £76,000 to his widow, son and two daughters, but stated that if any one of them should indulge they would lose their share of the inheritance. Likewise, should they challenge the terms of the will. Weston lived the life of a recluse in his later years and also banned 'loose sexual conduct, extravagance, ostentatious adornment, face powder, creams, paints, lip stain, nail lacquer, beauty hair treatment and anything beyond good soap and water, suitable diet and exercise.' The will added 'Any beneficiary who shall fail to observe the proprieties of good breeding, courtesy and friendliness in discussions, especially those relating to my will, or shall persist in maintaining an obviously unreasonable attitude, shall forfeit any benefit.'

Not only did American Christopher Janus inherit a third share of an Egyptian cotton plantation from his uncle but the old man's harem too! However, the four pretty young girls were of no interest to young Janus, and he left them to continue their lives near the Nile.

In 1953, Hollywood actress Virginia Field was left a 300-year-old boot by one family member and was delighted with the bequest. Apparently, it had been worn by an ancestor at the Battle of Worcester in 1651, and as a young girl Virginia had shown a great interest in the family heirloom.

Another strange bequest was left to Roy McFarland by Mrs Ida Jones of Kentucky, who left him the front doorbell of her house which he had rung with great fervour during his days as grocer's errand boy.

When Ernest Baker's will was read, in May 1960, local residents in Petersfield, Hampshire, were shocked to hear the bequests that the former butcher had made in favour of his nurse, leaving his own family in financial struggles. Having drawn up the document a year before he died, at the age of 93, Ernest left everything he possessed to Sister Ethel Broad. One passage in the will read: 'My son John has been intemperate in the past, and I consider that if I were to leave a lump sum of money to him, it would not be in his best interests. He receives the old age pension, and the income from his trust fund hereunder will be sufficient for his needs.'

A second son, Robert, was managing the family butcher's and fish shop in the High Street of the town, but under the will bequests, everything was to be turned over to Miss Broad, including the flat in which Robert resided. Ernest's youngest son was far more complacent about the terms of the will than his brothers, having made a success of his own business. He concluded that the nurse had been a great companion to both his mother and father and accepted that Ernest could decide to distribute his wealth in any way he wished.

Sometimes love really does conquer all, as was the case for one couple in Nicosia, Cyprus. On 10 March 1967, the adopted son of an American millionaire married the family chauffeur's daughter in a simple church service that cost him his inheritance. Mining millionaire Christian Gunther and his Cypriot wife Zena had previously announced that they were disinheriting their adopted son Theodore, aged 20, because of his determination to wed his childhood sweetheart, Christine Frangescou.

Contention of will bequests is on-going in recent times, sometimes with heart-breaking consequences. Cancer victim Malcolm Craig left an astonishing legacy when he died, bequeathing the family home to the Scottish National Party but leaving nothing to his widow. The shocking last wish was only revealed to the family when their lawyer formally read Mr. Craig's will after his death. Mrs. Craig and her daughter Morag found that they had been cut out completely and learned that the seafront property in Dunoon, Scotland, had been bequeathed to the SNP party with the residue of the estate going to Malcolm's half-sister, Florence Harris. SNP lawyers tried to realise their good fortune but discovered that widow Rita Craig still lived in the house. They offered to sell the family home back to Craig's widow for £34,000 and then dropped the price to £24,000 in a bid to settle the matter amicably. Mrs. Craig was quite determined in her counter claim and refused to leave the home that she had shared with her husband on Alexandria Parade. Malcolm, a former ship inspector, had become a keen cyclist since his retirement and made his will only a month before he died of cancer in 1986, aged 70. He married late in life, at the age of 64.

More recent cases of disappointed family include the children of pensioner Alexander Robinson, who died at the age of 82 leaving £276,000 to charity. He wrote, 'I hope you are disappointed. I detest the calculated approach of cultivating rich relatives for the sake of their money.' And also, that of journalist Anthony Hugh-Scott who added a clause which read, 'To my first wife Sue, whom I always promised to mention in my will: Hello, Sue.'

Another bequest was from a man who left a supposed friend £1 to buy a pint of beer 'in the sincere hope that while drinking it, he chokes himself.'

And finally, one man who died in 1990, leaving an estate valued at £1.8 million, ordered his wife be given 'one pound of pig manure, so that, to quote from Chaucer: 'She may be enshrined in an hogges turd.'

Chapter Five

Burial & Wake Wishes

History contains many instances of strange burial and funeral requests, with the romance of the heart of Robert the Bruce being one of the most familiar of them. The famous Scottish king wished that his heart be buried in the Holy Land and his followers set out to carry the precious cargo, enclosed in a silver casket, to Palestine. The sacred mission came to a tragic end when the crusader tasked with its journey was tragically killed in battle. Tradition states that the heart of Robert the Bruce was eventually taken back to Scotland and enshrined in Melrose Abbey.

Richard I, Duke of Normandy, commanded that he be buried under the porch of Fecamp Abbey when he died of natural causes on 20 November 996, 'in order that he might be trodden upon by all those who entered the sacred building.' This wish was complied with but a few years later an abbot had the body removed to the front of the altar. Richard's son, not to be outdone in humility, requested to be buried in the cemetery, but under the gutter-pipe of the church. However, in 2016, Norwegian researchers opened what they believed to be Richard's tomb but discovered that the remains were actually much older than expected and could not have been his. Records show that the body had been moved several times within Fecamp Abbey since Richard I's burial and the exact location of his present resting place remains a mystery.

Lord Ranulf Dacre, who died fighting for the Lancastrians at Towton in 1461, directed that if he was killed in battle, his favourite warhorse should be buried in the same grave with him. According to his wishes, when the interment took place in All Saint's Churchyard at Saxton, Yorkshire, a tremendous grave was dug. In it the noble warrior was buried, seated upright on his horse. This is the only case on record in the United Kingdom where a man has been buried on his horse. For many years speculation was cast upon the accuracy of this story, but at the end of the nineteenth century, while excavations for new graves were being made close to the reputed burial place of Lord Dacre, the pick of a dagger struck into a great bone, and upon a further search being made the skull of a large horse was brought to the surface. As this was found almost on the exact spot under which the body of Ranulf Dacre was said to lie, it was accepted as confirmation of the supposed manner of burial, especially as the horse's skull was found to be vertical in the soil. The skull was carefully replaced in its original position and the excavation site filled up. An enclosure of iron railings was provided for the grave of the nobleman, who sleeps in the company of his beloved loyal horse.

Numerous cases have been recorded of eccentric personages who have exhibited their oddity of character even in the arrangements for the final disposition of their remains. The obituary of *The Gentleman's Magazine* for 1788 contains an account of the funeral of John Underwood, of Whittlesea in Cambridgeshire. When the burial service was over, an arch was turned over the coffin, in which was placed a small piece of white marble with the Latin inscription 'Non Omnis Moriar (I shall not wholly die), 1738.' The six gentlemen who followed Underwood to the grave sang the last stanza of the Second Book of Horace. No bell was tolled, none but the six gentlemen were invited to the funeral and no relations followed the corpse. The coffin was painted green and the deceased lay in it with all his clothes on. Under his head was Sanadon's 'Horace', at his feet Bentley's 'Milton', in his right hand a small Greek Testament and in his left a miniature edition of 'Horace', lettered 'MVSISAMINS JU', and Bentley's 'Horace' under his back. After the ceremony was over, the six mourners went back to Underwood's house, where his sister had provided a cold supper. After the tablecloth was taken away, the men sang the 'Thirty-First Ode of the First Book of Horace', drank a glass of wine and went home about eight in the evening. John Underwood left nearly £6,000 to his sister, on condition of her observing his will, ordering her to give each of the gentlemen ten guineas. He also specially desired they would not come in black clothes. The will ended thus: 'Which done I would have them drink a cheerful glass and think no more of John Underwood.'

Also in 1788, the remains of Margaret, wife of Richard Coosins, of Gravesend, were deposited under a mural monument above ground in Ouxton Church, Kent. In the monument a glass door was fitted, covered with a green curtain, and having a lock and key. The coffin, which was mahogany, rested upon trestles and the lid was not nailed down. It was elaborately ornamented, and the lady was interred in an expensive dress of scarlet satin.

Surely there has been no request as uncommon as that of Major Peter Labelliere who died at the turn of the nineteenth century. He declared, 'The world is turning topsy-turvy, and it is only fitting that I should be buried so in order that I may be right at last.' Therefore, when the major died, he was buried in this manner in his grave. A little cubical stone marks his grave but lies hidden by thickets on the summit of the famous Surrey beauty spot, Box Hill. The epitaph reads 'Peter Labelliere, an eccentric character of Dorking was buried here head downwards, June 11, 1800.'

Clemenceau, the French statesman, left instructions that he should be buried in a vertical position and in his case the interment took place as though the dead man was standing upright. Another curious desire was that of a woman who directed that 'a bottle of chloroform be placed in my hands as soon after my death as practicable and before the closing of my coffin.'

From time to time, wills are found to contain very queer bequests, including that of an American who left a business colleague a pair of herrings a day for two years, together with a fish knife and fork!

An old lady, named Margaret Thompson, who died at the end of the eighteenth century, left one of the most extraordinary funeral requests on record, which was almost entirely taken up with directions for her burial. Margaret was a noted snuff-taker and was evidently determined to go to her grave with a liberal accompaniment of the fragrant dust. She instructed that her body, after it had been placed inside the coffin, should be covered with 'Scotch snuff.' The will went on to say,

> 'Six men to be my bearers who are known to be the greatest snuff-takers in the parish of St. James's, Westminster. Instead of mourning, each to wear a snuff-coloured beaver hat. Six maidens of my acquaintance (named) to bear my pall, and to carry a box filled with the best Scotch snuff, to take for their refreshment as they go along. Before my corpse I desire the minister may be invited to walk, and to take a certain quantity of the said snuff, not exceeding 1 lb. And I desire my old faithful servant, Sarah Stuart, to walk before the corpse, and to distribute every twenty yards a large handful of Scotch snuff on the ground and upon the crowd who may possibly follow me to my burial place. I also desire that at least two bushels of the said snuff may be distributed at the door of my house in Boyle Street.

An eccentric character named Pilkington, but better known in the neighbourhood as Squire Hawley, was buried in the early 1800s at Hatfield, near Doncaster, in his own garden amid graves of his rinderpest-stricken cattle. He was laid out in full hunting costume, including spurs and whip, and was placed in a stone coffin weighing upwards of a ton, which had to be lowered into the ground by means of a crane. Pilkington's old pony was shot and buried at his feet, and at his head were entombed the bodies of his favourite dog and an old fox. The deceased left the whole of his estate to his groom, John Vickers, on condition that the funeral arrangements were carried out according to his expressed wish. The Last Will and Testament stated that should Vickers fail to fulfil every last detail, the property was to go to the priest of Doncaster, for the benefit of the Roman Catholic religion.

From the 'Beauties of England and Wales', 1801, we glean our next instance. Mr. Tilly, once the owner of Pentilly House near Cotehele, in the parish of Calstock, Cornwall, was a celebrated atheist of the last age. He had by rote all the ribald jests against religion and scripture, but the brilliancy of his wit carried him a degree farther than is commonly met within the annals of profaneness. In ridicule of the resurrection, he directed his executors to place his dead body in his usual garb and in his elbow-chair upon the top of a hill, and to arrange on a table before him bottles, pipes and tobacco. In this situation he ordered himself to be immured in a tower, the dimensions of which he prescribed, where he proposed, he said, patiently to await the event. All this was done and for many years the tower enclosing its tenant remained as a monument of his impiety. The country folk were wont to shudder as they passed, as this local poem says:

The fear-struck hind with superstitious gaze,
Trembling and pale the unhallowed tomb surveys;
And half expected, while fear chill'd his breast,
To see the spectre of its impious guest.

An unusual case was noted by Brewer in his London and Middlesex, Vol iv, 1816. 'In a small apartment leading to the gallery at the west end of the parish church of Staines, are two unburied coffins containing human remains. They are covered with crimson velvet, and richly embellished, placed side by side on trestles; they severally contain all that is mortal of Jessie, the wife of Frederick Campbell Esquire, who died 1812, and of Henry Caulfield Esquire, who died 1806.' The volume does not explain whether the two deceased persons were related to one another, nor the reason for their remains not being interred in the usual manner.

On 24 March 1837, at Primrose Cottage, High Wycombe, Buckinghamshire, John Guy died at the age of 64. His remains were interred in a brick grave in the Hughenden churchyard. On a marble slab on the lid of the coffin is inscribed: 'Here without nail or shroud, doth lie, or covered with a pall, John Guy, Born May 17th, 1778, died May 24th, 1837.'

On his gravestone are the following lines:

In coffin made without a nail,
Without a shroud his limbs to hide;
For what can pomp or show avail,
Or velvet pall to swell the pride.

John Guy was possessed of considerable property and was a native of Gloucestershire. His grave and coffin were made under his own direction more than twelve months prior to his death. He wrote the inscriptions himself, gave the orders for his funeral and wrapped in separate pieces of paper were five shillings for each of the bearers. It was remarked by mourners that the coffin was very neatly made and actually looked more like a cabinet for the drawing-room than a receptacle for the dead.

The following is the convivial will of Samuel Purlewent, of Lincoln's Inn, who passed away in 1839:

It is my express will and desire that I may be buried at Western, in the county of Somerset, if I die there, if not, to be carried down there (but not in a hearse) nor will I have any parade or coach to attend upon me, but let me be carried in any vehicle, with all the expedition possible to Bath, so as the same does not exceed the sum of twenty-five pounds; and when I arrive there, I direct six poor people of Western do support me to the grave, and that six poor women and six poor men of Western do attend me to the grave, and that I may be buried at twelve at noon, and each of them to have half-a-guinea; and I hereby order and direct, that a good boiled ham, a dozen fowls, sirloin of beef, with plum puddings, may be provided at the Crown, in Western, for the said eighteen people besides the clerk and sexton. And I allow five guineas for the same; and request and hope they will be as merry and cheerful as possible, for I conceive it a mere farce to put on the grimace of weeping, crying, and snivelling, and the like, which can answer no good end, either to the living or the dead, and which I reprobate in the highest terms.

Codicil: I desire that after I am buried, there be a cold collation provided at the Crown, a sirloin of beef, potatoes, and a fillet of veal, with plenty of good ale, where I hope they will refresh themselves with decency and propriety. No friends or relatives whatever to attend my funeral.

In the nineteenth century there was still a great fear regarding premature burial, and quite rightly so. In 1871 French newspaper *Galignani* stated that amongst the papers of a wealthy old gentleman, who had died very suddenly in the gardens of the Tuileries, was the following note dating back to 1845: 'When I am dead, I desire that my face shall be covered with a pitch-plaster, closing entirely the nostrils, so as to prevent a return to life in the grave; and that afterwards a deep incision shall be made in my heart. I wish to be buried without any coffin and also desire that the earth shall be carefully trodden down on my body.'

When an old reclusive spinster died in Cologne, Germany, in 1863, her funeral was attended by an extraordinary number of people. On inquiry as to the cause of this honour being shown to a person of whom no one had ever heard before, it was found that in her will the woman had directed that everyone who followed her coffin to the grave should be given ten silver groschen (one shilling). It wasn't long before word spread of this bequest, especially amongst the poorest areas of the city, and crowds turned up to join the funeral procession.

In the will of celebrated Ukrainian composer and vocalist Hermine Kuchenmeister- Rudersdorff, who died in 1882, she directed that her body be buried in an oak coffin 'lined with zinc or lead, whichever is the cheapest.' The instructions continued, 'I wish to be buried in a chemise, skirt and wrapper. Everything must be of the cheapest character. There is a heap of stones by the lake of Lakeside. A hut must be built of these stones, and my coffin placed in it. A one-foot square of grass must be placed over my face. Captain Silas Sawyer will build the hut.' After several specified legacies. Madame Kuchenmeister-Rudersdorff left the whole of her property to her son, Richard Mansfield, at the time an actor living in London, on the condition that the money not be paid to him until he married, and that he not marry until December 1886.

In another odd request, an old man of seventy-five, who died near Tarascon, France, in May of 1882, left a clause in his will to the effect that all friends attending his funeral were to smoke pipes while following his remains to the grave. They were afterwards to adjourn to a café to spend in drink a sum of £12 specially bequeathed for that purpose. Three hundred men, headed by the mayor of the village, duly attended the obsequies, which took place without any religious rites. Every mourner had a lighted pipe in his mouth and after the interment the second portion of this curious testamentary disposition was carried out to the letter.

When Emma Markley died in September 1885, her body was buried at the Odd Fellows' Cemetery in Philadelphia, despite her express wishes that she be cremated due to a morbid fear that her body would be stolen for purposes of dissection. Sadly, her husband's limited means prevented him from carrying out Emma's dying wishes. A Philadelphia correspondent of the *New York Sun* gave the following particulars on Thursday, 10 September:

> Mrs Emma M. Markley, who was credited with being the heaviest woman in the country, was buried from her home, 526 Lombard Street, today. She was known to the amusement public as Madame Victoria. Her advertised weight was over 600 pounds and her actual weight about 550 pounds. She was born in Reading, Philadelphia, about thirty-three years ago, and was slim and delicate throughout her girlhood. At nineteen she weighed 90 pounds only, but from this age she began to gradually gain flesh. Between three and five years ago, when she made an application for an insurance policy, she weighed 280 pounds. Afterward her weight increased rapidly, until she gained the distinction of being the fattest woman in the country, if not in the world.

> A week ago last Sunday, while suffering great pain, she fell out of her bed. A number of strong men tried to lift her back, but failed. They placed her on a mattress on the floor, where she lay until her death. Her weight seemed to increase during her illness, and some time before her death measurements of several parts of her body were taken. The circumference of her arm at the biceps was thirty-six inches. Her waist measured sixty-two and a half inches, and from shoulder to shoulder she measured thirty-six and a half inches. The measurement across her hips was just four feet. On the night of her death it required the full strength

of nine men to carry her body from the second-storey front room to the parlour on the ground floor.

The body lay in a coffin that was probably the largest ever built. It was constructed of three-inch walnut planks and was stoutly braced on the inside with a dozen heavy iron bars. It was six feet long, forty-six inches wide and three feet deep. It was too large to pass through the door and was taken through the wide single window and carried to the undertaker's wagon by twelve stout men. There was not a hearse in the city large enough to contain the coffin.

Madame Victoria first placed herself on exhibition as a 'fat woman' in Trenton in 1876. She then made a contract with Adam Forepaugh's Circus, travelling with him for one season. Later she exhibited herself at a New York museum, and after leaving there retired from public life for a time after starting up a boarding-house for sailors. Doctor Samuel Ashton who had been Emma Markley's physician for the final two years of her life said that death was caused by haemorrhages and blood poisoning caused by a fall some weeks earlier.

On 16 October 1885, a very eccentric retired butcher known as 'Owd Bill' died at Chorley, Lancashire, aged 84. William Harrison, had very specific plans for his own funeral and how it was to be conducted, declaring in his will that carts should be used, and no relative was to attend the burial service wearing black clothes. Ten pounds in weight of sweets were to be given to the children of Blackrod town and twenty pounds in weight to his grandchildren. Finally, Bill requested that all those attending his wake have as much to eat and drink as they wanted.

Perhaps more concerned with keeping his memory alive than the actual funeral, the late Thaddeus F. Stewart of South Burlington wrote the following rather long-winded request just before his death in 1886:

I will to the Vermont conference of the Methodist church, $200 in trust to be kept at interest and the interest to be applied as follows: At each annual session of said Vermont conference, that body shall appoint one of its members on the first Sunday of June in each and every year to repair to my grave in Green Mount Cemetery or in any place where I may be buried within the state of Vermont, and standing at or on my grave, preach a full and free salvation to all that may attend to hear.

The stewards of said conference shall pay to the preacher that shall preach such annual sermon at my grave the sum of ten dollars. It shall be the duty of such preacher as may be appointed to preach such annual sermon to give due and timely notice of the hour when he will preach, to the churches and community that may attend.

A parish priest named the Abbe Beliard, living at Dole in France, died in May 1887, leaving instructions in his Last Will and Testament that he was to be buried with civil rites only, no prayers or church ceremonies on any account to be used. The friends and ecclesiastical colleagues of the defunct clergyman were, naturally, terribly scandalised at this news. Not so the Republicans, Radicals, Socialists and Freethinkers of the locality, who hailed the event with unbounded joy. The funeral was splendid and imposing, all the anti-clerical societies from far and near attending with their brass bands, tri-colour flags and ornamental banners. Prominent Radicals were even invited from Paris and Lyons to be present at the obsequies of the minister of religion who had declined benefit of clergy and determined to go to his tomb without being sprinkled with holy water and unaided by the prayers of local priests. At the graveside, a number of discourses were delivered and the deceased priest was held up as a model of rectitude and toleration.

John Redman termed himself a 'Citizen of the world' and some of the directions of his will, read in 1887, were:

My body to be buried in the ground in Bunhill Field, where my grandfather, Captain John Redman, of the Navy, in Queen Anne's reign, lies interred. My grave to be ten feet deep, neither gravestone, atchment (sic), escutcheon, mutes nor porters at the door; to be performed at seven o'clock in the morning. All my wine to be drunk on the premises, and to be shared by and between my four executors. Having then divided the bulk of his property between his nearest relatives, Redman continued: 'Holding my executors in such esteem, I desire them to pall all the legacies without the wicked swindling and base imposition that smell of blood and carnage.'

In his will, drawn up long before his death in 1893, saloon keeper Philip Jaeger from New York instructed that his body be cremated and the ashes scattered to the wind during an outing of the Sea Robbers' Fishing Club, of which he had been a devoted member for many years. On 22 July 1894, after Jaeger's demise the previous November, twenty of the club's members met in Clifton, Staten Island, to carry out his final wish, which was to be scattered on Romer Shoals, off the point of Sandy Hook. Lawyer Albert Goettman was on hand to ensure that proceedings were carried out to the letter and a cornet player accompanied the group. On board the club boat together with the canister of ashes were kegs of beer and a formidable picnic hamper. At noon, the ashes were distributed to the winds, which blew briskly that day, and a small cannon was fired to mark the occasion. The cornet player then struck up a German ballad, descriptive of the escape of a sea bass from the hook. The Sea Robbers sang loudly, the chorus of which was:

> It would no doubt have been fine to see,
> But it, alas! was not to be.

It was reported that the remainder of the day was spent in the pursuits of fishing, eating and drinking.

A rather more ostentatious affair was the interment of a French countess who died at the end of the nineteenth century. One of the provisions of this eccentric lady's will was that the equivalent of £40 be paid to the local band on condition that it played Chopin's *Funeral March* in every village, and before every inhabited house on the route covered by the funeral procession, a distance of twelve miles! The band earned the gratuity by playing the piece in relays, repeating it fifty-seven times in all. The musicians were reported as suffering from severe physical exhaustion by the time the graveside was reached. The deceased also insisted that she was entitled to wear the mourning colour of white, usually adopted for young girls in that period. She ordered the coffin, its pall, the flowers placed upon it, the hearse and the horses all to be white. Apparently, all of the conditions, with the exception of the colour of the horses, were complied with.

A French author who also died around the time issued even more astonishing orders with regard to the disposal of his mortal remains. 'Give my body to the Paris Gas Company,' was his last remark, 'I have always used my mental powers for the enlightenment of the public, and I desire that my body be used to enlighten the people after my death.'

His wishes, however, were not carried out. The Gas Company declined the offer of the body, and the mourning relatives were obliged to send it to the crematorium.

Consideration for her children and friends induced the widow of Sir Morell MacKenzie, the famous throat specialist, to insert a somewhat unusual clause in her dying wishes.

'I hope,' she said, 'that they will not shut themselves up, but go out among their friends, and visit places of amusement. I am not afraid of their forgetting me, but I want them to be happy.'

A wealthy and eccentric Swiss man who died in Moscow at the turn of the twentieth century, as the result of an accident, left behind him a novel will, one of the clauses of which directed that £1 a year should be paid to the editor of his favourite newspaper, 'to drink to my death.' The only condition attached to the bequest was that the toasting ceremony must take place on 1 January and 1 August every year until the editor's death.

The merriest funeral ever recorded was that of an Italian broker who, in departing this life, left instructions that at least 600 pints of the best wine should be doled out to all the mourners at his burial.

'If I order an ordinary funeral,' he argued, 'probably few will follow me to my grave, whereas if I order a merry one a crowd of poor beggars will enjoy a pleasant time.' His reasoning proved to be perfectly sound. Several thousand people flocked around the canteen wagon that followed the rear of the hearse. The procession halted every few minutes while drinks were served out all around. The 'mourners' were toasted and 'hurrahs' were given for the departed benefactor. The crowd sang comic songs and patriotic ditties, and the cortege took a full half a day to reach the place of interment. It is almost needless to add that the proceedings were totally devoid of ecclesiastical ceremony.

Herman Unger, of Boston, Massachusetts, who committed suicide in 1907, believed that his body would be revived in the form of some flowering growth, an idea that repulsed him. Unger therefore left instructions in his will that his body should be cremated, his ashes mixed with cement, and this compound to be pressed into a solid brick and then buried underground.

Two far less extraordinary requests were reported in the early part of the twentieth century. First was that of John Richard Farneux, a cycle dealer from Kensington Cottages, in Bath, who was found suffocated in his bed in November 1907, after having cut a hole in a gas pipe and allowed the fumes to poison him. Letters found in Farneux' possession revealed that he was disappointed because the government ignored suggestions he had made regarding the design and construction of airships. He left detailed directions as to the disposal of his body, which, he said, should be covered with salt and buried in a box inside a cave.

The second case came to light during an inquest in March 1920, in Croyde, North Devon, on Miss Margery Deakin, aged 49, from Liverpool, who was found dead at Baggy Point in Devon. Around her body were tied a will, some share certificates representing more than £2,000 and a quantity of jewellery in an old kid glove. The will stated that Miss Deakin wished her body to be placed in a fishing boat, taken out to sea 'without a gaping crowd' and buried off the Cornish fishing village of St. Austell, where she had spent many happy days.

Leo Tolstoy, the great Russian writer who died at the age of 82, wrote his last will and testament on the stump of a tree at his home in 1910 and requested, amongst other things, that he should be buried like a pauper. Renouncing his aristocratic lifestyle and privileged upbringing, Tolstoy left home one winter night and travelled south by train. At Astapovo railway station, a senior staff member took the ailing old man to his apartment where he called for a doctor, but despite applications of morphine and camphor the great writer died of pneumonia shortly afterwards.

When American-born actor and writer Herman Vezin died at the age of 80 in 1910, he left a codicil in his will directing the precise manner in which he wished his body to be disposed of.

> My wish is that my remains shall be reduced to ashes in the least expensive manner at the Golder's Green crematorium, near London, and in the afternoon, if, as I am informed is now the case, a lower charge now obtains than in the morning. That such process of cremation be attended by no formality or ceremony of any sort or kind, and particularly by no religious ceremony service of any description. That none of my ashes to which my remains are so reduced be preserved or kept by anyone, but that the same be spread as manure on the ground of one of the gardeners at the cemetery at Golder's Green. That no tombstone, urn, or other monument be erected or dedicated to my memory.

Vezin graced British stages for almost sixty years and died at his home at 10 Lancaster Place, Strand, on 12 June 1910.

Sometimes those who are close to death have very specific wishes concerning the way in which they are to be buried, occasionally citing the mode of dress for their corpse, as in the case of a woman in Rome who passed away in 1913. The will of Florence, daughter of the late William Ogle Hunt, and widow of Luigi, Marquis of Rocca Gradara, directed that she should be buried in her nightgown and a white blanket with a red border which her husband used to have. If the blanket was moth-eaten, her body was to be wrapped in a green plush table cover with embroidered stripes!

Unconventional directions for burial occurred in the will of Captain Walter Gordon-Cumming, who served with Bethune's Horse in the South African war, and who died on 20 February 1913, aged 56. The captain directed that if he should die in Great Britain his body was to be buried without a coffin on the banks of the Findhorn, near the Soldier's Hole, and a cairn of stones erected over him. He bequeathed £2,000 and an annuity of £52 to his nurse, Janet Tidey, and £100 to his servant, Ernest Jelks.

In July 1915, during the First World War, the *Matin* newspaper stated that a lady died in Marseilles and in her will the following remarkable clause was found: 'If I die before the end of hostilities, I ask that my body may be laid provisionally in the cellar, and that it shall eventually be interred in the field where the final decisive victory is gained. I also leave the whole of my fortune to the town which shall bear the name of this victory.'

One of the strangest burials ever known in England was that given to Wilfred Scawen Blunt, poet, diplomat, traveller and fierce opponent of British rule in Ireland, India and Egypt. 'I wish,' his will said, 'to be buried in the simplest manner, to be laid in the ground wrapped in my old Eastern travelling carpet, without coffin or casket.' These instructions were faithfully carried out when he was buried in Sussex in September 1922. Blunt's daughter, Lady Wentworth, his grandchildren and a few personal friends were present. The poet desired to be buried by men employed on his own estate and to the pallbearers he bequeathed £10 each. The will further requested that 'my nurse, Elizabeth Lawrence, shall accompany me and arrange me in the grave.'

Misers have, on more than one occasion, carried their characteristic penury into the arrangements for their interment. Edward Nokes, of Hornchurch, was buried in the following curious manner:

A short time before his death, which was hastened by excessive indulgence in ardent spirits, Nokes gave strict charge that his coffin should not have a nail in it, which order was actually carried into effect, the lid being made fast with hinges of cord. Instead of going to the expense of a coffin-plate, the initials 'E.N.' were cut into the wood of the lid. His shroud was made of a pound of wool. To avoid having to hire a pall, the coffin was covered with a sheet and was carried by six men, to each of whom, according to the directions of the deceased, was given half a crown. Also, by Edward Nokes' particular desire, no one who followed him to the grave was attired in mourning clothes. The undertaker had on a scarlet waistcoat and blue coat.

Another case was that of Thomas Pitt, a Warwickshire miser. It is said that some weeks prior to the sickness which terminated his despicable career, he went to several undertakers in quest of a cheap coffin. Yet at his death Thomas Pitt left £3,475 in the public funds.

The 5-year-old daughter of Mr and Mrs Bergson of Regent's Park, London, was buried at sea in October 1920. The child died of consumption and the unusual burial was by the wish of her mother. The body, enclosed in a white coffin, was taken by motor car from London to Burnham and then placed on board the boat *Island Queen*, which carried it fifteen miles down the River Crouch to the Channel, where it was lowered into the sea. The father and mother rode with the boatmen and an undertaker, who were the only people who witnessed the interment. It is understood that a religious service was held before the body left London.

Instructions as to the disposal of his body were contained in the will of Alexander Keller, of Gothland Villa, Isle of Wight, and also a resident of Edith Grove, Fulham Road, London, in October 1920. He directed that his body be placed in a lead-covered shell, provided with a face window of plate glass, such shell being placed in a coffin of durable hard wood, and his body kept so for a week, before the lid of the outer coffin be screwed down.

When the will of Elena Stanislaus Wolfskill Hulburt was filed for probate in January 1923, it revealed the deceased's fascination for everything purple. Mrs. Hulburt's will, which was read in court at Los Angeles, Southern California, and was valued at less than $10,000, gave minute details as to how she wished to be buried and the colours for her attire, including items to be burned. It read:

I wish to be buried in my dark purple plaid skirt, my wisteria waist with sailor collar and my purple jersey sport coat. I wish to have all my artificial bouquets, violets, orchids and all or any one of them buried with me. I wish that all my personal clothes – dress skirts, all of them, waists, ribbons, handkerchiefs, kimonos, stockings, slippers and my old red silk kimono and all my writing papers, envelopes and correspondence cards, scarfs, bags, purses, anything of mine that is purple or lavender or orchid, or any of those shades, to be burned – burned in a pile. If whoever this concerns does not do it, they will regret it!

When I am laid away, I wish you to put me away wearing my purple amethyst ring, pin, chain and amethyst pendant and other amethyst pin that are in my blanket I use for my pillow. I wish you to inter with me a purple silk bag with contents unopened, also an envelope like those from dry goods stores that is marked private – I wish these to be buried with me – and for no one to open them. These are my last wishes.

Sadly, it was learned later that the requests of the will were not carried out due to the fact that Elena Hulburt was buried before the document was opened.

Alfred Brooking, of Fort Villa, South Wonford, Exeter, who died on 15 December 1926, aged 77, left estate of the gross value of £10,222. The testator left his house and several other properties to his brother, on the condition that he pay £100 to a woman named Sarah Jane Bartlett, and a sum of £57 4s per annum for the duration of her life. The residue of his property he left to his niece, Mary Eleanor Smith. However, Brooking directed the trustees 'not to allow my body to be screwed down in the coffin until some surgeon has certified death and the cause thereof, and has opened the veins in my neck, and an open bottle of chloroform is to be placed in my coffin.'

Unusual directions concerning death and burial were contained in two wills published in August of 1927. The first was that of James Mott, aged 82, of Valentine Road, King's Heath, Birmingham, a retired brass founder who left an estate worth £19,088. He directed that two medical men should apply every test to prove that he was dead, that a strong dose of prussic acid should then be put in his mouth and that his body should then be decapitated. Prohibiting interment in any wooden, metallic or other kind of case, Mott asked to be buried at sea, wrapped only in sacking. His bequests included £300 for the care of animals and birds.

The second will that month belonged to Reverend Alfred Edward Alston, aged 64, rector of Framlingham in Norfolk since 1887. The vicar left £7,723 and desired to be buried in 'stuff vestment and appurtenances, with a small pewter chalice and paten' in his hands.

In accordance with her wishes, there was no mourning at the funeral of Mrs William Jones of Glandenys, Lampeter, Wales, in 1929. A member of the Quorn Hunt, the deceased's body was dressed in her riding habit and placed in a casket of polished oak. The hearse was a hay cart painted red, the estate colours, and covered in moss. The cortege accompanying the coffin included Mrs Jones' two favourite hunting horses, under the care of a groom who was also dressed in hunting attire. The cart proceeded up the slopes of a mountain situated between Llanfair and Llanddewi Brefi, with the burial taking place in a wild and desolate spot.

In September of the same year, a burial at sea under unusual circumstances took place in Ramsgate, on the Kent coast, England. Four women dressed in black, presumed to be a widow, her sister and two daughters, arrived from London carrying a casket. The little party walked along to the East Pier, where the widow inquired of a boatman if they could have a short trip out to sea, explaining that she wished to commit her husband's ashes to the deep. They then chartered a motor pleasure boat and, at a short distance from the harbour mouth, the casket was dropped into the waves. The women then returned to shore.

It is not unusual for the dying to be concerned about their own funeral expenses, but two sets of instructions published in wills in September 1930 raised a few eyebrows regarding their content. One man directed that £900 and a good luncheon should be provided at his burial, whilst the other stipulated that the cost of his funeral should not exceed £10.

The man who wanted the expensive funeral was Arnold Lupton, of Victoria Street, Westminster in London, a mining engineer and former Liberal MP for the Sleaford Division of Lincolnshire. He stated in his will that £400 be spent on cremation or burial and funeral expenses. 'If that is not enough,' he wrote, 'another £100 may be spent. If necessary, a new tomb might be made and a sum of £100 invested for maintenance.' Mr Lupton's ashes were buried in Sidmouth Parish churchyard with those of his mother and sister. He left £300 to his wife to pay her for the trouble of carrying out his wishes, saying, 'I wish her to offer a good luncheon at some convenient restaurant to all who come to the funeral.' Lupton's estate was valued at £5,896.

The man who directed that his funeral should not exceed £10 was George James White, of Laburnum Grove, Portsmouth, a retired commercial traveller.

In the same period an English vicar of the parish of Thurley stated to the *London Press* that he wished to be buried in a lidless wooden box, with a few bedside novels and a hot water bottle.

In May 1930, a prominent Australian doctor told of an instance where a dying woman in Adelaide tried to persuade him to allow her cat to be buried with her. The woman explained that the pet had kept her company throughout her long and lonely life and added that the creature would probably pine away and die after the burial of its mistress. The doctor refused to sanction the action, and the body of the old woman was buried without her beloved cat. It was adopted by some friends and, far from pining away, grew fatter than ever with its new owners and lived for many years afterwards.

Another incident happened in a southern suburb of Adelaide. A woman who was passionately fond of gardening lost her husband while he was on holiday in the far north of Australia. The man had gone on a fishing trip on an inland lake and the boat capsized, with him drowning before help could arrive. His body was never recovered. When the widow learned the tragic news, she had a plot in the centre of her garden dug the exact size of an adult grave. This plot was kept planted with bright flowers all year round and became the most striking feature in her garden.

There is something rather wholesome in the phrasing of the testament of Group Captain R.M. Pink, who died in 1933 after a distinguished career in the Royal Naval Air Service and Royal Air Force. After expressing the wish to be buried on land overlooking an aerodrome, he requested that

> Any funeral ceremony shall be as unostentatious and as little harrowing as possible… no firing party, or pomp or ceremony. I would like my personal friends just to say a quiet prayer for me. I request my wife that out of the numbers of silly little possessions of mine, which merely make additional weight to be cared round the place, she will make suitable gifts to my staff and friends who may desire to have them. Finally, I should like to place on record that I have been one of God's luckiest creatures, and that I can only wish that I had been more worthy of the affection lavished upon me from birth by my dear mother, father, uncles, relatives, and later by my very dear wife, my children, and my friends. I have had a wonderfully happy time, and I thank God for the boon of life.

Whether it be a burial at sea or to be interred next to a loved one, many of us have last wishes that we would like to see fulfilled. However, on occasion, some rather bizarre requests come along that do more than raise a few eyebrows. One woman in Southampton, in 1934, asked that a rag doll be placed inside her coffin when the time came, presumably as a kind of comfort in her final resting place.

The affection which a former Burnley woman had held for her late husband throughout her long years of widowhood resulted in an unusual scene in Burnley Cemetery in January 1935. Before Annie Swire, who was 86 years of age, died at Knutsford Hospital she pleaded with relatives for the cremation of her body and the interment of her heart alongside her late husband's coffin in the family vault. Mrs Swire's wish was fulfilled in every detail. Prior to her cremation at Manchester Crematorium, the heart was removed by a hospital surgeon and placed in a specially constructed casket. The casket was taken to Burnley and the interment, alongside her husband's coffin, was carried out quietly but impressively. Mrs. Swire, who was formerly a headmistress, had lived with her nephew, William Turner, at Lymn during her later years.

In his will, read in August of 1941, Sergeant-Pilot Robert Frederick Rose, Royal Air Force, of Colyton Road, East Dulwich, London, who died in war service leaving £1,163, stated: '£20 to be spent in a binge for members of 49 in the event of being reported missing; if I am killed flying, £20 to pay for a cheerful celebration by members of my section R.A.F. Reserve.' He left £250 to his wife to buy a trip to the Pyramids in Egypt and a new outfit of clothes, and also the residue of his property. Rose left his sports coats to Max Miller, the comedian.

The tomb of Daniel Heard is one of the most unusual in the United States. Situated on the edge of a Maine highway, far from any cemetery, it consists of a box-shaped vault made of hand-hewn granite. In this odd tomb, propped up in a wheelchair, is all that is mortal of Daniel Heard. This seemingly strange burial was at Heard's own request. For many years a helpless cripple, Daniel became fondly attached to his old wooden wheelchair. When he knew that death was finally going to overtake him, he summoned his family and expressed the wish that there be no casket but that he be permitted to repose in the chair in the centre of his burial place. His wishes were duly carried out, with the tomb erected on his own farm, located between the towns of Wells and Sanford. The corpse was rolled into the vault and wheeled about to face the entrance. It was then sealed and has never been opened since. In appearance, the tomb resembles an upright dry goods box, six feet in width and five feet in height. Plain granite steps, such as might adorn some old homestead, lead up to the entrance.

As the keepers of Portland Head Light in Maine were whitewashing the tower in April 1943, they had a visit from undertaker Lloyd Hay. Mr Hay produced a small box full of human ashes which he proceeded to scatter on the water, explaining that a man who had recently died requested that he be cremated, and his ashes thrown into the sea from the lighthouse cliffs. This was, to say the least, unusual, but nothing compared to some of the other strange burial requests in New England.

For example, George Leavitt, a veteran lobsterman of Casco Bay, who was very fond of beer and sardines, died of an infection caused by the nip of a lobster. In accordance with his wishes, a bottle of beer and a box of sardines were buried with him. 'I'll be hungry and thirsty by the time I cross the Styx,' he had said. Mrs. Martha Seymour, of Freeport, left instructions in her will that her cat be painlessly killed by a veterinarian and buried with her, 'So it can go to Heaven with me.' Quite the opposite view was taken by a Campobello, New Brunswick, fisherman who wanted his pet dog killed, 'Because I know I shall go to Hell and I want Spot with me to help fight my battles. He is a great little scrapper.' A St. John, New Brunswick, college professor had Webster's Dictionary substituted as his headrest instead of the conventional coffin pillow. A Great Island fisherman, unable to swim and who had always had a fear of drowning, died at the age of 82. Complying with his last wish, friends put a cork life preserver around his neck as he had told them, 'I may have to swim across the river.' A Woodford man always had a horror of being buried alive and asked that a cocked and loaded revolver be placed in his hand when he died, 'In case I should come to.' And finally, Lee Endicott, an old-time cornet player of Biddeford, asked that his instrument be interred with him because, 'Gabriel may want me to play in his band.'

A psychic experiment by a dead man, to knock a cylinder from the top of his coffin during his funeral, failed in June 1953. Cyril Thorne, a 53-year-old building contractor and student of psychic phenomena from Hollywood, who killed himself by inhaling carbon monoxide from a cylinder in a suitcase he was carrying, left instructions that some light metal object be placed on his open coffin in full view of the mourners, writing 'and I will knock it off if I can.' Doctor Hereward Carrington, of the American Psychical Institute, conducted the funeral service and the experiment. Forty witnesses waited in silence as Dr. Carrington said, 'Cy, we will now ask you to try to influence the object, as you said you would. Try, Cy.' There was another silent wait. The cylinder on the coffin remained motionless.

A Los Angeles millionairess who died in March 1977 was buried according to her last wishes after a judge considered her request to be unusual but not illegal. Sandra West, aged 37, left her $2.8 million estate to her brother-in-law on the proviso that she was dressed in a lace nightgown after death and buried in her blue 1964 Ferrari 300, both gifts from her late husband, a Texas oil baron. If he failed to carry out these instructions, the heir was to receive the much smaller sum of $10,000. Sandra West was lowered into the car with the seat slanted comfortably, packed into a wood and steel container, encased in concrete and then lowered into the family grave at Alamo Masonic Cemetery. A crowd of over 300 onlookers gathered to watch the burial.

A classic car fan took his beloved American Thunderbird to the grave with him in September 1994. When he was terminally ill, Bristol lorry driver Cliff Tanzell asked that his 1964 convertible be buried with him. His wife Cherilyn carried out those wishes by having the car crushed into a block and buried with her husband's ashes. Cemetery officials took a while to agree on the unusual burial. The car was Mr Tanzell's pride and joy for six years as he lovingly restored it, a task left unfinished because of his illness. He died in Bristol's Royal Infirmary in August 1994. At the time of death, a restored Thunderbird in top condition could fetch up to £30,000 according to experts.

The dying wish of Fredric John Baur was to be cremated and have some of his ashes buried inside an Original flavour Pringles can. An American organic chemist and food storage scientist, Baur patented the tubular Pringles container for stacked potato chips in 1971. He also developed frying oils and freeze-dried ice cream. Fredric died on 4 May 2008 at the age of 89 due to Alzheimer's disease and his family carried out the final request at his grave in Springfield Township, Ohio. The rest of his remains were placed in an urn and buried alongside.

Chapter Six

The Will of the Body

In 1720, a rather jovial Herefordshire farmer directed that 'as he was about to take a thirty years' nap, his coffin should be suspended from a beam in his barn but by no means nailed down.' On the man's death, the coffin was locked, with a hole in the side through which the key was pushed, so that the farmer might let himself out when he woke. In 1750, thirty years after his demise, the old gentleman showed no sign of waking and the coffin was taken down. A year later he was given a traditional burial in the local churchyard.

Eccentricity distinguished the will of grocer Henry Trigg in 1724, who directed that his body should be committed to the west end of his 'hovel', to be decently laid there upon a floor erected by his executors. It is said that the bones of Mr Trigg remained unburied in the rafters of his home until the 1830s.

A provision just as bizarre was made in the will of Jeremy Bentham, who died in 1832 and requested his executors to embalm his corpse, 'pickle it' and then dress the body in Bentham's regular clothes, so that it could form part of an annual lecture being delivered at a school of anatomy in Windmill Street, Haymarket, London. The request was carried out and the preserved skeleton and head were stored in a wooden cabinet called the 'auto-icon'. Bentham intended for the display to include his own mummified head, but after being placed under an air pump over sulfuric acid, the skull looked distastefully macabre and was later replaced with a wax head created by the famous miniaturist painter Margaret Gillies and fitted with some of Bentham's own hair. From 1833, it stood in Southwood Smith's Finsbury Square consulting rooms and more recently was moved to University College London where it sat on display at the entrance in Gordon Square.

On Wednesday, 17 March 1858 an inquiry of a very important public nature, relating to the scandalous sale of pauper bodies for anatomical purposes by the late master of Newington workhouse, took place before Mr. Elliott at Lambeth Police Court. Some days before a summons was applied for by Mr. Chester, clerk and solicitor to the guardians of the parish of St. Mary, Newington, against Alfred Feist, for having 'unlawfully taken away the dead body of a certain female, named Mary Whitehead, with intent to sell and dispose of it for gain and profit', and that summons having been returnable at 1 o'clock on Wednesday, 17 March, the court at that hour was crowded to excess. The following witnesses were examined in support of the charge.

Louisa Mixer said that she was the wife of John Mixer, and resided at 30 Pitt Street, Southwark. On 6 October 1857, she visited her mother, Mary Whitehead, at the Newington workhouse, where Mary remained up to the time of her death on 30 January. Louisa called at the workhouse on the day before her mother's demise and on the morning of her death. She asked Mr Feist if more than one person could follow her mother to the grave, and he replied that they could on the payment of one shilling and sixpence each. She also asked him when her mother would be buried, and Feist replied on the following Saturday or Monday, and referred her to the parish undertaker, Mr. Hogg. The funeral was arranged for the Monday and, on that day, Louisa Mixer accompanied her sister to the workhouse, where they were shown to the mortuary in the presence of both Feist and Hogg. Alfred Feist took the lid off one of the coffins at the request of the women, telling them not to go too near, and they witnessed the dead body of Mary Whitehead. Feist then told them to withdraw to the waiting-room and half an hour later told them to get in the coach, which they did, following the hearse to Mile End. At the graveyard two coffins were buried and both women were under the impression that one of them contained their mother's remains.

At this point the court called forward Robert Hogg, the undertaker, and showed him a bill in his own handwriting. These were the quarterly accounts from the beginning of the year for the burials undertaken by him for the parish of Newington. In that bill there was a charge for the burial of Mary Whitehead, even though he had removed the body from the workhouse and taken it to Guy's Hospital on 2 February.

Hogg told the court that from instructions received from Alfred Feist he received the necessary document from the inspector under the Anatomy Act for the removal of the body of Mary Whitehead to Guy's Hospital, having first carried the documents from Feist to the inspector. Mr. Robinson, prosecuting asked:

'Now, seeing these documents, and supposing it was a sham funeral, and after taking the body to Guy's Hospital, cannot you tell the court what was in the coffin?'

Hogg: 'I cannot. There might have been two bodies in the hearse when there ought to have been three. It was my duty to see the right number of coffins come out of the deadhouse.'

Robinson: 'What do you mean by telling us that there might have been three bodies that ought to have come out, when only two really came, and that the third was left for anatomical purposes?'

Hogg: 'I never go to the cemetery with parochial funerals. I leave it to my men, who get the names of the outdoor paupers from me, those of the indoor paupers from the master of the workhouse. When I have gone down of a morning and found four or five to be buried Mr. Feist has told me to leave certain of them.'

Robinson: 'Have you ever known an instance where some body has been substituted for another in the deadhouse?'

Hogg: 'I have, but I cannot say in how many instances.'

Robinson: 'You know they substitute bodies, or parts of bodies, for others – how often?'

Hogg: 'Ten or fifteen times within the last twelve months.'

Robinson: 'On these occasions has Mr. Feist been with you?'

Hogg: 'Yes. It was done by direction of Mr. Feist, but there were bodies or parts of bodies brought from the hospital for the purpose of interment.'

Mr. Robinson here remarked that it was the duty of the hospital to send the remains of bodies dissected direct to the place of interment, and not to the workhouse.

The witness then admitted that the coffins sent by him to the hospital were precisely the same as those furnished to the workhouse. When the bodies or parts of bodies were put into the coffins at the hospital, it was nailed down before he took it from there to the workhouse. Hogg insisted that he had never received any money from Alfred Feist and under cross-examination said that the removal of bodies was under warrant of the medical inspector. In this instance Feist was allowed bail at a cost of £40, and ordered to appear the following day.

In a Manchester museum, in the 1800s, lay the mummy of a lady in a glass case, labelled 'The Mummy of Miss Beswick.' It is highly probable that these are the remains referred to by Thomas de Quincey in his Autobiographic Sketches, 1868. He said that it was then in the possession of Mr Charles White FRS, an eminent Manchester surgeon and described it as that of a lady who had been attended medically for some years by Mr White and had owed much alleviation of her sufferings to his inventive skill'. She had therefore felt herself called upon to memorialise her gratitude by a very large bequest – not less, he had heard, than £25,000, but with the condition annexed to the gift, that she should be embalmed as perfectly as the resources of the art in London and Paris could accomplish, and that once a year Mr White, accompanied by two witnesses of credit, should withdraw the veil from her face. The lady was placed in a common English clock-case, having the usual glass face. On the death of Charles White in 1813, the greater part of his anatomical collection was presented to the museum of the Manchester Lying-In Hospital by his son and contained the mummy of Miss Beswick.

'Fantastic' is the only word for the will of another eminent woman of the nineteenth century, Harriet Martineau. She willed her body away in parts. It is said that when he heard of her intention James Payn, the novelist, endeavoured to stop her. 'I shall leave my ears,' she told him, 'to Toynbee, the aurist.' But here her surgeon chipped in: 'If you do that,' he said, 'your other legacy will be worthless.' For she had forgotten she had left her head to the Phrenological Society, and £10 to the surgeon for cutting it off!

In 1871, Mr Sanborn of Medford, Massachusetts, bequeathed his body to Professor Agassiz and his colleague Oliver Wendell Holmes, requesting that it should 'be prepared in the most scientific manner known to anatomic science' and placed in the museum at Harvard. He also directed that his skin should be made into two drumheads to be presented to his 'friend and patriotic fellow citizen, Warren Simpson,' on condition that he beat on them the national air of 'Yankee Doodle' at the foot of the monument on Bunker Hill at sunrise every 17th of June. On one drumhead was to be inscribed Pope's 'Universal Prayer' and on the other the Declaration of Independence. It is unclear as to what extent Sanborn's wishes were adhered to.

Thomas Hobson, at 78 years of age, committed suicide by hanging in Prestwich Union Workhouse in May 1881 and left a will in which he bequeathed his body to a Dr Titler of Lord Street, Cheetham, near Manchester. The document stated, 'In gratitude for his kindness and urbanity when under his treatment as a patient.' Should the doctor decline, the School of Anatomy at Owens College, Manchester, was selected. As to his motives for taking this unusual step, Hobson wrote: 'For the satisfaction of the curious:

1. I don't believe in the resurrection of the body.
2. I feel a repugnance at being put into a wooden box and stuck in a clay hole to rot and fester and be a unit in generating a nuisance injurious to the living.
3. It may be perhaps of some use and help, be it ever so little, towards the amelioration of mankind.

The deceased closed the unusual will hoping that his wishes would be carried out in their integrity and declaring that 'I shall ever remain a well-wisher of mankind.' However, both Doctor Titler and the Owens College authorities declined the responsibility of the bequest.

Doctor Everett Wagner, a physician living near Elmonton, Kentucky, was a man of peculiar habits and spent most of his life shunned by relatives. However, when the old man became ill in 1888, and evidently didn't have long to live, family appeared and started dropping hints that they would like to receive some small 'trinket' to remind them of their 'beloved Everett' after he had passed. On account of their former disinterest and treatment of him, Wagner made the following last will and testament: 'First, I give to my beloved brother, Napoleon Bonaparte Wagner, my left hand and arm. Second, I give to my beloved brother, George W. Wagner, my right hand and arm.'

Similarly, he disposed of eyes, nose and other body parts to other relations and stated that should anyone in the family be forgotten, the dissecting surgeon was to distribute further organs on a first come first served basis!

In 1889 the *Evening Tribune* (Pawtucket) reported that an English lover who had been jilted wrote out his will just before committing suicide. In it he directed that his body should be boiled down and all the fat extracted from it used for the purpose of making a candle. This was to be presented to his sweetheart together with a letter, the appointed delivery time at night, so that she could use the candle to read the reasons for his death. Apparently, the unnamed executor carried out these wishes to the letter!

An incredible incident occurred at the New York Medical College in September 1890, when a messenger arrived in the dissecting room of Professor James Walsh, announcing that a lady wished to see him. As it was a most unusual request, and the professor being unable to think which female acquaintance might be anxious to see him at his place of work, he bid her come in. A tall, angular woman, well past middle-age appeared. 'You are the superintendent here?' she asked, and without waiting for an answer added, 'I have a body at home to dispose of, and I am told you buy such things here.'

This was indeed in the professor's line of business, and he eagerly caught on to the opportunity.

'Yes, we buy bodies here,' he said, 'but they must be of the right kind – no mutilation, no infection, nothing of that sort, you know.'

'Oh', the woman replied, 'this body is all right, and I will be responsible for it. You see, my children are hungry and it will not do to starve while one can get bread. I do hate seeing them dying before my very eyes, while I am able to give them no help.'

'Perhaps then it is the body of one of your children you are going to sell,' interposed Professor Walsh, 'In that case it would be of no use, as we require adults alone.'

'On that score you may rest easy. It is not my child's body, but my own, for I can get bread now no other way, and you can have it as soon as I receive the money, for I can die easy when I know the little ones have something to eat.'

The professor looked up into the face of the distraught mother and immediately saw a look of earnestness and truth that went down into the very depths of his heart. Professor Walsh drew a $5 bill from his pocket and placed it in the poor woman's hands. She naturally overwhelmed the doctor with her thanks.

Professor Hoppe, an academic from the University of Basle, left his heirs protesting against bequests in the old man's will when he left half a million francs to a scientific society. The money was to be prepared as prizes for research into the human soul, a subject that the professor had studied and was fascinated by. Understandably, Hoppe's family threatened legal action against the society should they accept the funds and with representatives advising that the body stood little chance in court the bequest was willingly forfeited.

Champion billiard player Frank Ives was recorded as being able to strike a ball with a cue harder than any man in the world. The unbeaten American claimed that there was no trick in his methods, he merely was able to strike the billiard balls squarely in the centre. Ives' abilities became so renowned that he consulted physicians who told him that he had developed muscles in his arm that other sportsmen rarely used, although they were unable to be more specific. With the question unsettled in Frank's mind, he took steps to enlighten the world after his death and, in 1896, wrote a will in which he ordered his right arm to be severed from his body and sent to a surgeon for dissection in order to reveal the secret of his skills. The rest of his body was directed to be cremated.

Seven embalmed thumbs of notorious murderers of the eighteenth century were the gruesome relics bequeathed to policeman John Corry of Philadelphia by his father who died in May 1904. The digits were cut from the hands of the famous murderers who were executed in a prison where one of Corry's ancestors was the jailor.

In 1905 a miser by the name of Monecke died in Mexico and could not be interred until a court was consulted due to the fact that he had tattooed his will all over his chest in red pigment ink. The judge decided that the remarkable 'human document' should be copied and duly attested to in the presence of witnesses. This was done and satisfied relatives were able to both put Monecke's body to rest and receive their share of his estate.

A scene reminiscent of an Edgar Allan Poe novel was witnessed in the village churchyard of St. Servais, a sleepy French hamlet of 700 inhabitants in the district of Finistere. St. Servais is famous for two reasons. Its weather-beaten church stood siege against the 'blues' in the troublesome days of the Revolution, and it was the birthplace of the famous painter, Jean-Edouard Dargent, known as Yan. It was in connection with the artist that it found itself the most talked about village in all of France in 1907.

Yan Dargent was a true Breton, and his paintings adorn the walls of many Breton churches. He died in 1899 from a pulmonary embolism, at the age of 75. In his day Dargent had arrived in Paris poor and unknown, and it was when he finally quit the city to retire in Brittany that he acquired fame and wealth. The artist's mother and grandfather were interred in the cemetery at St. Servais and Yan had their graves opened, bones gathered together and placed in a vault within the church. When Dargent found himself on his deathbed he summoned his son, Ernest, and his wife and bade them swear that they would scrupulously carry out his last wishes. The couple took the required oath and Dargent then ordered that after he had been dead for a certain number of years his grave should be opened, his skull removed, enclosed in a casket, and placed beside those containing his mother and grandfather.

Eight years elapsed before Ernest and his wife once more stood beside his father's open grave, determined to carry out the terms of the oath. Yan Dargent's body had originally been interred in a zinc casket, and this in turn enclosed in an oaken case. When the coffins were opened, instead of finding a skeleton in a state of decay, they found the body in an excellent state of preservation. The head was intact, and the shroud still not discoloured by the years of interment. This was a most unexpected dilemma. It was suggested that the operation of removing the skull should be postponed for several more years until decomposition had done its work.

'No,' said Ernest firmly, 'I have an exhumation order today, five years hence I may not be able to obtain another.'

Then, turning to the gravedigger he ordered him to cut off the head. The man was aghast at the proposal, immediately throwing down his shovel and fleeing. Ernest, feeling bound by this strange oath, approached the curate, Abbot Guivarch, and implored him to help. Throwing aside his cassock, the priest descended into the grave and sought to sever Yan Dargent's head from his body. However, the pocket-knife he was using was blunt and he had to borrow a second one. Presently, he emerged from the hole carrying the freshly-severed head, at the sight of which the local peasants, who had been mute spectators to the scene, fled terror-stricken. The head was firstly placed in a bucket of water and, after being carefully washed by the curate, was wrapped in linen and placed in a zinc box, which was then sealed. Later in the day there was a funeral procession to the church. The local mayor and several villagers attended, and the zinc box was borne to its resting place in the church vault.

Afterwards a great outcry was caused by the mutilation of the painter's body. Yan Dargent still had a living brother and sister, who professed ignorance of the terms of the pact in which Ernest saw fit to decapitate his father's body. They lodged a complaint with police authorities and asked that everyone concerned with the desecration of Dargent's tomb be prosecuted. Ernest Dargent had already taken legal advice and was advised that he had acted perfectly within his rights when carrying out his father's last wishes. The trial lasted for a full six months and on 26 June 1908, the Morlaix Tribunal issued a not guilty verdict. Sadly, the legal process had a profound effect upon Ernest Dargent's health and he died four days after the acquittal.

In 1908 Thomas Bunker, a tinsmith, committed suicide with a rifle at Cobbora, New South Wales, Australia. He left a letter in which he wrote:

My body I wish handed over to Dr McReady for to cut and carve about for the benefit of medical science. There is a skin disease which I have been in great fear of, lest it should be the first stage of leprosy. I think this skin is the cause of my action. I am lately penniless.

Determined that humanity should benefit from his sufferings, Henry H. Hooper of Whittier, who died of an ailment of the spleen, willed that organ to five medical friends for experimental purposes. This strange bequest became known on 23 September 1909, following the probating of Hooper's will. The first clause of the will read as follows:

I order that at my death, should there be any trace of my present ailment, enlargement of the spleen, I give and bequeath to Doctors W.H. Stokes, F.H. Hadley, J.F. Bold, and H.P. Wolsin, of Whittier, and Dr Theodore G. Davis, of Los Angeles, the before mentioned spleen and any other of my internal organisms, if they should like to study the existing ailment, with the object of learning, if possible, some treatment that would cure the complaint.

The following remarkable clause appeared in a will, which was admitted to probate in Melbourne, Australia in March 1911:

Being at this time in sound bodily and mental health, I hereby appoint my wise and most excellent wife sole executrix, trustee, and legatee of this my will. Having promised my dead body to the medical school for anatomical purposes at the Melbourne University, I desire that it be handed over to the order of the head of that school whom I have requested to secure the destruction of the debris by fire before final disposal, according to regulation. This seems the only way (1) it can be made to secure a useful purpose, and (2) besides will bear witness to my strong opinion that the state should exercise its admitted right to enforce a careful post-mortem examination of every dead body to ascertain the cause of death. My third reason is to my mind my protest against the foolish prevalent antipathy to giving over a body for this purpose. Very little consideration should suffice to convince anyone that were it publicly known that every dead body must undergo a strict autopsy to ascertain the cause of death before its disposal in any manner, murderers who have often entirely escaped notice by the neglect of this precaution would find it impossible to continue their nefarious practices with impunity. Universal autopsy would thus be the best preventive of secret murder, and a decreased death rate would perhaps show the extent of the need, as well as the efficacy of the expedient. Having no property but my furniture, apparel, tools, watch and library books, I have made a catalogue so as to facilitate the sale.

The document was unsigned.

One of the most astounding ceremonies ever witnessed in the history of the Church of England was presented by the venerable Archdeacon Colley for the 'edification' of his parishioners in the Church of St. Michael and All Angels, at Stockton, Warwickshire, in 1912. At the close of an evening service the archdeacon stepped into the coffin in which he intended to be buried and had himself carried around the church in full view of the congregation.

After the sermon, which was preached on the text '*Set Thy House in Order*', the eccentric clergyman amazed the throng by saying:

Not feeling that I am getting younger every day, I have had my coffin, which many of you for some years have known has been made for me, brought over from the rectory music room, and now it is before you in the chancel. On May 1st, 1904, I bequeathed my body to the University of Birmingham for medical students' use and to be cut up in the interests of anatomical and surgical science when I have done with it.

Then, calling for his 'bearers', the archdeacon stepped into the coffin, which stood on end, and a glass cover fixed in front of him. Carried at breast height by four bearers, so that all the congregation might see, the priest was steadily borne up and down the church aisle. As it passed seat after seat the startled parishioners gazed spellbound at the unusual spectacle. Some were so overcome that they wept, others giggled, while a few, shocked by this display of mockery of death, fled.

Returning to the chancel, the glass cover was removed from the coffin and the archdeacon was heard to say, 'For this relief much thanks.'

Then, still standing in the coffin, Archdeacon Colley joined in singing the hymn *Praise God From Whom All Blessings Flow*. These extraordinary proceedings closed with the benediction in the customary form, and the congregation filed out, obviously relieved from a strain that was, to most of them, almost unbearable.

In December 1912 Florence Foster, a trained nurse from Westcliff-on-Sea, Essex, shot herself and made elaborate preparations for her own cremation before she did so. Shortly after noon on the fateful day, Miss Foster arrived at Woking station, having travelled up from Southend. On leaving the station she engaged a taxi and was driven to the post office, then onwards to Woking Crematorium. Arriving at the entrance gates she got out and went to the superintendent's office. Here she handed Mr Sargent a large sealed envelope, with the request that it should not be opened for a little while. Re-entering the taxi, Florence Foster asked to be driven into the countryside and, when passing through Hermitage Woods, told the driver to stop. She then walked into the woods, saying that she would be back in quarter of an hour. However, while waiting for Miss Foster to return, the driver heard the sound of a shot but, owing to a military presence in the neighbourhood, it did not arouse his suspicion. Later, when his passenger had failed to return after quite some time, the driver left his cab and walked into the woods where he discovered the woman's body. Florence had partly removed her clothes and had a bullet wound in the lower part of her stomach. Two revolvers were close at hand.

Meanwhile, when Mr Sargent opened the letter left at the crematorium, he found that it contained £13 and a letter dated from Westcliff-on-Sea, which read:

I have enclosed two £5 notes and a PO for £3, a total of £13, out of which to purchase me a 5ft 3inch shell – just the light wood you like for cremation. I request you to hold the money until I have been cremated, and in no wise to give it up, as I desire my body to be cremated. The ashes can be put in a white urn until December 26, 1912, and then blown to the four winds. A perforated casket at the top of a tree will do very well.

If there is any funeral service, I suggest the Fifteenth Psalm in the Book of Common Prayer, and the 21st hymn in the Ancient and Modern Hymn Book to be used. I have written to the London Crematorium Company and informed them of the aforementioned fact. If there is any superfluous money please send it in my name to the treasurer of the Royal Ophthalmic Hospital, City Road, London. Apologising for troubling you, believe me, yours very truly.

FLORENCE FOSTER.

Bowman Mansion, Vermont.
(*Detroit Evening Times*,
26 August 1945)

Right: Mrs Arthur Timleck &
youngest child. (*International News
Press*, 1938)

Below: Isabel McHie (Mrs Sidmon
McHie). (*Detroit Evening Times*,
13 August 1944)

Above left: RSPCA historical poster. (Horsham Museum)

Above right: Robert Louis Stevenson, 1893. (State Library of New South Wales)

Below: SS *Schiller*, 1875. (Public domain)

Above left: Louis Landrock.
(*The Bismarck Tribune*,
7 July 1921)

Above right: Wedding of
Anna Bolchi Benjamin and
Arthur Fullman. (*Age Herald*,
19 July 1923)

Right: Madame Rudersdorff.
(Carte De Visite Collection,
Boston Public Library)

Above left: Maine Cemetery Record for Daniel Heard. (Cemetery Association, 1977)

Above right: Portrait of Einstein, Princeton, 1935. (Public domain)

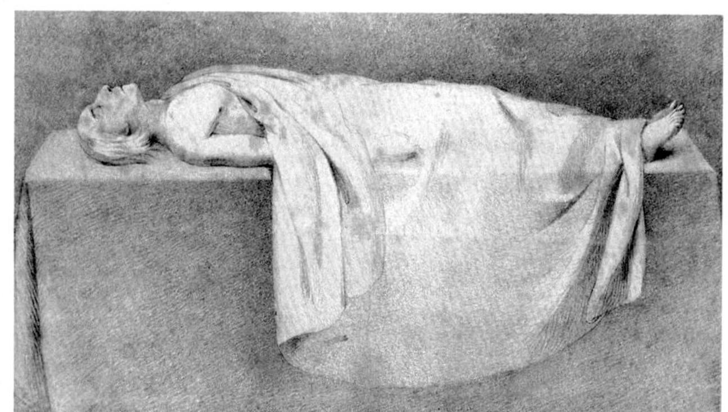

Mortal remains of Jeremy Bentham, 1832. (H.H. Pickersgill, Wellcome Collection Gallery)

Elvis Presley with Ginger Alden. (*Daily Mirror*, 1981)

Above left: Mickey Rooney, 1941. (Public domain)

Above right: Marie Dressler, 1908. (J. Willis Sayre Collection, Public domain)

Below: St. Lucia Map, West Indies. (Thomas Bowen, Boston Public Library)

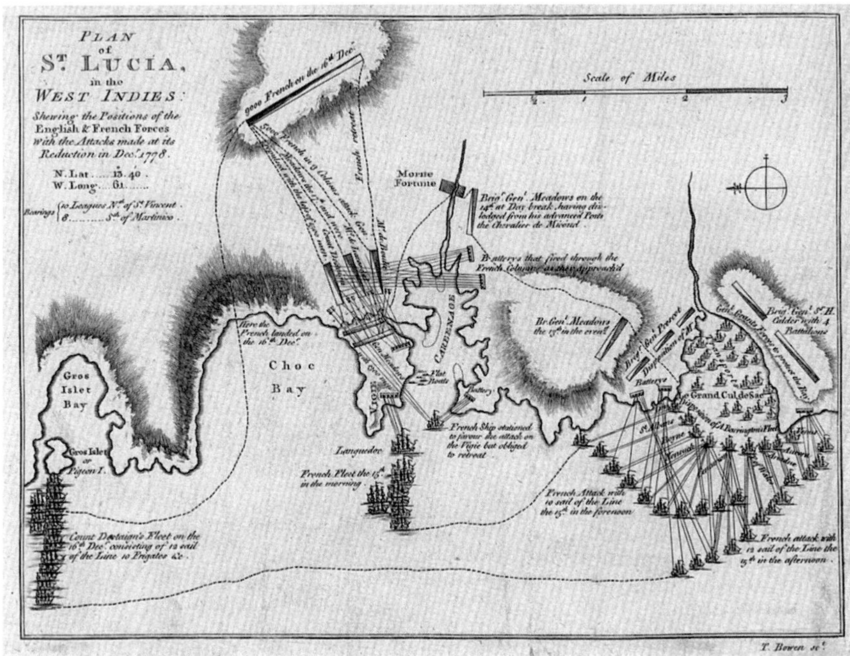

Left: The Burial Of Louis A. Thiel. (*The Brownsville Herald*, 30 June 1930)

Below: Bomb Damage To St. George's Cathedral, Southwark. (Imperial War Museum 1942, Public domain)

Right: Caricature Of Charles Peace. (Victorian Publication, Public domain)

Below: Aerial View Of Sing Sing Prison, 1937. (US National Archives & Records Administration, Public domain)

Above: Shelagh Tennant & Reginald Conrad. (*Sunday People*, 2 March 1975)

Left: L'egalite by Paul Andre Basset. (Musee Carnavalet, Public domain)

Bantu Migration. (*The Illustrated London News*, 27 February 1960)

Miss Foster was possessed of considerable means and had, on previous occasions, corresponded with the crematorium authorities with reference to the disposal of her remains after cremation. A jury at the inquest found that Florence Foster had committed suicide whilst in a state of unsound mind caused by overwork. They returned a verdict accordingly.

John D. Gleeson, an old age pensioner, who lived in Myers Street, Geelong, Australia, drowned himself in the bath in 1920. He left behind three letters showing that it was a case of deliberate suicide. In one of his letters, Gleeson requested that his body be handed over to the warden of the university for the use of the medical school. The police communicated with the warden, who agreed to accept the body.

In 1924 Tom Birkett, a County Councillor and magistrate of Lapworth, Warwickshire, left £64,643 and directed: 'That my body be sent to the General Hospital, Birmingham, and post-mortem thereof made to ascertain if any information may be obtained as to the origin, mitigation or cure of the scourge of headache, the unmerciful disaster that has wrecked my happiness from my earliest recollection.'

Birkett's body was afterwards to be cremated, and the ashes disposed of in accordance with instructions left with his papers.

In concluding an extraordinary letter to the City Coroner in Sydney, Australia, in 1925, William Green, aged 71, wrote:

'I am sorry to trouble you, and I bequeath my body to the students at the R.P.A. Hospital.' He added, 'I have taken strychnine to end my pain and suffering.' Green lived with his wife in Smith Street, Marrickville. On 15 January, his wife found him suffering from the effects of poison. He was taken to the Royal Prince Alfred Hospital, where he died. The widow told the coroner that her husband was a chemist but had not practised for years. After an accident involving a tram, William suffered great pain in his stomach and spine and also had diabetes. A verdict of suicide was returned.

In 1926, Sir Robert Chas Brown left £76, 974, of which he bequeathed £1,000, together with his body to Cambridge University Research Hospital, requesting that they keep any organs desired, also his ashes after cremation of the remainder. He added:

I believe in the resurrection of the dead, life in the world to come and that when the body dies my soul will go to heaven where I shall be allowed in an intensified form those pleasures enjoyed on earth. There is no death, sorrow, crime or pain. I believe Christ's death on the cross made atonement for my sins.

A strange will was left by Percival James Grant Smith, aged 57, who lived alone for thirty years and committed suicide on 28 July 1928, in his two-roomed cottage at Cregneish on the windswept headland overlooking Fort Eain, on the Isle of Man. Smith left the residue of his estate to a widow named Esther Annie Callister, on condition that she obeyed the direction that after death his body be destroyed by fire on a pyre in the open air, the pyre to be built of wood taken from the garden fence. Mr. Smith also asked that his ashes be dispersed or covered lightly with soil somewhere on the coast. After some debate, Percival Smith was buried in the parish churchyard, but no steps were taken to affect the will or personal estate valued at £25. Moorland Cottage, where Smith had lived all his life, was on Mull Hills, an area where, in olden times, funeral pyres were lit for incinerating bodies of the dead.

Unemployed labourer John Richard Watts, of Palmers Road, New Southgate, left a letter asking that his body be given to a doctor at the Royal Northern Hospital in London. Apparently, Watts, aged 61, had been operated on several times by the named surgeon, previous to his committing suicide by taking spirit of salts in 1929.

The fulfilment of one of the three last requests made by the late Professor H. Turner, professor of astronomy, was made possible on 29 August 1930. Professor Turner, who died a few weeks earlier at Stockholm, requested that his body should be used for scientific purposes after his death, and left his body to Stockholm Hospital. His second request, however, precluded the hospital from accepting the bequest. He asked that no ceremony, religious or civil, should be held in connection with his burial. Swedish law at the time directed that a ceremony of some kind must follow death. Stockholm Hospital communicated with London Hospital who eventually agreed to accept it.

The body, enclosed in a lead coffin, arrived in London on the steamer *Frecia*. It remained in the ship overnight and was called for by one of the hospital's undertakers, who carried it by hearse to the Medical School. The body was then immediately injected and put into the hospital cold store. The Secretary of the College, E.J. Burdon, said that the body would probably remain in the College for two or three months. 'There is a time limit of nine months beyond which we may not keep a body for dissecting purposes,' he said.

'As a matter of fact, bodies are never kept as long as that. Three months is usually the limit we observe. The body will remain in the cold store until the Director of the Anatomical School, Professor Wright, returns from Canada. It will then be in his entire charge. He may decide to extract certain organs for analysis, but it is unlikely that he will make an extensive dismemberment.

'It is very unusual for a distinguished man to leave his body to a hospital for scientific purposes. I do not remember a similar case in this hospital. Most of our bodies are obtained from infirmaries and workhouses through a government officer. Mrs. Turner has not yet signified her wishes in regard to the burial of her husband, but I understand that it will probably be in London.'

Professor Turner's third wish was that his friends should drink to his memory. He added that he preferred that they should do so with strong ale.

For two decades Seth Stratton of Chicago carried around one of the strangest bequests ever written, as he lived in constant fear of death.

It read: 'I, Seth Stratton, being of sound mind and being affected with an unusual disease of the oesophagus, do hereby bequeath my stomach and oesophagus to Doctor Frank Smithies in appreciation of his professional services so that the true status of my oesophagus may be observed.'

The unusual document came about twenty years earlier when Dr Smithies discovered that his patient had two stomachs but was unable to swallow enough food to satisfy his double hunger. In addition to this dilemma, the passage between the larger stomach in Stratton's chest and the normal one in his abdomen was obstructed. All hope of Seth leading a normal life was dashed until the surgeon struck upon the idea of passing a silk thread attached to an air pressure ampoule down through the throat and into the stomach. By this means, the opening was gradually cleared. By the age of 72, Seth Stratton was still living a relatively normal life, spending his time playing golf and hunting. However, it had been understood by doctor and patient that it was imperative for Stratton to attend six-monthly medical appointments in order to have his stomach stretched, a matter that Seth apparently didn't adhere to, missing his final appointment, which resulted in him dying.

The late Archibald Siddall, a retired banker from Sydney, Australia, directed in his will that, after death, a test should be carried out to his eyes by applying capsicum or cayenne on his eyeballs 'to make sure that life was extinct.' His body was then to be cremated, his ashes placed in a grave at Waverley Cemetery and a headstone erected bearing his name, age and the words 'Saved by Grace', repeated over and over again. Mr Siddall left an estate of £4,794 in 1936, mainly for the benefit of his wife and other members of the family. He also left his wife two booklets which he said he had printed to give away or sell, one of them being entitled *Brandy and Salt – A Medicine for the good of the People's Health.'* Siddall also made religious and other bequests.

To be suspected of murder and to have his ears assailed by the disturbing cry 'body snatcher', were the unpleasant experiences of Frederick Tubb of Pine Island, near Auckland, New Zealand. When his wife died in 1942, Tubb decided to carry out her last wish and have the remains embalmed. These he since kept in a shed on his property. When interviewed, Tubb said his motive, apart from his wife's request, was that he and their children might be able to revere her memory by close contact. It was his intention, he said, to eventually place the body in a mausoleum. However, owing to the war he was unable to secure the necessary materials, but had planned to spend £500 on the project. Admitting that the action was unusual, Frederick Tubb reminded a reporter that Abraham laid his wife, Sarah, to rest in a rock cave. He therefore saw no reason why he should not have his wife's remains embalmed and kept at home pending a more permanent arrangement.

In 1945 Tubb was sent for by the local police, who showed him a letter from a neighbour. She stated that her suspicions had been aroused by seeing a young lady enter the shed on Sundays carrying flowers. The woman investigated and saw a coffin in a shed, by coincidence around the time that Mrs. Tubb had died in Auckland. The author of the letter then disappeared and in spite of efforts by the police no trace was ever found. They did, however, eventually follow up on the letter but found that Tubb had no difficulty in clearing himself.

Well-known Australian horticulturalist Thomas Henry Storr, who died in Newcastle Hospital on 27 August 1948, aged 63, requested in his will that his body be neither buried nor cremated. Instead, Storr asked that his body be sent to Sydney University for research and 'in the hope of helping suffering humanity.' A short service was held at Meighan's Funeral Home the day after Thomas' death and the body was then transported to Sydney by train.

The body of Albert Barker, aged 60, of Bellevue Hill, Sydney, Australia, who was killed in a road crash in 1949, was accepted by the Sydney University. A letter found in Barker's car after the crash bequeathed his body to the University and directed that the corneas of his eyes should be given to some person who was blind. The letter was written three years earlier. However, sadly the offer of the corneas could not be accepted as they needed to be removed immediately after death to be of service to the recipient.

A similar bequest was made by a Brisbane estate agent before he took an overdose of sedatives, it was revealed at the inquest in May 1953. John Robert Clarkson, aged sixty-four, died on 13 March as a result of pentobarbitone poisoning. Clarkson was found dead in his bed in Kangaroo Point while his wife was away on holiday in New Zealand. Police found a note dated 12 March on a table in the lounge. It read: 'In the event of my death, I bequeath my body to the Queensland University for scientific research. My wife will confirm that this has always been my intention.'

At the inquest it was recorded that Clarkson suffered from insomnia.

When Professor Albert Einstein died from internal bleeding in April 1955, he was cremated at Trenton, New Jersey, and his ashes privately disposed of at an undisclosed location. The renowned scientist's lawyer told newspapers that any plans for memorials or dedications should be dropped. Details of where and how the ashes were disposed of were not revealed.

'The ultimate fact is that no physical traces are left anywhere. The disposition of the remains was made in conformity with the wishes of Doctor Einstein,' said the late scientist's lawyer, David Levy.

During his brief hospital stay, Einstein refused surgery and was quoted as saying, 'I want to go when I want. It is tasteless to prolong life artificially. I have done my share, it's time to go. I will do it elegantly.'

Parts of Einstein's body, including his brain, were preserved for scientific study during an autopsy by pathologist Thomas Stoltz Harvey, without permission of the Einstein family, in the hope that the neuroscience of the future would be able to analyse exactly what it was that made Albert Einstein such a genius. All of Albert's personal archives, library and intellectual assets were bequeathed to the Hebrew University of Jerusalem in Israel.

Chapter Seven

Matters of the Heart

The post-mortem humour found in many wills has caused amusement to many a reader, but it often becomes quite a serious matter to the parties involved, especially when conditions contained in the document refer to matters of the heart. It is not uncommon for those on their deathbed to suddenly recall an unrequited love, a broken heart or a long-distance admiration, as the following cases will show. One case in particular that caused a dilemma for the heir was the will of a Pittsburgh woman who left half a million dollars to an old sweetheart, so long as he divorced the wife to whom he was happily married. It does seem that some people, having suffered a broken heart in life, try to fix the damage by causing more disruption after death.

In 1610 a French merchant left a large legacy to the lady who had jilted him, apparently in order to express his gratitude to her for her forbearance and his admiration for her sagacity in leaving him to a happy bachelor life!

Mrs. Van Hanrigh, in 1868, among other positive things obviously worried a great deal that her spouse should be looked after on her demise. She said in her will 'It is also my earnest wish that my darling husband should marry ere long a nice, pretty girl who is a good housewife, and, above all, to be careful that she is of good temper.' Such documented sentiments are all too rare nowadays.

In the Court of Chancery, before Vice-Chancellor Malins, in July 1872, a petition arose under the trusts of the will of the late Nathaniel Bates, of Milbourn Hall, Northumberland. The testator was possessed of large landed and other estates being worth £19,000 a year. By his will he left £1,000 to 'the person whom I might have wished to marry.' In another clause he said, 'if she dies before me, I direct my trustees to pay £1,000 to the three eldest children, being girls, of three agricultural hands residing nearest Milbourn Hall, within a mile measured in a straight line.'

The petitioner, Ellen Wilson, claimed this money as being the person whom Bates desired to marry. She had resided in his family for some years in the capacity of cook, and there was evidence to show that on more than one occasion Bates had offered her marriage, which she had consistently declined for one reason or another. The testator's surviving sister, Sarah Bates, appeared by counsel. She was residuary legatee and had paid the amount of the bequest into Court. The facts as stated were confirmed by her and also the fact that the marriage of Ellen and Nathaniel was approved of and desired by his family as they were very fond of the woman. The petition was opposed by the parties claiming under the devise to be three eldest daughters of the agricultural labourers. The Vice-Chancellor said that the case was a most extraordinary one, the wonderful part being that a woman in the position of a cook should refuse to marry a man as wealthy as the testator, and not only so but that the family should do all in their power to bring about the marriage.

His Honour had no doubt that the description in the will was perfectly sufficient, there could be no doubt about the person whom the testator was desirous of marrying, still, as the name was not expressed, there might be a difficulty, and he strongly advised the parties who claimed the money to divide it between them. It was then agreed that the case should stand over to allow his Honour's suggestion to be considered.

A fortune estimated at between £4,000 to £6,000 a year was bequeathed to Mr Rogers of Staffordshire under unusual circumstances in August 1872. A widower, Rogers was a former baker and had retired to a small village where he had lived happily with his wife until her death. The couple did not have any children and lived fairly modestly but comfortably. A few years after his wife's demise, Rogers became acquainted with a wealthy lady in Cumberland who formed a rather ardent attachment to him, offering him marriage and money. However, Rogers did not reciprocate the feelings and declined marriage, with wealth being of little interest to him. Nevertheless, the woman persisted in her romantic yearnings towards him. In April 1872, the lady was taken to her bed suffering from a terminal illness and requested the presence of Rogers at her side to give comfort in her last days. The former baker declined politely, instead sending a letter expressing his sorrow on hearing of her situation. Not even this rebuff abated the woman's affections and, passing by her nephews and nieces, she had a will drawn up in which she bequeathed the bulk of her property to Mr Rogers, the lady's state of mind and signature being attested by a lawyer and witnessed by two doctors who were called to her bedside. Unfortunately, there is no record of Mr Rogers reaction to his sudden wealth.

In the same year, a very personal bequest was made. Around 1852, the daughter of a professional gentleman in London ran away with her father's coachman, a man named Smith, and soon afterwards married him. As a result of her elopement, the young woman was disinherited by her irate father. The couple settled in Jersey where Smith earned twelve shillings a week in service, just enough for the couple to live on. Twenty years later, while digging potatoes in his garden, Smith was informed that his father-in-law had died and left the pair a property valued at £20,000.

A case of forbidden love resulted in Mrs Lincoln of Portland, Maine, becoming heir to $175,000 in September 1882, the estate of her cousin Erven Noughton of California. In their youth Mrs Lincoln and Noughton were intimate friends and fell in love and would have been married had it not been for the intervention of disagreeable relatives. As a result of the break-up, Noughton headed West and vowed never to return to his hometown. He kept his word, prospering in business and becoming wealthy but never marrying. Meanwhile, his beloved cousin married Captain James Lincoln, who died in 1877, leaving his widow $25,000, a sum that ensured a comfortable retirement. The additional bequest from Noughton was said to have come as a great surprise to his cousin.

It was in 1885 that Laura Gregory, of Buckingham County, Virginia, contributed several articles on the Education of Women, and Women's Suffrage, to the *Kansas City Times*. At the time, her writing attracted the attention of Charles Wilmot, general superintendent of a large gold mining company in Colorado, who wrote and asked for the honour of corresponding with Miss Gregory. Over a period of thirteen years, the pair came to know each other well and eventually became engaged to be married. During this time, Wilmot gifted his fiancée a precious ring and several other pieces of gold and silver from the far West. Over the years, Charles Wilmot planned many trips to Virginia to claim his bride, but for reasons unknown these were always postponed and after several years his letters ceased to arrive. In 1902 it was discovered that he had travelled to Alaska in search of greater wealth, where he died. However, Wilmot had not forgotten his love and administrators of his estate wrote to Buckingham County authorities to find out the address of Laura Gregory. On 3 May of the same year, Charles Wilmot's fortune of $60,000 was divided equally between his fiancée, a nephew and niece.

In April 1889, Bessie MacDonald, of Glasgow, was on a visit to Cardiff when she received the rather gratifying news that she had become entitled to the sum of £2,000 and an hotel in New York. Some years before, Bessie had become engaged to Harry McLeod, a native Glaswegian who had resided in America for many years and was the proprietor of the Great Eastern Eagle at Turner's

Falls. On many occasions Harry had pressed Bessie to join him in New York, with a view to getting wed, but on each occasion she made excuses to delay the marriage, having a great dread of the sea voyage across the Atlantic. Sadly, Miss MacDonald deferred her betrothal for too long, and on 15 March 1889 Harry McLeod suddenly passed away. The deceased's last surviving relative, an elderly aunt, had died in Glasgow some three months prior, leaving Bessie as the sole heir according to the wishes of Harry's will held by his New York lawyer. Unfortunately, it was by receiving a letter and copy of the will from her late fiancé's lawyer that the young woman learned of his death.

A very sad case of unrequited love was reported from Paris in November 1893. Madame Milher was a very good-looking widow, a little over 30 years of age, who fell deeply in love with a neighbouring tradesman who was slightly older than herself. Unfortunately, the widow's attention was not reciprocated and no matter how much the lady's determined advances increased, the gentleman repelled each and every one. Devastated, Madame Milher travelled to Metz, in the district of Lorraine, where she had friends who endeavoured to help her forget about the man who remained impervious to her charms. After a while, she returned to Nogent in the Parisian suburbs. On the Sunday morning after her arrival, the widow's body was found on the footpath outside the tradesman's house. Madame Milher had swallowed a dose of vitriol, commonly known as sulphuric acid, and in order to make certain of death had entwined two pocket handkerchiefs tightly around her neck. In her dress pockets were found several letters intended for the man she loved, and a quantity of gold and silver. Before committing suicide, Madame Milher had thrown a pocketbook into the man's garden, which was found to contain bank notes and Credit Foncier Bonds, together with her last will and testament, by which she had made the tradesman sole heir and universal legatee to her estate.

The bequest of Mr J.S. Alexander's estate to a Miss Young, dispossessing his lineal heir, caused great excitement in the newspapers all over Northern Ireland in 1901. The will was drawn up five years previous to the death of Alexander by a solicitor of the High Court of Judicature in Ireland and was attested by two witnesses. It left all of the wealthy gentleman's property, without reservation, to Miss Young, and included over 800 acres of land. Apparently, Mr Alexander had proposed marriage to Miss Young, whose family was related to his by another tie, but she refused and told him that she preferred to remain single. Alexander chose bachelorhood but still cherished affection for his lost love for the rest of his days. The grounds of Portglenone House, which Miss Young inherited, were described as being 'beautifully wooded, with the River Bann at the back of the property. There was also good salmon and trout fishing and excellent shooting. The whole farm was large and well cultivated and was a source of great interest and pride to its late owner.'

From an income of $45 a month as an oiler on the Burlington railroad to the sole ownership of two gold and silver mines in Montana, estimated to be worth $5 million, was a dream that came true for George Gunter of Lincoln, Nebraska, in 1903. The bequest arrived out of the blue from a former sweetheart to whom Gunter was engaged many years before. Although there was no bad feeling towards one another when the pair separated, they had simply drifted apart, the young woman married a man who became wealthy in the Montana gold fields. In 1902, the man died, just a short time after George Gunter had married for a second time. In a strange twist, the widow of the prospector, Mrs. Pingen, paid a visit to Gunter a few months before her death and left him everything as a token of their early love. Official confirmation of the bequest was given by the court.

When Stephen Salisbury died in 1906 it was revealed that the aged philanthropist had led a life full of sadness. A millionaire twenty times over, Salisbury, from Worcester, Massachusetts, was envied by the rich and beloved by the poor. However, the foundation of the man's great wealth had been bestowed upon him by his father, who heaped estates and money on his son with one very cruel stipulation, that Stephen Salisbury should never marry. Should he violate the agreement, all property, wealth and funds were to be forfeited. Stephen was a popular young man with many friends, attending Harvard University, and with vast amounts of money at his disposal, he resolved to travel. Having explored Europe, the young man ventured south and arrived in Yucatan, where he met a dark-eyed Spanish girl. As time passed, affection turned into love, but the conditions of his fortune nagged greatly at young Salisbury's conscience. Faced with a choice between betrothal and poverty, or a fancy life of continued wealth, Stephen chose the latter and returned home to the family mansion. It wasn't until his death many years later that the tragic story of lost love was discovered in his diaries, perhaps a good example of the old adage that money can't buy happiness.

The reading of Colonel Isaac Wing's will at Washburn, Wisconsin, in September 1907 brought to light a touch of romance in the late man's life. By the terms of the will Miss Catherine Rittenhouse of Jamestown, North Dakota, inherited $20,000 in cash. The young woman was the daughter of an old sweetheart of the late Colonel Wing, he had been a rival for her hand in marriage, but the woman favoured Mr. Rittenhouse, who later became her husband. Colonel Wing never married and, when the will was read, he had made the girl's father executor, showing that there was no hard feeling toward the man who had won his youthful sweetheart. Colonel Wing's entire estate was estimated at between $500,000 and $800,000 dollars at the time of his death, with investments in the West. The majority of the estate went to his sister, Abby Benjamin, who was asked to put the money into trust for her two children, Jeanette and Alice. Various smaller amounts were bequeathed to cousins and friends.

In May 1907, a young woman from Bristol became richer by £15,757 after a man with whom she was only slightly acquainted left her money in his will. The testator was Edward Garraway Cope-Proctor, of Pembroke Road, Clifton, the son of a city alderman who had apparently fallen in love with the girl at first sight. A year earlier he had spotted Mercy Lilian Large on the way to the Bethesda Chapel, at Almavale, and was so attracted to the young woman that he followed her and became a member of the same congregation. An introduction was made but the young woman gave him little encouragement. It was said that the pair occasionally walked home together but that the woman only regarded her companion as a casual acquaintance. Sometime afterwards, the young man became ill and was advised to travel abroad for his health but sadly died in Berne, Switzerland, before he could return home. Having inherited money from his mother, the man bequeathed his fortune to the love that he never could have, also leaving Miss Large his writing cabinets, books, watch, travel clock and several pictures.

A painfully dramatic story of inheritance was revealed in South Africa in 1907 after a divorce was granted by the Supreme Court of Cape Colony. It began some years earlier when magnate Pieter Marias, reputed to be worth the equivalent of £9 million, opposed the marriage of his son, Belfield, to Madame Philippe, a French widow with two grown-up daughters. Believing that his father would eventually relent, Belfield married the woman. Nevertheless, Pieter Marias was resolute in his decision and soon after altered his will, under which each of his nine children were to inherit one million sterling, except for the offending son who was cut off without a shilling. Belfield, whose charming disposition made him a great favourite in social circles, obtained a position as surveyor under the Cape Government, but the £500 a year salary proved inadequate to maintain his new family in the style to which they were accustomed. Gradually the couple drifted apart, the wife brooding over the financial situation, causing the estranged Mrs. Marias to threaten vengeance on her father-in-law. Learning that Pieter Marias and his family were staying at the Mount Nelson Hotel in Cape Town, she drove there with her 15-year-old daughter, Aileen, and requested a table for dinner next to that of the Marias family. The dining room was crowded and at the end of the meal Aileen rose from her seat, approached Pieter Marias and threw a quantity of vitriol, or sulphuric acid, in his face, while her mother shouted, 'That man has wronged me, and this is my revenge.'

Marias was severely injured, and his sight impaired as a result. The mother and daughter were immediately arrested with Mrs. Marias being sentenced to eighteen months imprisonment. Aileen was released on remand as the judge considered her to have been acting purely under her mother's influence. After her release, the Frenchwoman moved to London and instituted an action for the restitution of her conjugal rights, since her husband had not contributed anything towards maintenance since her arrest. In her evidence Mrs. Marias claimed that she had become entirely dependent upon friends and had been forced to accept a £200 cheque, in order to return to Cape Town to take part in court proceedings. Belfield Marias was ordered to return to his wife by a certain date, but he failed to comply which entitled her, under South African law, to a divorce. As soon as he was released from the marriage contract Pieter Marias restored his son to favour and changed his will accordingly.

In November 1909, widow Alpha Mack was preparing to travel from her home in Indianapolis to Asheville, North Carolina, to take charge of an estate valued at between $40 - $50,000, which was left to her by John Hastings. The testator was an old sweetheart whose advances Mrs. Mack had refused but, evidently, he still held a soft spot for her in his heart. The pair had become acquainted when Mack took her son to Asheville while he was suffering from tuberculosis.

After a two-week hunt for a bride, Charlie Schluter, a waiter from Missouri Valley, remained single. According to conditions in a relative's will, if Charlie failed to marry by 1 October 1915, he would forfeit a legacy of $17,000. The unusual bequest containing the marriage proviso was made by his uncle, Charles D. Schultz of New York City. Following the reading of the will, Schluter invited a board of advisers to tell him how to distinguish between true love and avarice on the part of the girls. 'A few want me,' he said, 'lots of them want my coin. I'll try to find a little old-fashioned girl, but she must be cute!'

As the result of a romance which started in Dublin, Ireland, during the Easter week rebellion of 1916, Mary O'Sullivan, a nurse from Providence, United

States, received a legacy of $2,000 and deeds to a property in Dublin in 1920. The house was bequeathed by her fiancé, Peter Dunn, a young businessman, who died from the results of gassing received in the First World War.

The entire estate of the ex-soldier was willed to his American sweetheart and a cheque for the money and property deeds were forwarded to the young woman by a firm of Dublin attorneys. A warm sympathiser of the cause for a free Ireland, Mary O'Sullivan invested part of her inheritance in Irish bonds. Early in the war, Mary entered the Red Cross service in Europe where she spent two years. When uprisings began between Irish patriots and English military she asked to be transferred to Ireland where she grew up as a girl. It was then that she met Sergeant Dunn, and it wasn't long before a promise of marriage was forthcoming. Subsequently, Dunn fell ill after being severely gassed on the western front and succumbed to the effects some time afterwards.

When Charles Hamilton of Chicago died in 1919, he willed his former sweetheart, Eleanor Berlin, a trust fund of $60,000 on condition that she live with his mother and never marry. The unusual bequest was the result of a wartime romance that started in the south, where Hamilton was an officer in the air force, and ended when he was killed in a plane crash at Ellington airfield. Described as tall, handsome and athletic, Charles Hamilton presented a striking figure in his military uniform. At the same time, Miss Berlin was doing war work in Galveston, Texas, greeting the trains of enlisted men with coffee and sandwiches as they embarked on their way overseas. As soon as the pair met, a romance was sparked and continued until the day that Hamilton was fatally injured in a crash. Eleanor was able to visit Charles in hospital, at which point he took her hand and asked his beloved to swear that she would never marry.

'I promised I would do as he wished,' Eleanor said. 'Then, while he was dying, he had his will drawn up, leaving his money to me, and stating the conditions. He signed it and died with a smile on his face.'

However, by 1922, Eleanor Berlin was torn between her emotions, obeying her former lover's request or spurning the money and following her heart, for she had fallen in love again. Eleanor chose the latter course, and married Raymond Goding, a wealthy real estate broker from Worcester. Massachusetts, who with his own sizeable fortune was able to relieve his new bride of the necessity of worrying about the loss of hers.

In April 1921 a fortune of £60,000 and a large ranch in Queensland was left to Maisie Major, a 19-year-old from Lincolnshire, England. Apparently, during the First World War, the young woman had met Captain Donald Bonds of the Australian Air Force, and the pair became engaged. However, some time not long after returning home, Captain Bonds died from pneumonia and left his entire estate to his betrothed. Maisy expressed her wishes to take her parents to Australia and to live on the ranch as soon as probate on the estate was granted.

A story of goodwill was related in the London press in December 1912, regarding the bequest of a large sum of money to Mrs Longeon, the wife of a shipyard labourer at Gateshead. It appeared that ten years before, Mrs Longeon gave shelter and food to a seafaring youth who was in need of assistance and the young lad, on emigrating to Australia, assured his benefactress that he would never forget the kindness that she had shown him. While in Australia, where other members of his family joined him, the young man successfully set up a farm and made a considerable fortune. However, his relatives died and in June 1911 the man met with an accident, sustaining injuries that subsequently proved fatal. It was after the man's death that his will showed a bequest of estate and stock worth £25,000 to Mrs Longeon. The surprised woman expressed her intention of travelling to Australia to claim the property and on return proposed to settle in Chile, her husband's native country.

On being taken to hospital in January 1924, the first words of Jonathan Draycott, who had been buried by the fall of a mine roof in England, were: 'I want paper.'

On being giving a piece, Draycott made a will upon it, leaving his £1400 life savings to his sweetheart. He signed the document and then fell back, dead.

On the death of Cleveland Masterman, of South Shields, a cousin of the Bishop Suffragan of Plymouth, a secret wedding which took place thirty-seven years before was revealed. In 1924, Masterman left estate to the gross value of over £130,000. Among the bequests was one of £10,000 in trust for life, his wines and furniture, and the income from two houses to his housekeeper, Martha Mary Ann Broom. However, at probate it was revealed that 'Mrs Broom' was actually Mrs Masterman.

The marriage had taken place at Carlisle register office on 4 May 1886. Since that day, Mrs Masterman always called herself Mrs Broom, and Mr Masterman referred to her as his housekeeper. By all accounts the marriage was a happy one. The only other living person who was in on the secret was Annie Turner, Mrs Masterman's niece, who was witness at the wedding. Cleveland Masterman was a well-read man, interested in archaeology, and a devout churchgoer. He was eighty-two at his time of death, and the widow eighty. The reason behind the couple's well-kept secret remains a complete mystery.

Husbands and wives have been recorded as acting in the extreme when news of being disinherited by a spouse has been revealed, as was the case of a cattle dealer in Australia in 1925. Mr Fraysee and his mother arrived at the notary office to learn the contents of his deceased wife's will, only to find that he had been left nothing at all. An angry scene followed, in which the ageing mother suddenly snatched the will from the notary and passed it to her son, who promptly crumpled it up, popped it into his mouth and swallowed it! The astonished lawyer could do nothing but look on, thereafter calling the police to have Fraysee and his mother arrested.

Heinrich Sten was born in Tyrnau, Austria, but emigrated to Australia, where he married. Despite being from a good family, Sten served five years in prison for theft, blaming his wife's extravagance for his actions. During his time in prison, Heinrich's wife died, leaving him a broken man and forcing a decision to move to Hungary to look for employment. However, not long afterwards, in July 1927, Sten received documents conveying a bequest of £100,000 upon him from the estate of John Charles Midwood, of Sydney. It turned out that Sten's wife had been involved with Midwood before her marriage to Sten and then went back to him after her husband's incarceration. A letter enclosed in the generous testator's bequest read: 'I wanted at first to commit suicide, but instead decided to try to steal your wife, and succeeded in winning her affections. I did not find courage during my lifetime to make the reparation that my testament now makes.'

In February 1927, a servant girl in Saxony was notified of a shock bequest from an uncle who died in Milwaukee, United States. Marie Draxdorf, whose family were in the butcher's trade, was left $1 million, and soon afterwards became inundated with offers of marriage from strangers. However, despite the very tempting love notes, Marie stayed faithful to her fiancé, a local bricklayer.

In the same year, an abrupt termination was brought to the action of penniless widower Edward Smith Wilkinson at Nottingham Assizes. Wilkinson's deceased wife was dubbed 'the world's best dressed woman' before she died in 1924, leaving an estate valued at £17,000 but not a penny to her husband. Wilkinson intended to sue the trustees to recover the value of jewellery, an oil painting of himself and £500, but Justice Shearman, presiding, refused to try the case. Mrs. Wilkinson was aged 50 when the couple married, with her much younger husband being just twenty-two. It was reputed that she spent a sum of over £30,000 on dresses in just two years.

Finally in 1927, the price of love was fixed at a sum of $25,000. John Russell Boggess was a struggling artist who worked as a clerk at the cigar counter in the Chicago Club, Illinois, due to his paintings not paying any dividends. He was also a great friend and protégé of wealthy consultant engineer Robert Forsyth. Every fortnight the men dined together, discussing many subjects but never women. Forsyth was a misogynist in the extreme and even refused to give direct orders to his housekeeper, instead leaving written notes, so that he might avoid personal contact with her. A few months before Forsyth died John Boggess married, a circumstance which created a great rift in the friendship. Subsequently, when Robert Forsyth's will was read, it was found that a $25,000 bequest to Boggess had been taken out a short time before. Boggess' only comment to the press was that it was a cheap price to pay for love.

Sometimes a will can be baffling to outsiders but completely rational to the partners involved, such as the concluding sentence of William W. Champton's last will and testament read in Australia, in 1928, that stated:

'I make no provision for my wife, because she has ample property of her own. As was mutually agreed between us prior to marriage, neither was to look for any properties from the other, either during life or after death.' The will instead made the bequest of £800 each to the District Grand Lodge of North Queensland, Freemasons, and Thornburgh College, Charters Towers, £400 to the Charters Towers Hospital and several bequests of £30 and all residue of the estate to the United Grand Lodge of Masons for the Aged Masons Home in Brisbane.

A tragic inquest in April 1929 heard how 28-year-old Archibald Leonard Holdstock, of Reading, left everything to the young woman who rejected him. It was stated that Mr Holdstock frequently met up with Doris Blackford without her parents' knowledge and had recently proposed to her. Later he was found shot through the mouth with a suicide note addressed to Miss Blackford nearby. The coroner announced that the letter was a will leaving everything to Doris and returned a verdict of suicide with no evidence to show the young man's state of mind.

A direct contradiction to the many wills forbidding spouses to remarry on pain of disinheritance, is the will of Elizabeth Lys, aged 60, wife of the Provost of Worcester College. In her will it is stated: 'I leave my diamond wedding ring to his wife if he marries again after my death, as I hope he will.' Mrs Lys left an estate of £12,000 to her husband.

Henry Frederick Holland Coward, a wealthy grazier, was killed in a motor accident near Mount Wilson, New South Wales, Australia, on Christmas Eve 1932. In his will he left his wife the income from £40,000 but then revoked the bequest in a series of codicils. In May 1933 probate was granted on the will and the codicils, showing that Coward's total estate was valued at £86,516. The will itself was dated 10 July 1923, with three codicils dated 26 April 1929, 1 March 1932, and 25 May 1932 respectively. In the will Coward left his wife, Decima Harriette, all his household effects, jewellery, and motor cars, in addition to the income from £40,000. Upon his wife's death this portion of the fortune was to go to their children. Of the residue, half was bequeathed to the children and, subject to certain legacies, the remaining half was left in trust to three brothers and a sister. However, by the first codicil Coward revoked all the gifts to his wife, directing that the £40,000 should be disposed of as directed by the will in the event of her death. In the second codicil he left his wife an annuity of £300 for life, but in a third codicil revoked every provision. Obviously a man who was indecisive when it came to his spousal affections!

A wealthy middle-aged woman's secret betrothal a few months before her death was revealed in October 1935 by the publication of her will. Norah Cecilia de Vahl, of Westbourne Park, London, left £154,584, with £22,500 on trust for her 'beloved fiancé Vivian Godwin Robert'. The news that Miss de Vahl was engaged to be married came as a great surprise to those who knew her. A member of the 53-year-old's household said that they knew of a friendship between the pair but had no idea of any romantic involvement. The fiancé in question held the rank of captain after serving with distinction during the First World War. Mr Robert was overseas at the time of his betrothed's death, but it was generally believed that Miss de Vahl had suffered from ill health for most of her life.

Another case the same month in 1935 was rather more selfish in nature. George Johnson Marples, a bachelor and barrister of the Inner Temple, London, died on 24 December the previous year, aged 84. He left the bulk of his fortune of £49,160 to his fiancée, Dorothy Ethel Green 'as long as she remains a spinster.' The will also stipulated that Miss Green must assume the surname of 'Marples' within one year of George's death.

It was a very sad state of affairs that surrounded the death of assistant rate collector Jack Harding Douglas on 5 June 1936. Aged just 26, Douglas was found in Victoria Park, Melbourne with a bullet wound in his chest and a revolver lying next him to him. At an inquest Doris Wright told the Deputy

Coroner that she was engaged to marry Jack Douglas but broke off their relationship on 29 May after a disagreement. The day before Douglas' suicide, the couple made up again, and made a decision to get married the following Christmas. However, on the day of his death, Jack addressed a letter to Doris, including £7, his bank book and an authorisation to the bank manager inside the envelope. The letter was reported to have been very affectionate but also asked Doris to receive all the money from what he termed 'our savings', and to use it to regain her health by way of taking a good holiday.

Childhood friendship that developed into love was undoubtedly the key to a bequest of a young Englishwoman. Margaret Ann Watney died at the age of 21 after a short illness in December 1936, leaving £52,476. From this she bequeathed £400 a year for five years and then the capital sum absolutely to Patrick Stevenson Blackwood, a medical student of Goodge Street, London. Of this sum, Miss Watney requested that Blackwood devote £300 a year to continue his medical studies. Margaret inherited the money on her 21st birthday, only a few weeks before she died, from her grandfather, who was a son of the founder of Watney's brewing company, founded in 1837. Sadly, Patrick Blackwood was overseas when Margaret was taken ill but returned as soon as he heard the news. The young man was described as being heartbroken on the death of his beloved.

In the late 1890s, London barmaid Norah Ryan fell in love with a champion boxer known as Cast Iron Man. She followed him to America where he was pursuing a prosperous career, but the couple quarrelled, and subsequently the young man returned to England. In 1937, the 66-year-old ex-fighter found himself living in Wales, almost blind, completely deaf and living in poverty. Imagine the surprise when he learned that Norah Ryan had died in the United States, still unmarried, and had left her ex-lover £1,800.

Sergeant Stuart Norman Saunders, a 22-year-old RAF pilot who was killed in a flying accident during the Second World War in 1939, left half his worldly possessions to his sweetheart 'in token of a love that will never die.' His total estate was £208.

There was a tale of unrequited love spanning fifty years when Mary Ann Brown of Macclesfield, England, died at the age of 83 and left a £310 legacy to her housekeeper, Beatrice Laurie. Whilst in her teens, Mary Ann had been employed at the local silk mills and during that time a fellow worker named Davis had fallen in love with her. The young man proposed marriage, but Mary

Ann refused, despite him persistently trying to woo her. Davis vowed that he would never marry and, when he died many years later, left £100 to Mary Ann in his will. Miss Brown never touched the money, despite living in an almshouse and relying on her pension and few savings for her daily needs and put it in the bank. The interest grew over the intervening fifty years until it reached the £310 that she bequeathed to Beatrice. However, Miss Laurie told the *Daily Mail*, 'I will never touch it. It is as sacred to me as it was to Miss Brown. She rarely talked to me of her broken romance, and I cannot say why she did not marry. She was the only friend I had.'

It was reported in the *Sunday Mirror*, dated 25 February 1940, that textile worker James Entwistle was living on an old age pension of 10 shillings a week sick pay for a broken wrist after his wealthy wife had died and left him nothing. Without the means to instruct solicitors, 68-year-old Mr Entwistle was aided by his local trade union in putting forward a claim to a part of the £14,000 estate. The deceased spouse was said to have been living in fairly humble circumstances despite her fortune, doing her own cleaning and upkeep in the family grocery shop which she had worked in for years. It became apparent that Mrs Entwistle had left everything to her nephew, Mr Band, of Leek, when she died at her home in Staffordshire after having heart trouble. Her husband, from whom the late woman was separated, staked his claim based on the laws of the Inheritance Act and duly received a share of the pot.

In March 1942, a girl who allegedly never existed was left a fortune by a man who believed he was her father. This extraordinary case was heard in Chancery, where it was revealed that the late Walter Langley left considerable property in British Colombia to one Peggy Doggett, supposedly the daughter of Mary Doggett of Hereford. Justice Simmonds heard that Mary Doggett had made a statutory declaration that she had been Mr. Langley's housekeeper for forty years and misled him into believing that she had given birth to a daughter, of whom he was the father. Lloyd's Bank, trustees of Langley's estate, asked for a ruling as to the disposal of the property, prompting the Court to order an official inquiry to find out whether or not Peggy Doggett existed, and where she might be living. An investigation proved that the girl had never existed, it was simply a case of Mary Doggett stringing along a former lover.

I leave £25 to my dearest, unseen friend whose letters have given me great comfort – Miss Grace Ferguson, of Martyn Street, Airdrie, Lanark.

This clause in the will of Corporal Charles Henry George, Royal Air Force, marked the end of a strange romantic attachment to a girl he had never met. When Corporal George was stationed at the lonely RAF base at Lochinver, Sutherland, he often visited the home of the Ferguson family, having struck up a close friendship with them. There, on the mantelpiece, he saw the photograph of Grace Ferguson, but never actually talked to the girl herself. Mr and Mrs Ferguson frequently talked about their daughter to the mild-mannered airman, whose home was in Battersea, London, and when he was seconded to India the young man decided to write to her. George told the Fergusons that he would spend his leave with them on his return, but sadly he never came back, instead dying in India in 1946. On the opening of his will, it was found that he had left the sum of £25 to Grace, the girl in the photograph.

Manuel Antonio Luzarraga of Geneva, formerly of London, left an estate in England valued at £25,989 when he died in 1947. He bequeathed everything to Lady Diana Duff Cooper, including 'whatever I may possess in the Banque Cantonale Vaudoise, Lausanne.' This mysterious gentleman's will disclosed that he had written to Lady Diana once a week for over fifteen years, after once seeing her at a ball and taking quite a fancy to the young woman. He then spoke to her in the street but was met with not the slightest encouragement, after which he wrote to her once a month. Born Lady Diana Manners, she was the wife of the British Ambassador in Paris, former Cabinet Minister and author Mr A. Duff Cooper. She was the daughter of the eighth Duke of Rutland.

Although disinherited by her husband, Agnes Copper Miller, aged 62, was awarded 17s 6d a week from her late husband's £5,300 estate. In the Manchester Chancery Court, England, Sir Leonard Stone noted that the wife complained that during their marriage the late Robert McQueen Miller had cut her housekeeping money from £3 down to £2 a week. As a result of his miserly ways, Agnes left home in August 1942. The following October Robert added a codicil to his will revoking his bequest of a life interest in his estate to his wife. Mr Miller then committed suicide in 1946. A solicitor in court was quoted as saying that the late Miller was 'honest but morose and miserable.' His brother testified and called the deceased man 'mean.' Sir Leonard decided that in the circumstances of the separation it was unreasonable that the widow should get nothing and made his award. It is interesting to note that the case wasn't deliberated upon in court until 1950, four years after Robert Miller took his own life.

In 1951 wealthy businessman Tommy Manville, of New York, made a will leaving $10 million to help young medical students, as he had been married eight times and was determined that none of his former spouses should get anything from his fortune after his death. Manville was reported to have spent almost four million in divorce settlements from his first seven wives with the eighth, Georgina Campbell, refusing a divorce on her husband's terms. Tommy often clashed with his multi-millionaire father, especially over his romances, and was disinherited at the age of 17 when he married Floreen Huber, whom he met at the theatre, after a whirlwind three day liaison. The couple lived together for seven years. However, after a change of heart, Manville's father left him $10 million, plus a $2 million trust fund, one million of which he used to divorce Floreen. Tommy then married his father's former secretary, divorced her and paid out another million in settlement soon afterwards. The subsequent wives weren't quite so lucky and received no more than $250,000 each. After drawing up his will, at the age of 56, Tommy Manville said, 'In future I'm washing my hands of women, unless they're under twenty-one, funny, and don't know anything about legal processes.'

With her 21st birthday just two weeks away, Jean Tanburn from Park Avenue, New York, faced a very difficult choice as part of a court ruling in May 1953. If Jean was to go ahead with her plans to marry Donelson Kelly, she would forfeit the right to a $10,000 cash inheritance, and a $6,500-a-year income from a $675,000 trust fund. The dilemma resulted from a clause in her great-grandfather's will that stated no descendant who marries a person 'not of the Jewish faith and not of Jewish blood' could benefit from the will. Donelson Kelly, a Princeton University senior, was not Jewish and intended to marry Jean before he reported to the Army Training Camp at Fort Sill, Oklahoma. When the problem was raised with judge Surrogate William Collins, he said that Miss Tanburn's situation commanded the court's sympathy. Despite deeming the will as discriminatory, the judge upheld the clause saying, 'A testator may exclude a child or other descendant from participation in his estate for sound reason, or because of whim or prejudice which might seem unreasonable to others.'

Jean Tanburn's great-grandfather, Abraham Rosenthal, was a silk importer who died in 1938, leaving bequests totalling $5 million. Despite the loss of a great fortune, it was reported that the couple planned to go ahead with their nuptials. In a strange twist of fate, Jean Tanburn and her mother Ruth found themselves back in court a month later when they tried to block attempts by other family members to bury the ashes of Jean's father in the family mausoleum. The other relatives claimed that mother and daughter should have no say in deciding the place of interment as they were both estranged from the deceased. Jean Tanburn said that she found it impossible to be friendly with her father as he demanded that she also be on good terms with his mistress too.

Music legend and ladies' man Elvis Presley excluded both his former wife and his fiancée from his will it was learned in August 1977 when the document was made public in Probate Court. The singer stipulated that his estate, thought to be worth many millions of dollars, be used for the benefit of his 9-year-old daughter, Lisa Marie, his grandmother, Minnie Mae Presley, and his father, Vernon Presley, who was also appointed executor. Elvis divorced Lisa Marie's mother, Priscilla, in 1973. His girlfriend, Ginger Alden, said that when the singer died, she was engaged to marry him. Presley also stated in his will that on the death of his father and grandmother all assets would revert to Lisa Marie when she reached the age of 25. No charities were named as beneficiaries.

When Hollywood actor Mickey Rooney died at the age of 93, in April 2014, his will revealed that, not only had he disinherited his estranged wife Jan Rooney and her children, but all of his own children as well. The only person to benefit from the legend's will was his stepson, Mark, who was the actor's personal caretaker during the final two years of his life. Despite a long and very successful Hollywood career, Rooney's entire estate was valued at just $18,000.

Chapter Eight

Loyal Servants

It is rare to find an employer as generous in life bequests and testamentary wishes as the late Henry Pierce, of Massachusetts. Not only was he renowned for his remarkable encouragement and support to hundreds of employees during his long career, but in his will left $750,000 to be divided between the officers and employees of the corporation of which he was the head. Out of an estate valued at $5 million, the poet Thomas Bailey Aldrich, close friend of Pierce, was bequeathed $200,000, a similar sum to his wife and their two sons received $100,000 each.

When Monsieur Chanteloup, brass founder of Montreal, Canada, died in February 1890, he left his entire fortune to his employees, except for a few thousand dollars which were bequeathed to charities. The estate was valued at $500,000. Each of the 500 workmen received $400 and the balance was left to three foremen who were tasked with carrying on the business with the funds provided. M. Chanteloup was a Frenchman who had been forced to flee from his native Paris during the riots. He settled in Canada and built up a large business shortly afterwards.

At the turn of the twentieth century, it was not unusual for some kind employer to leave a token gesture of appreciation in their will, remembering the loyal staff, caring nurses and diligent gardeners who had taken care of their daily needs in ageing years. However, one benefactor who showed her appreciation in great swathes was Emma Schley of New York. Dispensing of the bequests in 1900, lawyers found that the millionairess had left monetary gifts to seventy-five different people. The sums included $5,000 left to a local shop girl who had pleasantly attended to Mrs. Schley, $5,000 to each of her household cooks, $5,000 to a nurse who had attended her brother-in-law after a fatal stroke and $5,000 to 'the niece of Mrs. Harris', whose name she apparently couldn't recall. Emma Schley's wealth was accumulated from the death of a former husband, Henry Keep, and the nurses and attendants who cared for him during illness were also remembered in the same way. Mrs. Schley also left $10,000 to her maid, with the proviso that she take good care of the deceased's cats and dogs for the remainder of their natural lives.

As a reward for having carefully cared for an invalid through a trying siege of sickness, a servant girl fell heir to $3 million in 1900. Seven years earlier, Erna Ihde had been employed to nurse a wealthy patient in a German hospital in Berlin. She had apparently received a marriage proposal from him, which she supposed was out of kindness, but her parents refused to give their permission to the union on the basis that the man was consumptive. Fraulein Ihde then left the hospital, was employed as a maid for a royal family, and then eventually made her way to America, where she was taken on in the household of cracker manufacturer R.A. Johnston in Milwaukee. The last information obtained by Erna about her old patient, a clothier to the aristocracy, was that he had accumulated a vast fortune. Fraulein Ihde refused to name her benefactor on the advice of lawyers, due to the fact that the deceased had a brother with whom he had differed but had not been mentioned in the will. Erna made passage to Europe on the *Auguste Victoria* where she claimed her legacy in Berlin.

A very unusual case was brought to probate in 1901 regarding the will of a former slave. Before the civil war Louisa Grant worked for a prominent Louisiana planter in Donaldsonville and became his wife's favourite maid. After the war, Louisa was given her freedom and managed to set up her own business taking in laundry. She saved her money and accumulated considerable wealth, investing in real estate. It was widely known that Louisa remained fond of Mrs. Grant, her 'old missus', and her admiration was proven when she left all her belongings and an estate worth $12,000 to her former mistress, despite having a large family of her own.

In October 1902 the will of Belgian Queen Marie Henrietta was opened, and in it she stipulated that her body should not be embalmed or lie in state, but that her funeral should be conducted with the utmost simplicity and that she be laid to rest close to her son. The unhappy queen, who left to her children only what was required by law, was singularly thoughtful of a few friends who were near to her affection. Her twelve horses were bequeathed to Baron Gofflinch, Secretary of Orders, whom the King, in grateful recognition of his devotion to the Queen, named commander of the Order of Leopold. To her god-daughter Marie Henrietta left all her jewels. The Dean of Spa, Baron La Fontaine, was remembered with a reliquary, a container for holy relics, and considerable sums of money were left to faithful servants of the family household.

Much astonishment was caused in Manchester by the magnitude of the estate left by John Port, who died in March 1903, as well as by his disposition of it. It was generally known that he was a wealthy man, though Port lived in quite a modest style in Richmond House, Chorlton-on-Medlock, with only three servants, but no one was prepared for the huge figure of £532,562, with a net of £377,095. Still less were people prepared for the news that practically the whole of the fortune was bestowed upon a 9-year-old girl named Jane Lofts, the daughter of a lady who for some years had been the testator's housekeeper.

In 1915, Miss Lofts took possession of the inheritance after a lengthy term of probate in the Manchester courts. The will stated that if she did not survive, the bequest would fall to her mother, together with Richmond House. All furniture was to pass to Mary Ellen Kershaw, the testator's niece. The late John Port began business in a very small way at Hazel Grove, near Stockport, making bedsteads, but his shrewdness and thrifty habits soon enabled him to open more extensive premises in the Ancoats district of Manchester. In later years Port added the manufacture of iron safes and other articles to his business. The industry and trade was carried on by a number of specified executors.

By the will of William Lysaght of Monroe, Wisconsin, a labourer named Frank Mackey received a bequest of a farm worth $25,000 in November 1904. The conditions attached to the gift were that Mackey keep widow Lysaght's carriage clean and that he continue to supply her with fresh milk every day during the remainder of her life.

It took more than a substantial legacy to disturb the equanimity of Ellen Devaney, a grey-haired servant employed for 25 years by the late Mrs. A.C. McClurg. Despite the fact that she became comparatively wealthy after her employer's death, Miss Devaney refused to relinquish her control over the household at the McClurg residence on Lake Shore Drive, Chicago. When the will of the late Mrs McClurg was filed for probate in Judge Cutting's court in November 1905, it was found that Miss Devaney had been left $15,000 in recognition of faithful care of McClurg's son, Ogden. The will stated that the money was to be held in trust and an income to be received.

'And what should an old woman like me be wanting with so much money?' said Miss Devaney, when the news was brought to her. 'I have always had enough and to spare, have I not? But it was the will of the good mistress, and I will take it.'

'Of course, you will give up working and take a nice little home for yourself?' suggested a friend.

'Indeed, I won't,' responded Miss Devaney. 'How could I rest easy, knowing that the mansion was kept by strangers?'

And so, Miss Devaney remained to keep a critical eye upon the work of everyone from the butler to the hall boy. When she died one-third of the sum of the legacy was given to her relatives and the other two-thirds returned to the trust fund.

Another curious clause was contained in the will of the Reverend G.W. Ireland, for fifty years the rector of Sampford Peverall, near Tiverton in Devon, who died in 1908 leaving an estate of £21,526. The testator left £500 to Elizabeth Needs, a domestic servant at the rectory, on condition that at the time of his death, she remained in the services of the vicar's nephew, Henry Charles Rossiter, curate at the rectory, and that she should not marry a certain person whose name was given. Miss Needs was also requested to give Rossiter security not to leave his service without his written consent, and not to intermarry with the person already mentioned. Reverend Ireland also left a sum of money for the erection of a memorial tablet to himself.

The story of a 45-year-old romance between a barrister-poet and his domestic was revealed in the will of Arthur Joseph Munby of Fig Tree Court, Temple Bar, London, when he died at the age of 81 in January 1910, leaving estate to the gross value of £25,867. The codicil written by Munby reads:

Whereas Hannah Cullwick, servant, born at Shifnal, Salop, and bred in the charity school at Aston Brook, Shifnal, has been for 45 years and upwards beloved by me with a pure and honourable love, and not otherwise, and she, the said Hannah, has during all that time been as faithful and loving and devoted to me as ever woman was to man, and whereas after trying vainly to explain this state of things to my father, I married the said Hannah (she being then in my service) publicly in the presence of all her kindred who could be got together in the parish of Clerkenwell, in the County of Middlesex, on 14 January 1873.

And whereas there is no issue of the said marriage, and whereas notwithstanding her said marriage the said Hannah has always refused and still refuses to have the position which as my wife she might and could have had, and has always insisted, and still insists, on being my servant as well as my wife, her one grievance being that she cannot be my only servant, and whereas owing chiefly to this noble and unselfish resolve of hers I have never been able to make known my said marriage to my family, or to the world at large, and the same is known only to her kindred and three of my most intimate college friends, of whom Robert Spencer Borland knows the full circumstances, and knows her personally.

Arthur Munby stated that his wife lived at Hadley, Shropshire, and that he had made a practice of spending as much of every year as possible with her. 'During her years of servitude for hire,' he wrote, 'she did from time to time, of her own accord, hand over to me the savings of her wages, and never asked what I did with them.'

He added that he invested those savings, which amounted to £300, in railways stocks. He proceeded:

> Whereas it is my desire that my most dear and beloved wife and servant shall be (as she now and always has been) provided for comfortable and in that state of life which she prefers to another, and desiring as she does also that she shall not have any claim as my wife on my estate other than that given to her in my will, I leave her £300, her savings of wages as a hired servant, a life annuity of £70, and my household effects in the residence occupied by her.

Arthur Joseph Munby died at the house in Shifnal, his wife's native birthplace, and was buried in the churchyard there. He had expressed the desire to be buried wherever he might die, 'but in a consecrated churchyard, and not in any so-called cemetery.' He also made a curious bequest to the British Museum in London. He left to the trustees, two deed boxes with their contents, manuscripts and photographs, with a proviso that they were not be opened until 1 January 1950.

Under the will of R.M. Gullick, manager of the Bijou and Lyceum Theatres in Pittsburg for thirty years, and a widely known theatrical promoter, a fortune of $300,000 was left to his housekeeper, Florence Housewright, who nursed him through his last illness. Mr. Gullick died in August 1911. To a son, living in California, he bequeathed $100,000, but his father, sister and two brothers were not mentioned in the will.

The will of Dr. Edwin G. Stemmetz, of Hokendauqua, Pennsylvania, gave a piece of woodland to his brother and his books and medicines to Margaret Kreglow. The residue of his estate, valued at $100,000, was given for life to Jennie Faulkner, who was his housekeeper for eighteen years, and then to descend to Miss Kreglow, her niece, afterwards. Dr. Stemmetz was 68 when he died in August 1912 and was one of the most prominent physicians in the area. He had made his fortune primarily through banking and investments. The doctor's wife was great friends with Jennie Faulkner before she died twenty years earlier, although it was said that the two women quarrelled like cat and dog. Lawsuits were threatened by Stemmetz' relatives, who were all ordered out of the house prior to his demise, but local courts ruled that the original will benefitting Miss Faulkner should stand.

Even the promise of a bequest of $5,000 in the will of Henry C. Hurlbert, a paper manufacturer who died on 24 April 1912, failed to solve the regular quitting of servants problem in his home. Margaret Moore was a cook in the household and Mr. Hurlbert promised her the money in his will if she would continue in the family employ until his death. Mr. Hurlbert kept his promise and made a provision of $5,000 in his will for the cook. However, executors refused to pay the bequest because Mrs. Moore left the Hurlbert family home shortly before the death of her employer.

A German merchant named Hinkel, who was for some years resident in Moscow, bequeathed a fortune amounting to half a million pounds to his employees in 1912. Through the deceased man's generosity several dozen clerks, book-keepers, packers, porters and doormen suddenly found themselves raised to affluence and partnership in a well-established and lucrative business. All members of staff who had worked with the testator for at least five years shared in the bequest, said the *Daily Mail*'s Berlin correspondent. Their portions were to be reckoned on the basis of the first annual wage multiplied by the number of years they had been in service. Those who had worked for the company less than five years received a joint sum of £10,000 which was divided according to wages and length of service. It was reported that staff decided to organise the business inherited by them into a joint stock company. They also built a handsome tombstone over their benefactor's grave, built an asylum bearing his name and continued to contribute to various charities which Herr Hinkel had supported during his lifetime.

For thirty years the late Francis Jones Heseltine lived as a guest at the Westminster Palace Hotel, London, and on his death, in 1913, he left bequests to the hotel manager and his wife, and to members of the hotel staff. The final estate was valued at £50,615. Hotel life obviously held a strong appeal to Heseltine, who preferred the smooth running of the hotel to the responsibilities of running a private household. When his wife died thirty years before, Francis Heseltine took two rooms at the Westminster Palace Hotel and lived there until the end of his days. To his valet, Henry Jones, the old gentleman left £2,000 for his long and faithful service. Other bequests were:

£50 each to George Jenkins Brinkworth, manager of the hotel, and his wife, 'as a slight acknowledgment of their attention to me while residing under their management.'

£50 each 'to Nurse Mills, Beale, "who has been my waiter", and Sam, head porter at the Westminster Palace Hotel'.

£50 for distribution among the servants at the Westminster Palace Hotel, £50 to the servants of the Grand Hotel, Eastbourne, and £50 to the attending nurses.

For helping 'to smooth life's difficulties,' to quote the words of the testator, £2,500 was left to Annie Norman in September 1913, a servant of Mr. Wardale of Bognor, England, who considered that those who minister to one's comforts 'are more entitled to such recognition than blood relations one seldom sees.'

This is just one of the many displays of gratitude shown by wealthy employers. Another was the will of W.T.C. Pardoe of Hove, who left £15,000 and all his clothes to his butler and £10,000 to the valet. The previous year the late Lord Llangattock made handsome provision for several of his servants, leaving £5,000 and a life annuity of £250 to his butler, £5,000 to his estate manager and £500 each to his valet, head gardener, fireman, coachman and engineer.

Another remarkable will at the same time was that left by Rowland Ward, a Piccadilly taxidermist, who left an estate to the gross value of £735,835 and bequeathed his business to the members of staff who worked for him, contingent on them continuing their employment at the establishment. There were seven heirs in total, including a porter.

Even King Edward left some extremely generous legacies to his old servants. His personal valet benefitted to the extent of £25,000 under his royal master's will and several other royal household employees received sums varying from £5,000 to £1,500 each. However, undoubtedly the most generous bequest to an employee must certainly fall to a Mr. Pelly, assistant to wealthy London architect Mr. Grunnor, who inherited to the tune of £940,000 and his employer's firm as a going concern.

A handsome reward for faithful service befell Elizabeth Lake Richings in 1913. Under the will of her employer, Dr Evan Abraham Morgan, of Hove, she benefitted to the extent of £26,000. Morgan, who died on 3 May, granted his housekeeper the sole executrix. The doctor also left a life annuity to his brother, Richard, but all the property unexpectedly went to Miss Richings. Morgan testified in his will that his servant had 'served me honestly and faithfully for about twenty years as a domestic and housekeeper, only taking about eight days holiday during that time.'

A month later, in June 1913, a case of the wrong person inheriting money was discovered. The Duke of Devonshire's head gardener passed away in 1908, and it was supposed that the old gentleman had died intestate. An Australian relative came forward claiming to be the next of kin and was given a sum of £5,000. However, five years later a will was discovered in the ceiling of the former gardener's house, in which he left everything to his housekeeper.

For putting off her marriage for three years, and for serving her employer faithfully for fifteen years, Kathryn Tully received $50,000 under the terms of a will. Housekeeper to William Runkle, iron founder, who died on 31 January 1914, Kathryn had put her own plans on hold to fulfil the wishes of her employer's late wife. Three years previously, shortly before Mrs. Runkle's death, Tully was to be married to the family's head coachman, but knowing that her husband needed caring for, Mrs. Runkle pleaded with Kathryn to defer her marriage, insisting that she would be well provided for.

It is not often that a railway guard is rewarded for being polite to passengers, but that is exactly what happened to Frank Bunnell in 1915. A guard on the American railways, Bunnell happened to punch the ticket of a wealthy widow one day, bowing politely as he handed it back to her. The woman was so impressed with his politeness that she took an interest in Frank's career and left him her entire fortune when she died.

A rather unusual scenario occurred in 1915, when Mary Watkins left the very considerable sum of £1,300 to a former employer, Miss Lewis, of Milford Haven. Mary was in her nineties when she died and, by a codicil in her will, also left £400 to the vicar of St. Mary's Church in Haverfordwest. A box found in the old lady's room also contained £290 in gold. Friends and neighbours believed that Miss Watkins was extremely poor, due to the fact that she lived in a most frugal manner, denying herself luxuries and many of life's necessities, even insisting on doing her own washing. Mary Watkins spent nearly all of her life in domestic service with well-known families. It appeared that she had always hoarded gold and, when war broke out, guarded her box of sovereigns most vigilantly, never allowing anyone to disturb her room.

When Septimus Curtis, of Fletchwood, died on 1 December 1916, he left a sum of £1,750 in trust for his servant John Joseph Boyce. He also left his trusted employee £315, his pigeon-house, a tin house erected on Curtis' land, the corner field facing his residence, an old armchair and cushions habitually used by the testator, his pigs, agricultural implements, dairy utensils, growing crops and a motor car!

Grey-haired and rheumatic housekeeper Kate Mulcahy became heir to a fortune of almost $200,000 in 1917. The money was left by Mrs John McCabe, whom Kate had served for forty-one years. When Kate went to work for the couple, Mr McCabe was a prosperous physician, but he died leaving very little property and his widow kept the housekeeper in her employ at a significant financial sacrifice. Mrs McCabe promised Kate that she would be sole heir to her mistress' estate if she stuck by her until death and kept her word. However, during Mrs McCabe's latter years, oil was struck on the property, and she became one of the richest women in Clinton County. The will went to probate, and everything was left to Kate Mulcahy, although relatives of the McCabes tried their best to break the agreement.

Sir Thomas Sutherland, chairman and managing director of the P&O Steam Navigation Company, and senior vice-president of the Suez Canal Company, left £723, 075 when he died on 1 January 1922. A striking bequest was £10,000 and half of the proceeds of two freehold properties, plus household effects and cars, to Marjory Sinclair McKay. Sutherland wrote: 'She has been acting as my private secretary for many months. I give this sum to her in order to secure her independence and freedom from ordinary work unless of a voluntary kind.'

He left to his daughter, Helen, £40,000 and family portraits, silver trophies and cars, writing 'and nothing more, as she was already provided for.' Sir Thomas also bequeathed £20,000 to various friends and staff, and directed that the remainder of his property should go to King Edward's Hospital Fund in London.

In 1919, an interesting and perhaps insightful article on the subject of leaving money to servants was written by Sophie Irene Loeb for *The New York Evening World*. It reads:

For faithful and devoted service to my beloved wife and myself.

These are the words in the will which gives $50,000 to Bessie Stern by her employer, who died recently in South Orange, N.J. At the same time the public press tells of another servant who, for similar services, is the recipient of $25,000. Her name is Annie Blackton, colored.

These two instances of faithfulness rewarded are worthwhile recording and thinking about. I can't help wishing that others who have money and who have servants will read about these wills and will reflect on what they have done in this connection. I believe that many more such wills are sure to come.

Long and faithful service is not so easy to get and a keener appreciation of such is bound to come. Besides, the war has taught us to look at real service, especially menial work, from a very different viewpoint than ever before.

I know of wealthy individuals who have died and left their money to relatives whom they have never seen – relatives who have not contributed one iota of pleasure or happiness to the person whose money they have enjoyed – relatives who have waited for years for this dead man's shoes, contributing nothing themselves to his good.

As against this there has been the splendid cook or the fine man-servant who has toiled night and day, giving energy and enthusiasm and youth in the interest of that self-same individual. Often they have been left but a paltry legacy.

One of the big things that the war has developed and that will come more and more in the reconstruction period is reciprocity. Faithful service is bound to be appreciated and more such rewards as are mentioned will surely materialise.

Harry Zeitun was a retired army officer, aged 50, who received £3 million under the will of American Julia Davies, 'In token of his affectionate care and protection of myself.' In January 1922, Zeitun was visiting Rome where he met Mrs. Davies, who was feeling unwell. He secured her the best care and medical advice, kept in contact with Mrs Davies and on his return to England was appointed as the lady's secretary. She returned to America a short time later, where she died in December of the same year. Zeitun first learned of his good fortune when he inquired whether wages owing to him could be covered by the deceased woman's estate. Mrs. Davies' will stipulated that her husband should have no claim on her estate after a disagreement between the pair when she had both English and American solicitors draw up a new will. Captain Zeitun was educated in Italy and fought with the Foreign Legion in the First World War, where he was badly wounded. He was reported to have spoken fourteen languages and for many years was interpreter at the West London and Bow Street police courts. He also apparently had an adventurous career and at one time claimed bankruptcy, owing £40,000.

Later the same year, in August 1922, when Lord Swansea's will was read in London, it was revealed he had directed that none of his half-blood relatives should attend his funeral. He bequeathed to his servant, Daniel Ellis, £2,000. Together with a further £2,000 legacy under the will, the peer's aunt also gave Ellis his coronet, coronation robes and all his papers and documents.

Charles Freeman, of New Jersey, who died in March 1923, left a will in which he cut off his wife, Mary Wilkins Freeman, a widely known novelist, with $1. Freeman left $200 to each of his four sisters and gave the remainder of his $100,000 estate to his chauffeur, Harry Mohring. The will was drawn up the previous July but no details of a rift between the couple were forthcoming. Mrs Freeman and her sisters-in-law announced that they would contest the will.

Frederick Rolph, a former chief petty officer in the Royal Navy was left a fortune of over £40,000 in 1927. The bequest came from his former employer Charles Bagge Penn, of Victoria Street, London, a stockbroker who died at the age of 69. Having employed Rolph as a manservant, Mr. Penn left his entire estate and property to his faithful friend. Rolph, aged 50, was still residing at the flat formerly occupied by Penn but declined to discuss his good fortune with reporters. The extent of Penn's bequest came as something as a surprise to neighbours, as Penn was not a communicative man, and his former place of residence was unknown.

The value of the New South Wales estate in Australia belonging to Alexander Busby, of Surrey, England, was sworn at £121,489 in August 1927. Mr. Busby, who was seventy-one when he died, directed that a year's wages should be paid to each employee on his estate at Cassilis as long as they had been in his employ for a period of over five years. The testator also left £500 to his valet, to be increased to £1,000 if his widow agreed, £250 to the Christian Science Benevolent Association, Boston, and £250 to the Christian Science Home for the Aged, Boston. The balance of the estate was left to relatives.

A Czechoslovakian immigrant who, up until 1927, was making beds and sweeping floors in the mansion of Frank W. Savin at Port Chester, United States, became the heiress to $5 million in January 1930. Anna Mary Schleis, aged 47, married her employer, a retired broker, and became his fourth wife. Slavin died from an appendicitis, aged 79, and left Anna his whole estate. She had at her command eight Rolls Royce cars and a staff of twenty servants, ironically all of whom were her former associates.

A year later, in October 1928, after a few minor bequests, Reverend Tertius Buzzard, of Grimsargh, Lancashire, left the residue of his estate to his housekeeper, Jane Hayes, for her long and faithful service. The clergy's heir was also fortunate that a few days before Reverend Buzzard's death, his sister died and left him a considerable sum. As a result, Hayes received a total sum of almost £26,000.

The late Samuel Crabtree Helm, aged 71, who made a fortune in the Bradford wool trade in England, left to his housekeeper, Catherine Ann Geech, the use of his residence and £1,000 a year in 1929 while she remained unmarried and in occupation of the house. Miss Geech told a newspaper correspondent:

Mr. Helm advertised for a companion-housekeeper, but I did not see the advertisement. A friend of mine at Huddersfield replied to it and at the same time applied for another post in Scarborough. She was offered both positions and decided to go to Scarborough. She asked me to answer Mr. Helm's letter. Rather reluctantly I did so, because never before had I undertaken a similar position outside my family. I explained this to Mr. Helm but he engaged me. His generosity was unbounded. You should have seen his list of Christmas gifts. Nobody was forgotten.

Catherine Geech added that she proposed to continue living at Mr. Helm's house.

In September 1930 a Berlin Court decided on the fate of a huge fortune, estimated at almost £10 million, left by German financier, jeweller and art dealer, Albert Loeske. The judge found in favour of Loeske's manager, Herr Oppenheimer, his wife Frau Oppenheimer, and a life-long friend, Frau Rosa Blaustein, leaving the 300 blood relations who had contested the will to go away empty handed. The family of the eccentric bachelor, who had refused to have anything to do with his relations during his lifetime, put forward the alternative pleas that the will was a forgery, that the testator was of unsound mind and under undue influence when he executed it, and that the beneficiaries were unworthy to succeed. The Court, however, made very short work of the allegations, for the judgement was the result of barely five minutes recess.

The defending counsel made the interesting statement that the moving spirit behind the disappointed family members was a Russian living in Paris, who described himself on his own notepaper as a 'specialist in inheritance cases' and that a handwriting expert who declared the will to be a forgery had been promised a fee equivalent to £2,500 if his opinion was accepted by the Court.

Albert Loeske, who died in October 1929, dined daily in a modest pothouse for just sevenpence, despite his great wealth. He owned valuable property in Berlin and other German towns, oil wells in Romania, clock factories in Switzerland, six art dealer outlets, and three shops of Magraf & Co, the best-known jewellers in Berlin at the time.

His neglected relatives, who had hoped that he would remember them in his final wishes, found that nothing at all had been left to them, while Loeske's manager, Oppenheimer, was authorised to select pictures from the galleries worth £15,000. The clock manufacturing business was to be divided among certain members of staff and every employee was left a year's salary. The residue of the estate was divided between the three aforementioned legatees. Loeske was for some time the biggest taxpayer in Berlin. It was said of him that he was the only millionaire in Germany who filled up his income tax return with scrupulous precision.

Thought for a beloved pet was a feature of the will of Mary Woodgate of St. Leonard's-on-Sea, England, who left an estate valued at £7,875. Miss Woodgate bequeathed her dog and £15 for him to her maid 'Grace Wood if still in my service. Otherwise, the dog is to be painlessly put to sleep.'

Leaving £7,368 in her will in 1933, Eleanor Catherine Cholmeley Russell, of Tower House, Bletchingley, Surrey, gave £100 a year, certain furniture, the use of a cottage, six of her hens and one cock, to her maid Alice Cox. She also bequeathed the proceeds of the sale of the remaining chickens and chicken run to her parlourmaid Annie Fairman. Mrs Russell also gave annuities of £100 each to her secretary, chauffeur and two maidservants, with a further £200 to Annie Childs 'in grateful recognition of the care which she has taken of me about my enforced diet for many years.'

In the same year, Mr G. Guthrie Dunn, a wealthy Scotsman, was returning from Australia in his yacht when he died in an accident at St. Helena in the South Atlantic Ocean. Dunn, 26, had derived his fortune from a Glasgow tobacco firm and left £1.2 million, of which £491,000 was paid in death duties. The sole beneficiary was the young man's housekeeper, Agnes Stevens, who looked after his home, Knock Castle, on the Isle of Skye.

Two faithful servants inherited $50,000 and valuable personal property from the estate of actress Marie Dressler in 1934. The actual value of property left by the star, who reputedly earned $3,000 per week, was not given when the will was filed for probate, but it was estimated to be worth over $300,000. To Mamie Cox, the coloured maid who had served her for many years, Marie Dressler left $35,000 and her clothes. The maid's husband, Jerry Cox, was bequeathed $15,000 and the actress's automobile. The couple were also given Dressler's silverware. There was also a bequest of $10,000 to the American Women's Association and various gifts to friends. The bulk of the estate went to the testator's sister, Bonita Ganthony, who lived in England, and to block any possible lawsuits Miss Dressler willed $1 to all persons coming forward to claim blood or legal relationship with her.

When Katherine Sweeney left her position of housekeeper in the employ of George French in 1934, little did she realise that she was leaving behind a bequest of $75,000. Seventeen days before his death, on 26 February, Mr French made a codicil wiping out a trust fund of $50,000 and a cash bequest of $25,000 made to his housekeeper after she left 'without ascribing any definite reason therefore.' French instead left Miss Sweeney $1,000. The money that she was to have originally received was distributed amongst various charities.

Also in 1934, a year of some very generous bequests, three employees inherited a prosperous building and decorating business in the West End of London under the will of their employer. Head clerk Harry Rowell, head plumber Richard Dennis and painting foreman William Hawkins had all worked for the firm for thirty years. The testator was their employer, Tom Henwood, of Portman Square who died, aged 59, leaving estate valued at £82,819.

'If you stay in my service and look after my house and myself until I die, I will make it worth your while'

Axel Walfrid Raberg, a Scandinavian shipowner of West Park, Eltham, South London, made this offer to his cook, Mabel Holmes, in 1931 when his second wife died. Mabel had already spent eight years in devoted service to the Rabergs and agreed to stay. She saw middle-age approaching and possibly dreamed that she would be left a small annuity by her employer. Axel Raberg died on 29 June 1935 and when the will was read Mabel was told:

'To my cook, Mabel Holmes, I leave the sum of £25,000.'

Overwhelmed by her good fortune, Mabel left at once for a quiet holiday to decide her future, leaving the whole of Eltham to discuss Raberg's will. The remainder of the estate was divided thus: £35,000 in trust and Raberg's property to his stepdaughter, Nellie Zethrin, and £40,000 in trust to her son, Walfrid.

A close friend of Axel Raberg's family described the qualities which the testator admired in his cook. 'Although a wealthy man and very generous, he had simple tastes. He hated to see money wasted, and Mabel was thrifty. She never attempted to serve him elaborate meals. But I think the most remarkable of her abilities was that when Mr Raberg became deaf, she was able to make him understand just what people were saying. She was his constant companion.'

On 11 November 1935 Polly Rawstron of St. James' Avenue, Thorpe Bay, Essex, stood before Southend magistrates on a summons for non-payment of property rates. The circumstances were most unusual, however, as the house in question had been left to Miss Rawstron by her former mistress, together with an annuity of £76, which was nowhere near enough to cover the upkeep of such a property. By terms of the will, the former lady's maid explained, if she were to sell or lease out the house, the annuity reverted to the RSPCA. In light of the circumstances, the society waived their rights in court, allowing Polly Rawstron to sub-let or sell the property in order to pay her debt.

In March 1935, a chauffeur and his wife, the household cook, and a maid became owners of an estate in which the week before they were servants. The will of their late employer, Jessie A. Goddard, left the trio her stately mansion to do with as they saw fit. Heirs to the estate were William Wilson, for twenty-five years Mrs. Goddard's chauffeur, his wife Annie, cook Margaret Macauley and maid Jane Douglas. Other bequests in the will were: $40,000 to Charles Dunham, a cousin from Boston, $25,000 to Ralph Whitney, another cousin from New York, $10,000 to Reverend Henry Goddard of Portland and $10,000 to Mannie Fields of Buffalo, New York.

For thirty-five years an elderly woman lived alone with only her maid for company. When she died of old age, it was found that in her will she had left to her faithful helper a large sum of money, the house they had shared for many years, and the right to be buried in the same grave! The old lady was Ann Haynes, her will being published in 1936. The bequest read:

To my good and faithful servant, Charlotte Pearson Wood, my residence, Trevor Lodge, certain furniture and £2,000 and if living in the neighbourhood of St. Peter's, Thanet, at her death, she may be buried in the grave belonging to the testatrix in the churchyard at St. Peter's, Thanet.' Another of the legatees, Dr. W.E. Pimbury, a Birmingham dentist, said: 'I have known Miss Wood for many years. She was more like a friend than a servant to Miss Haynes. She was absolutely devoted to her mistress.

The housekeeper of Ellis Merry, of Cambridge, was nothing short of stunned when her employer's will was disclosed in 1937. Instead of a token bequest, Merry had shown his appreciation of the woman's service by leaving her seven houses and a third of his $18,146 estate, the rest being distributed amongst relatives.

In the same year, a Weymouth physician, John Ernest Ransford, died leaving £200 to his only son, despite his estate being worth £10,190. Doctor Ransford stated in his will that his only child was amply provided for and the residue of the property was to go to his housekeeper, Hilda Mullard. In a statement to the *Nottingham Journal*, Miss Mullard said: 'It is quite true that Dr Ransford's only son, Major E.M. Ransford, was left only £200. He told me three weeks ago that he approved of the terms of his father's will and said that the doctor had done the right thing. If the will had been otherwise, he himself would have done it.'

In the same year, Lord Ormathwaite, King George V's Master of Ceremonies from 1910 to 1920, left his entire property of £107,351 equally to Rose Spary, his former housekeeper and wife of his valet, and her sons, aged 19 and 14. Mrs. Spary told news reporters that the Lord had been almost blind for ten years. 'We helped him in every way possible,' she said. 'He was very good to us and was godfather to our sons, but we were unaware that he was rich as he lived at the rate of £600 a year.' She went on to describe how Queen Mary regularly sent Lord Ormathwaite Christmas presents and had last visited him the previous year. The Queen had found him sitting in an invalid chair and had tucked a gift of a warm rug around him while they chatted for an hour.

However, the housekeeper's husband claimed that the late Baron was no hero regarding his bequest and didn't expect his wife and sons to receive a farthing, the estate being mortgaged up to the hilt. Mr Spary said that Lord Ormathwaite had been unlucky in his investments and had lost large sums of money on the turf and the gambling tables of Monte Carlo. The Third Baron Ormathwaite, born in London in 1859, served in the 1st Life Guards from 1878 until 1886, and was MP for Radnorshire for seven years. The heir to the title, but apparently not the property, was his brother, The Honourable George Harry Walsh.

When the will of the Reverend John Ledbrooke Broad, one-time vicar of Aintree, Liverpool, was read in 1939, white-haired Jane Tickle, who had served in his household for forty years, was surprised to find that he had left her most of his £23,000 fortune. She also received his Lakeland villa at Coniston, where she was residing at the time of her employer's death. Mrs. Tickle's sister, Mary Abram, of Liverpool, served twelve years with the minister and received £2,000 in the will. Reverend Broad had been a widower for over twenty years and had no children. 'He was a man in a million – reserved, but kindness itself,' declared Jane Tickle. 'I was surprised at the legacy and have not made up my mind what to do with the fortune.'

Ann Hutchinson Convery left her humble home in Sunderland at the age of 20 to work as a servant to Dr Charles William Graham at his home in the hamlet of Skinburness, near Carlisle. In 1945, at the age of 36, she became mistress of the palatial 'Windy Ridge' mansion in which she had worked for so long, and possessor of a fortune of nearly £30,000. Her 'Cinderella' story was revealed when the will of the doctor, who died in June 1945 at the age of 81, was published the following August. The only other bequest was one of £200 to Carlisle Dispensary, the residue being left to housekeeper Ann 'Nancy' Convery. However, the legacy came as no surprise to the young woman.

Dr Graham took me to his solicitor and showed me a copy of his will in May 1943, I went to work for   Dr Graham and his wife sixteen years ago and they were like parents to me. Mrs Graham died in 1932 and I became his sole companion and secretary in addition to running the house.

He has a brother and sister who live somewhere in the south, but no children. He called me 'Nancy' because he liked the sound of the name.

I have no coupons so I can't buy any clothes, and no petrol is available, So I can't use the car Dr Graham left. My main concern now is to try to make things comfortable for my mother for the rest of her years. Quite frankly, I'm perfectly happy as I am. Excepting for providing for one or two luxuries that have always been out of my reach, the money will not make any difference whatsoever to my way of living.

When Mary Sheldon Lyons died at the age of 81 in October 1946, she left half a million dollars to a preacher that she hardly knew. Father Divine was the leader of a widespread religious sect, was called 'God' by his followers and was already very wealthy at the time of the bequest. Mrs Lyons was a member of an old and distinguished New York family and dismissed six relatives in her will with $100 each, left $500 to a brother, and left the remainder of her fortune to two of Father Divine's 'palace missions.' A motor car, jewellery and valuable antique furniture were left to the old lady's maid, Patience Budd. It was reported that Mary Lyons met Father Divine when Mrs Budd took her from her home to various 'Kingdom Heavens and Promised Lands' services at church.

A bachelor curate who took lodgings for a fortnight in the home of a Liverpool woman was so pleased with her cooking that he stayed with her for fifty years, in fact right up until his death, at the age of 80, in 1948. It was revealed in his will that clergyman Canon Sydney Arthur John Barrett, vicar of St. Anne's in Liverpool, left £17,000 to 'my friend Annie Howard of St. Anne's Vicarage, as a token of my appreciation for her many acts of kindness to me.'

When former typist Mary Dugdale arrived at a Salford engineering works and took the governing director's chair, as she was entitled to do under the will of the former owner who appointed her to the position, all the 180 employees stopped work. The founder of the business, John Anderson, left Miss Dugdale most of his £132,000 estate and directed that she should have his position at a salary of £1,000 a year. The first time that the typist had visited the works since the will was published was 29 March 1949. After a conference with the employees, the company secretary told Mary Dugdale that they were strongly opposed to her interference until the legal position was clarified and that the strike would continue if she returned to the premises.

On Mothering Sunday in 1908, 10-year-old Mary Fowler delivered milk and helped Alice Griffiths in her cake shop at Wellinghall in Staffordshire. Mary continued to deliver milk around the community for thirty-two years and, because Miss Griffiths was lonely, she moved in with her in 1933. When the old lady died in October 1949, she bequeathed her shop and £30,000 to Mary. The *Daily Mirror* reported the new heir as saying: 'I shall carry on the same way because I love this business. In the last twelve years I have not had five days holiday and not a day's illness.'

The late William Effey, managing director of Rowes Café in Brisbane, Australia, left an estate of £104,817 in 1950, a great part of which was bequeathed in shares to current and former employees of the company. The café was a very popular social centre for locals and Effey expressed a wish that business be carried on with as little change of management and control as possible.

His will stated: 'My mother used to say: William if we make twelvepence in the business, we can only take threepence, ninepence must go back again, that is the foundation on which Rowes is built. I believe that the beneficiaries named in my will, will harmoniously pull together and further the success of the company.'

Gifts of shares to people who then resided in southern States included 1,500 to widow Alice Falconer of Sydney and 500 to Roy Sellars of the Hotel Australia in Melbourne. Other beneficiaries included relatives, a solicitor, a manageress, a private secretary, office girl, head cook, chef, waiter and cleaner.

At London in 1951 Mildred Smith, who was left £1,000 in the £727, 277 will of her mistress, Lady Lilian Francis Hind, said, 'I shall contest the will.'

Miss Smith, aged 72, added,

My mistress owed me hundreds of pounds. The housekeeping money she gave me was never half enough and I had to spend my own money so that she and the staff had enough to eat. I worked for Lady Lilian for twenty-nine years and had to do all sorts of jobs. I started as her personal maid. Then I had to learn sewing and I made practically all the linen in the house. Then because she couldn't get a cook to stay, I had to take on the kitchen work as well.

Originally, she said, a staff of eight servants and a charwoman used to run Lady Lilian's thirty-roomed mansion at Newcastle Circus, Nottingham. The staff was reduced to four in 1946, when Sir Jesse Hind, Lady Lilian's husband died.

A maid in Sacramento, California, was named by her late employee as sole heir to an estate valued at $200,000 in 1951. A sign of changing times, it was notable that white Ida Meyer cut off all of her relatives in favour of her coloured home help, Josephine Elston, the only named beneficiary.

Ernest Mooring was often called the 'perfect butler' by his employer, British painter and playwright Graham Robertson, of whom he was in the employ for fifty years. When Robertson died at his home in Witley, Surrey, in 1948, he bequeathed his faithful servant £7,500 and a cottage. Mooring subsequently left over £13,000 in his will when he passed away in 1951, with friends commenting that the deceased was a 'very thrifty man.'

In September of the same year, six employees of the Australian Optical Company were left almost £50,000 by their late employer, Lawrence Dickens Colechin. The employees had all been with the company for over twenty years and were unanimous in their views that most of the money should be reinvested back into the business 'to lift it to greater heights.' One third of Mr. Colechin's estate, valued at £148, 407 went to his secretary, Una Burns, and a friend from New South Wales received £400 a year until his death.

Another wealthy Australian businessman who appreciated his staff was the later Peter Mathieson who died in February 1953, aged 90. The elderly gent left an estate of £259,349, of which he left £20,000 to housekeeper Mrs. Moore, £5,000 to solicitor Mr. Shipway and £5,000 each to three faithful employees, each with more than forty years' service. The residue was left to Mathieson's great-grandchildren. With extensive interests in electrical goods, grocery and tobacco businesses, it is little wonder that Peter Mathieson was described as 'the ideal boss.'

For most of his 41 years, James Dolphus Cabler had never handled more money than the weekly pay doled out by his undertaker boss in a broken-down funeral parlour in Baton Rouge, the sleepy sunny capital of Louisiana. However, when rich cattle rancher James Harris Baughman fell ill at the age of 75, Cabler answered an advert and arrived at the impressive family home with a recommendation as a nurse. Although Cabler tended to the old gentleman for only three days before his death, Mrs Laura Baughman said that it was her husband's dying wish that Cabler remained at the property to care for her. He did so and was constantly at her side. Socialite friends to whom she introduced him winced when she referred to him as 'My Sonny Boy' and he affectionately called her 'Marm.'

As the dear friend of a wealthy widow, Sonny Boy could not be expected to run errands on foot and was provided with a new Mercury Sedan with a two-way radio. Mrs Baughman's cousins in Kentucky developed cold anger when they learned that Cousin Laura had bought an Italian marble monument and had three names carved on it – hers, her late husband's and Sonny Boy's! Laura Baughman died suddenly on 30 July 1949 and left James Cabler everything, except small bequests which gave the eleven cousins about £200 each.

As an ex-embalmer, Cabler handled the funeral arrangements with practised efficiency. He hired a fashionable preacher who was just clearing his throat to launch into the eulogy when the sheriff strode in with a court order for an immediate autopsy. Baton Rouge general hospital's head pathologist made the post-mortem examination and announced that Mrs Baughman had died from natural causes.

Starting legal action to contest their cousin's will, the frustrated relatives alleged that Cabler had induced Laura to leave him her fortune by fraud, threat, duress, deceit and other vile practices in an elaborate premeditated scheme. Cabler in turn declared that his relationship with his benefactor had been 'a lofty one.'

Cabler said, 'She was a sweet, wonderful woman. After all, I didn't ask for any of this. In fact, no one was more surprised than I.'

Both sides engaged private detectives to ferret for damaging evidence and Cabler employed a bodyguard. As the marathon court proceedings dragged on, James Cabler took leave long enough to woo and wed beautician Lena Bookter, the woman who had cared for Laura Baughman's hair. For two years Laura's cousins' sued Cabler for the £213,000 and mansion that she had left him in gratitude of his constant care. Finally, in January 1952, the court decreed that none of the relatives' charges against James Cabler could be proved and he, together with his new bride, were allowed to enjoy their inherited home in peace.

The same year Audrey Housman inherited £31,000 from the Duke of Bedford but insisted that she would continue to work at her moderately paid position at St. George's Hospital, London. Miss Housman was the duke's private secretary for fifteen years and said she was shocked at the amount her former employer left to her. Living with her parents and happy in her position as a distributor of alms for the hospital, 44-year-old Audrey had previously worked for Gillet and Johnston, the famous Croydon bell-making firm and had tuned many of the finest church bells and carillons. The Duke of Bedford was killed in an accident, aged 64, and left an £800,000 estate.

Said to have been one of the richest women in the world at the time of her death on 29 January 1952, the late Anne Morgan willed almost half her estate to her personal secretary, Daisy Rogers. The will was filed for probate in New York on 7 February. Anne, aged 78, was the daughter of J. Pierpont Morgan and reputedly had a three-million-dollar trust fund. The will stipulated that half of the residuary estate should go to Miss Rogers, with the remainder going to other employees and charitable organisations.

In 1954 a former chambermaid, who was promoted to manageress of a London hotel on the suggestion of a wealthy ex-diplomat who was staying there, inherited £20,000 in his will. Joan Aveling, 37 years old, from Folkestone, Kent, changed her name by deed poll in 1950 at the instigation of Arthur Aveling, who was 24 years older than her. In June 1953, Mr. Aveling, a former First Secretary at the British Embassy in China and subsequently a leading diplomat in Europe, was cited co-respondent in the young woman's divorce suit. He was ordered to pay the costs of the court case and £200 damages to Joan's husband, Harry Taylor, a boiler room attendant. In court it was noted that Joan Taylor had changed her name to Aveling, although both she and Arthur Aveling denied adultery. The judge heard that some time after the Taylor's separated, Aveling began to take Joan out, when she worked as chambermaid at his hotel. Arthur Aveling then suggested to the hotel manager that it was not right that one of the principal guests was walking out with a junior member of staff, and asked that she be promoted to manageress, which she was. Eventually Joan left the hotel and joined Arthur at his home in Folkestone as nurse-companion. He gave her a ring, which she wore on her wedding finger. Arthur Aveling died at the age of 61, leaving an estate valued at £111, 711.

A Filipino who served a Philadelphia couple for twenty years received a large inheritance from the widow's estate, with a rather unusual proviso. Paulino Dominisac had become like a son to the Mitchell family and inherited more than $200,000, with the string attached to his bequest that he not fall in love with any non-Filipino woman who might try to marry him for the money. As it turned out, Paulino already had his eye upon a lady named Dorothy Korpuze, whose father was a native Filipino. The terms binding Mr. Dominisac were clearly set out in the will of Adeline Mitchell, widow of T. Carlisle Mitchell, part-owner of a shipping container company. It stated that should Paulino marry a non-Filipino, the trust should be reverted to Jefferson

Hospital instead. Mr. Mitchell died in 1948, with his widow passing on 17 September 1958, aged 70.

According to the directions of the will, Dominisac was to get the income from two-thirds of the estate being held in trust, the Mitchells' home in Coral Gables, Florida, an expensive sedan and contents from both the Florida and Philadelphia homes. He was also to receive twenty acres of land near Fowlerton in Texas, where the drilling for oil was being undertaken. In addition, the trusted housekeeper, Paulino, was to receive the final third of the estate on the death of Ethel Poppleton, Adeline Mitchell's sister, which had been held in trust for her benefit. Finally, the will specified that Dominisac be well looked after through the years, but enough money should be kept in trust to ensure that he never be without funds in his lifetime. Always, of course, with the matrimonial proviso.

When the will of Eugene R. Phillips was read in February 1955, three of his servants unexpectedly became richer overnight. The millionaire manufacturer from Rhode Island left $100,000 each to his secretary Andrew Hlafter and housekeeper Jeanne Claghorn, and $50,000 to chauffeur James Hughes. The retired owner of a Providence cable-making firm, 84-year old Phillips also willed $200,000 to his daughter, Ruth Estelle, and $5,000 each to four grandchildren.

When retired farmer Walter George Sumption died in March 1962, aged 87, the details of his will conjured up images of cosy afternoon teas with his housekeeper, Sarah Berryman. Mr Sumption left £300, his silver teapot and the use of his bungalow, including furnishings, to his faithful help under condition that she was still in his service at the time of his death. However, it was also specified that the period of occupancy should not exceed five years after Sumption's death, and that Mrs Berryman remain a widow.

For forty-seven years Walter Wooding tended the rambling gardens at The Homestead, Stoneleigh, Warwickshire, as if they were his own. Walter was gardener and occasional chauffeur to the Hill family who owned the nine-bedroom house, and his wife was employed as housekeeper. When Evelyn Hill, whose father was the founder of the Hillman motor company in Coventry, died in December 1966 she left £10,000 and the house to the Woodings. Included in the bequest was a four-storey holiday home in Aberdovey and £500 in trust to the couple's daughter, Evelyn, who was named after the generous employer. Walter Wooding told a reporter that Mrs. Hill was always helping old people and children in the village and on the day before her death she had been copying books for the blind on a Braille typewriter.

It came as a great shock to his family when the will of multi-millionaire 3rd Baron Lord Glenconner, Colin Tennant, revealed that he had changed his will just twelve months before his death, cutting out his entire family. Lord Glenconner died in 2010, aged 83, at his Caribbean home in St Lucia, leaving everything to the West Indian servant who had cared for him. Kent Adonai was driver and companion to the eccentric Scottish aristocrat and was bequeathed the entire estate, including contents. As of 2023, the bequest was part of a legal battle between Adonai and the Glenconner family, and the entire estate was put up for sale, after Kent agreed to give the Lord's family their half of the inheritance. Beau House, the grand whitewashed property at the centre of the island, and its 95-acre estate went up for sale at a remarkable sum of £19 million.

Other bequests to faithful employees were made by a woman who died in Buckinghamshire at the age of 89 and left a fortune of £80,000 to her coachman; Lord Burton left £40,000 in annuities to his servants; while the proprietor of a Leicester Square restaurant left his female bookkeeper close to £100,000. The Dowager Duchess of Wilton left several large bequests to her servants, including the sum of £20,000 to her maid.

A Hove surgeon left his entire fortune to his housekeeper and the very same year a lady in the North of England left her companion £40,000.

A Liverpool shipowner left £1 million and remembered every person in his employ, both at home and in the offices, in his will. His legacies ranged from £50,000 to his manager to £100 to the office boy.

Some years ago, a British magnate, after leading his wife to believe herself sole legatee, left her one shilling and bequeathed £72,000 to others, including £3,500 to a servant whom his wife especially disliked.

Of all forms of petty spite, the vindictive will is the meanest, but now and then someone gets a reward for short service. A Scottish ironmaster who died just after the turn of the twentieth century had been entertained in his sick room by a Scottish piper who played his favourite reels and laments to his satisfaction. The piper was left £10,000 in the ironmaster's will.

Chapter Nine

Generous Benefactors

Over 300 years ago a benevolent, if somewhat eccentric, gentleman named Henry Greene directed that a certain portion of his property should be set aside to ensure that 'there should be given annually to four poor women, four green waistcoats to be lined with green galloon lace, and to be delivered to the women on or before December 21, so that they may be worn on Christmas Day.'

That curious bequest was made in 1709, and it is interesting to compare it with one made by James Moss, of Manchester, just four years before. The amount of this was £100, which was 'to be laid out in the purchase of real property, the profits of which should be yearly bestowed towards buying five gowns for five aged men, living in Manchester, to be of housewife's kersey, of a sad blue colour, and to be given on Christmas Day morning, before prayers, in the south porch of the Parish Church of Manchester.'

No less whimsical were the ancient bequests which more particularly concerned what may be called the 'inner man' at Christmas time. By the will of William Robinson, who had served as Sheriff of Hull, it was provided that every Christmas Day there should be given 'twelve loaves of bread to as many poor widows' of the town. But it was specially directed that the loaves should be delivered to the applicants at the side of the benefactor's grave in Holy Trinity Churchyard, possibly with the object of perpetuating his memory.

For a great many years, bread and cheese were regularly thrown from the belfry of Paddington Church on the Sunday morning closest to Christmas Eve and scrambled for by the people below. However, owing to the disorderly scenes which this novel distribution of Christmas cheer produced, a more sensible method was ultimately adopted. This interesting tradition was described in the December Edition of *The London Magazine* in 1737: 'This day, according to annual custom, bread and cheese were thrown from Paddington steeple to the populace, agreeable o' the will of two women, who were relieved there with bread and cheese when they were almost starved; and Providence afterwards favouring them, they left an estate in that parish to continue the custom forever on that day.'

Three pieces of land situated in the parish were certainly left by two maiden ladies, whose names are unknown, and their charity was distributed as described up until the Sunday before Christmas in 1834, when the bread (consisting of three or four dozen penny rolls, and the same quantity in pieces of cheese) were thrown for the very last time from the belfry of St. Mary's Church by William Hogg, the parish clerk. After that date the rent arising from the 'bread and cheese lands' as they were called, was distributed to the poorest families in the parish in the form of coal, blankets and food. To distinguish the most in need, an annual list was made out and presented to the church wardens, stating each family's residence, occupation and number of children under the age of 10.

The arrangements for their 'long rest' of two Dutch painters showed their love of life and distinguished them as worthy of their fellow artists' appreciation. Shortly before his death at the beginning of the eighteenth century, the celebrated Dutch seascape painter Ludolf Backhuysen (born Bakhuizen) purchased several gallons of the best wine procurable, then had it bottled and sealed. When his will was opened, a purse of sixty-eight gold pieces was found to be left to his friends on the condition that they give a grand dinner and drink the wine until there wasn't a single drop left. The second Dutch painter, Martin Heemskerk, left his fortune to be divided into parts, each one to be given as a dowry to a maiden of his native village, on the condition that the wedding festivities take place on his grave.

Another artist who directed in his will that his estate benefit other artists was Louis Lang who died a bachelor in May 1893. He was a member of the Artists' Fund Society and the Century Club and left around $50,000. Lang's will, dated May 1889 and May 1990, was written in his own hand and divided into two parts. He referred to them as 'Part American' and 'Part German,' with respective American and German executors for each half. Louis Lang left all his paintings and sketches to the Artists' Fund Society, in addition to many bequests to relatives. The residue of the estate was directed to go to the poor and disabled residents of Stadt Waldsee, in Wurtemberg, Germany. Lang's brother, Nepomuck, contested the will on the ground of mental incapacity, but when it was submitted for probate Surrogate Fitzgerald found that evidence failed to prove this.

A very benevolent benefactor was Spanish General Riquelme. He left a sum equivalent to £40,000, which in today's currency would total over three million, to establish a home in Grenada for penniless widows and daughters of officers. However, the bequest restricted its field of usefulness to those only of good looks, good figure and youth. Preference of admission was to be given to fine physical development over every other claim for assistance. The old General explained his strange limitation upon a philanthropic basis before his death. In the course of his wanderings, he said that he had observed that 'the greater the beauty that a woman is possessed of, so much more is she exposed to the temptations and misfortunes of the world.'

A remarkable case of charity going begging is to be found in the failure of a fund that for years appealed in vain to ministers of the Presbyterian faith. The story began in 1884 when Anne Jane Mercer, of Ambler, Pennsylvania, died and bequeathed her fortune, together with a fine house and grounds, for the use of infirm ministers of the Presbyterian Church. It was a very grand property, and the will was read amid the despairing comments of relatives who hoped that a very different disposition would be made of the Mercer wealth.

The house and grounds were ideal for an institution such as Anne Mercer contemplated, being in a picturesque part of the Keystone State. As the amount in cash to be used for the maintenance of the institution was $100,000, it seemed that the legatee had done everything possible to ensure the comfort for the declining lives of a good number of ministers. However, as a report stated in the *New York Daily Tribune* in 1909, the home willed by Mrs. Mercer housed just one lone occupant and, despite the efforts of the trustees and directors, no more Presbyterian clergymen could be induced to spend the winter of their lives within its walls.

Some light was shed on the mystery of this unsuccessful charity by the items in a bill asking for relief from the terms of the will and for some other project to be brought forward for the expenditure of the Mercer fortune. It was asserted in the bill that only thirty-five ministers had made application for admission to the home in the twenty-five-year period that its doors remained open to the men who could qualify. Twelve were found to be ineligible, fifteen were taken in and the rest were not heard from again. Of the lucky fifteen, ten left for various reasons, four of the remainder died, leaving just one, who in 1909 was the sole beneficiary of the accommodation under the terms of the will.

The lone survivor of the fifteen was asked why he thought that the charity had failed but could give no valid reason other than the home being too lonesome. It cannot be denied that this ancient minister's life was a lonely one, eating, sleeping and living in a great house with nobody to speak to except the servants who waited upon him. It would certainly not have been such a solitary life had he been blessed with the company of another hundred ministers like himself. The 'help' had an easy time of it, reads the report, consisting of three big men and one woman. With only one inmate to wait upon, it may be supposed that time hung rather heavily on their hands.

By the will of George Heigham, silversmith, of High Holborn, London, the bulk of his property valued at £100,576 was left to charity in 1906. King Edward's Hospital received the ultimate residue, which amounted to many thousands of pounds. Among the bequests were £100 each to the Silver Trade Pension Society and the Children's Hospital in Great Ormond Street, and £500 each to National Refuges for Children, Charing Cross, Royal Free, University College, Guy's, King's College, Great Northern, Middlesex, London Fever and London Hospitals.

John Steward Kennedy, one of America's little-known millionaires, left bequests of more than $25 million to religious, charitable and educational institutions when he died of whooping cough at his New York residence in November 1909. At the time, it was recorded as the largest single contribution, with the beneficiaries including fifty-nine schools and churches across the United States and abroad. Almost half of the money was donated to organisations connected to the Presbyterian Church, of which Kennedy had been an active member for many years. Others included the American Bible Society, the Metropolitan Museum of Art, the New York Public Library, the United Charities of New York, Colombia University and Robert College, Constantinople. Apart from these very generous bequests, Kennedy left another $15 million to his wife and $20 million to be shared between relatives, friends and employees.

One of the strangest wills ever recorded in Mason City, Iowa, was that of the late Ole Cloven, a bachelor who died at Lake Mills in August 1911. Cloven was sixty-one when he left $50,000 worth of property for the erection of a home for the aged poor on the middle of his farmland. The remaining balance of $1,000 was divided between six of Ole's relatives.

The following month an extraordinary surprise was bestowed upon Canada by the announcement that a Frenchman, Gustave Meurling of Mentone, had left hundreds of thousands of dollars to the poor of Montreal. Meurling was a cultured man of seventy, who had been married twice and inherited money from both wives. Early in 1911 he visited Stibbard and Gibson, a firm of London solicitors, and told them that he was childless and without relatives, then asked for their advice as to the disposal of his fortune. The city firm suggested that he should leave his money to a London hospital interested in caring for children. To this Meurling objected on the ground that he was not sufficiently in touch with them to do such an act. Nor would he leave his money to French charities, as he had never been able to reconcile himself to his native people's ideas upon morals and religion. He finally announced that he would like to leave his money to the poor of Montreal, as he found the Canadians 'a wholesome, moral and God-fearing people.'

In the will of Henry Beekman Armstrong who died at Red Hook, New York, in 1912, his property was bequeathed to charity. The residuary estate valued at $200,000 was left to his brother, James, with instructions that 'the whole sum is to be used for philanthropic purposes.' Armstrong lived as a recluse for many years after an unrequited romance in his early youth caused his retirement from society. Henry spent most of his life alone on his farm.

In the same year heroic Emil Brandeis, who gave up his life so that women and children could be saved from the sinking *Titanic*, left $5,000 to charity and $100,000 to be equally divided between his five nieces and nephews. The balance of his estate went to his brothers Arthur and Hugo Brandeis. The family owned a large department store in Nebraska and Emil had been travelling on the liner as a first-class passenger. Born in Manitowoc on 15 March 1864, Emil was the son of Jewish immigrants from Bohemia. Unmarried, Brandeis was in the habit of travelling to Europe to visit his niece in Italy. Having left his Omaha home in January 1912, Emil was due to return to the United States in May of the same year but changed his plans to sail two weeks earlier, boarding the *Titanic* at Cherbourg, occupying Cabin B10. Records show that Emil had stood on deck with other male passengers as the women were lowered into lifeboats. His body was later recovered.

A man of faith, Edward Trounson of The Square, Redruth, Cornwall, left a generous bequest of 200 £5 'A' Preference company shares in his will, the proceeds of which when sold were to benefit the pastor regularly officiating in the Fore Street United Methodist Chapel in his hometown. A former director of the Redruth Foundry Company, Mr. Trounson included a specific clause that the church should receive the money but 'only so long as such minister shall not take part in party politics, whether on the platform or in committee rooms or elsewhere.' Details went on to say that if the residing pastor of the chapel should venture to participate in political interaction, the income connected to the bequest should be handed over to the West Cornwall Miners' and Women's

Hospital, to which the testator also left £1,000. Edward Trounson's total estate was valued at £106,877.

There have been some very strange charitable bequests recorded over the years but a certain mission to Jews, it was discovered in 1914, had a very singular origin when a pious lady living in South Devon directed in her will that a particular tree on her estate should not be cut down till the Jews returned to Palestine. This circumstance becoming known in the district, a gentleman was so impressed by it that he left the whole of his fortune to found a society for the conversion of the Jews.

Subscribers to charities are, as the secretaries of such bodies often contend, some of the most eccentric people on earth. For instance, the National Lifeboat Institution once had a very curious bequest when a lady left them the residue of her estate valued at £400, payable on the death of her favourite tabby cat. For a year the animal showed no signs of departing this life, but then the lady who had charge of it changed her residence and the cat, after wandering away several times and being recovered, finally disappeared. As it was presumably dead, the solicitor to the estate paid the institution on the committee of management undertaking to provide for the cat should it at any time be recovered. The cat remained missing. Charles Dibdin, the late secretary of the RNLI, used to tell a story of another eccentric benefactor. A gentleman called at the office one day and introduced himself by remarking that he had dropped in to see if the institution wanted any money.

'Oh, we never refuse it,' said Mr. Dibdin.

So, after a short conversation, the visitor put down a roll of notes containing about £1,000 and, declining to give his name, departed. His identity was never discovered.

For some years another anonymous benefactor puzzled the officials of charities in and around Dudley in the West Midlands. On one occasion this person sent £500 to the Guest Hospital by registered post, 7 vanloads of furniture, much of it new, 4 pianos and 100 pictures valued at £350. Included in a gift the same person made to another charity organisation in the area were several more vanloads of furniture and three ricks of hay!

No charity had more experience of eccentric donors than the London Hospital and in the course of a few months three remarkable letters were received at that famous building. The writer of one requested a loan of £30, kindly adding that if it could be advanced, £5 might be retained for the hospital. Another of the correspondents sent fifty shillings, with the explanation that while out fishing he made a vow to contribute to a charity if he caught a fish within ten minutes. The third, an old lady, promised a donation if the name of the hospital could be changed. She wanted it named in the memory of her late husband!

According to the *New Britain Herald*, 21 January 1920 was set aside by the National Thrift Week Committee of the Young Men's Christian Association, in Connecticut, as National 'Make-a-Will Day.' The article read as follows:

On this day the attention of people throughout the country is being directed to the importance of making a Will.

In the event of unforeseen accident and death, a Will is of the greatest value in the protection of property and loved ones. By Will, property may be left largely according to your own wishes. If you do not leave a Will your property will be disposed of according to the inheritance laws of the State, in a manner which you might not have desired.

Almost everyone realizes the value of a Will, and plans at some time to make one. In a great many cases this plan is never carried out. Today, while the matter is before your mind, is the time to have your Will drawn. Tomorrow you may not think of it. See your lawyer today, and observe 'Make-a-Will Day' by having YOUR Will drawn.

In your Will you may name a Trust Company to carry out your last wishes and administer your estate. By naming a Trust Company you can be assured that your Executor will not die or become incapacitated. The duties of the Trust Company will be to collect the assets of your estate, protect and preserve them, pay claims and taxes, and finally distribute your property according to the terms of your Will.

The Trust Company is experienced in the work of administration, and is responsible, dependable, trustworthy and economical in the handling of your affairs. It is under the direct supervision of the State. The fees received by the Trust Company, being fixed by law, are the same as received by others for similar services. The cost to your estate is no greater, and often less, than where no Will is left. When you see your lawyer today, ask to have your Will drawn, appointing a Trust Company as your Executor.

In 1925, President Calvin Coolidge brought the matter of inheritance tax, as well as other high rates of tax, to the attention of the American public. The 30th President of the United States pointed out that inheritance and estate taxes were abominable with, in some cases, the taxes amounting to more than the property value. Coolidge was hoping to stir up sufficient public interest on the topic to put a stop to the overlapping and multiplying of inheritance taxation which the politicians had written into law. Some startling facts were revealed on the subject during the proceedings of the National Conference on Inheritance and Estate Taxation in February 1925, with the purpose being to discuss the negative impact of the situation, to invite remedies and invite intelligent discussion. In reality the law was complex, with forty-five of the forty-eight States having some kind of inheritance or estate tax, the exceptions being Florida, Alabama and Nevada. Added to the maze of litigation was the Federal Estate Tax.

Complications were discussed regarding the multiple taxation of individuals, according to where they held property, bonds, companies and shares, which could all be taxed by each one of the States staking a claim. A striking example of a victim of these laws was the estate of John Wanamaker, who owned several companies and homes in different States, where the taxes levied ate up every single dollar of the deceased's legacy.

A clear example of how inheritance tax laws differed from State to State can be seen in the case of Anthony N. Brady, who left an estimated estate of between $70 to $100 million. Under the inheritance tax laws in New York in 1915, when he died, the state claimed $5 million. However, if this estate had been in Illinois and under the operation of inheritance tax laws there, it would have been $6 million.

In order to show how inheritance tax laws benefitted the government in the United States, we need to compare these figures with what would have taken place under similar circumstances in England, where the estate would have been taxed three times as much, to the equivalent of $15 million. In Switzerland the laws were higher still, with eight times as much being held back from the estate, totalling $40 million.

The inheritance taxes in the United States played a strange trick with the estate of a millionaire hardware store owner in May 1924. The majority of his holdings were left to charity, but he also left $600,000 to his son with instructions that his only child should meet the inheritance taxes on the whole estate. As a result, the young man stated that he would be forced into bankruptcy because the total levies amounted to well over $1million.

Mr Justice Romer, in the Chancery Division Courts, in January 1925, was asked to determine whether certain bequests by the late Ada Louisa Reckless, of Attercliffe, Sheffield, were valid charitable gifts. She left the residue of her estate, about £1,600, to the Reverend John Russell Darbyshire, Archdeacon of Sheffield, and to the Vicar of Attercliffe, the Reverend Arthur Robinson, and to apply as follows:

A sermon to be preached annually on 16 June at the Old Chapel, Attercliffe, and one guinea to be paid to the vicar who preached it.

£1 a year to the caretaker of the Old Chapel

£1 a year to the sexton of the cemetery

The erection of a white marble pulpit in the Old Chapel in memory of the first vicar

£1 a year to 50 poor persons in Attercliffe, to be paid on 16 June, after the sermon

The erection of a stained-glass window in the Old Chapel, depicting the Lord feeding the multitude and bearing the inscription, 'Gather up the fragments that remain, so that nothing be lost'.

The balance to be devoted to the maintenance of the clergy and services in connection with the chapel

In the event of the gifts being held to be invalid, Mrs Reckless directed the money should go to the Attercliffe Nursing Association.

The evidence given at court was that the chapel, which had deteriorated through damp and neglect, had not been used for public worship for five years, and that the windows had been boarded up in order to protect them. It could be re-opened, but it would be an utter waste of money to erect a marble pulpit or stained-glass window. The major part of the cemetery had been made over to the Corporation of Sheffield as an open space, and was being used as a public park, so there was no sexton employed there at the time of the bequest.

Mr Dighton Pollock, for the Attorney-General, said that apart from the sexton, who was non-existent, the gifts were all charitable, but it would be incongruous and ridiculous to carry them out. The judge agreed and, in directing a scheme to be framed in Chambers, expressed the hope that the Nursing Association would receive the benefit of the whole residuary estate.

In March 1929, great surprise was caused in the Surrey district of Farnham by a strange bequest of £9,976 announced in the will of a local chaplain. Reverend John Gwyon, of the Rectory, Bisley, a man who had always represented himself as an impoverished man, living a frugal and pious life, committed suicide in December of 1928 by hanging himself from the skylight of the rectory. Reverend Gwyon left the whole of his estate for the foundation of a clothing trust, the yearly income of which to be applied for the purpose of providing boys, whose parents lived in the Farnham district, with knickers and 'for no other purpose whatsoever whether educational or other.' The conditions under which a boy could receive a garment were: 'He should not be under the age of 10 and not over 18, must not be a black boy, his parents must not be in receipt of parochial relief, must not belong to or be supported by a charitable institution.' The bequest went on to state that 'Each successful applicant will receive one garment once a year on which will be written 'in capital letters' the words 'Gwyon's Present.' A special clause directing that no sporting or fancy knickers of any kind, such as football, cricket, Boy Scout, riding or semi-riding knickers should be given, was also contained in the will.

Ensuring that he went out with a bang, and leaving a token reminder of his generosity, Louis A. Thiel was buried in Chicago in June 1930 surrounded by many benefactors of his will. Each received between $5 and $20 at the graveside according to Thiel's wishes, including fellow Lodge members and relatives.

In 1931, two charities in Cardiff, South Wales, benefitted substantially from the will of a Scottish sea captain named Robertson. When the old man died in July of that year, he left a fortune estimated to be nearly a quarter of a million. However, it was not from his own pocket that the legatee earned the huge sum. In 1927, Robertson was living at the Cardiff Poor Law Institution when news arrived from China that his brother had passed away, leaving his sibling as sole benefactor to a rather handsome estate. For the next few years, the pensioner lived a very comfortable life and wished to repay the kindness shown to him by the charities by bequeathing his money to them. The residue of the estate, amounting to £18,000, was divided between the Welsh division of the British Legion and the District Nursing Association. Robertson had become a cripple later in life and found himself having to rely on the generosity of a local institute, but after receiving his brother's bequest built a grand house and a specially adapted motor car.

In the same year, estate valued at £3,515 was left by Owen Williams of Solva, Pembrokeshire, who made a bequest of £200 to form a fund known as the 'Catherine Williams Charity', to perpetuate the memory of his mother as follows:

> During the week preceding Christmas, a new penny is to be given to each child on the register of the council school at Solva, and the balance of the income expended on suitable commodities with the tradespeople of Solva, and distributed between seven or more deserving persons of my native parish of Whitchurch (Shropshire) on the anniversary of mother's birthday, February 26, in each year.

When Julius Rosenwald, one of America's greatest philanthropists, died in 1932, his will was probated in Chicago and revealed charity donations amounting to $11 million, taking his lifetime gifts to the neighbourhood to a total of $70 million! In fact, Rosenwald is said to have given away four times as much money as he finally left to his heirs. Benefitting organisations included the Julius Rosenwald Fund ($20 million), $5 million to fund an industrial museum in Chicago, $6 million for Jewish colonisation work in Russia, $3 million to the University of Chicago, $2.5 million to build model tenements for negroes in Chicago, $5 million to the American-Jewish Agricultural Corporation, $5 million to the Jewish Theological Seminary and $500,000 to aid German war orphans and widows, amongst others.

Julius Rosenwald was born in Springfield, Illinois, the son of a small shopkeeper. He attended public school until the age of 16 and then entered into business, operating a clothing store for some years. Rosenwald entered the mail order field in 1895, building up a huge organisation from his initial investment of $35,000. Before the crash of 1929, the holdings had increased to over $150 million. In his one-page will, Rosenwald simply directed payment of his debts and then the remainder of his fortune, after the charitable bequests, be equally divided between his five children.

In stark contrast to Julius Rosenwald's generosity was the Last Will and Testament of Doctor John T. Dorrance, who died in the autumn of 1930. Dorrance bequeathed his entire fortune to his immediate family, leaving nothing to the household's faithful staff or any local charities. John Dorrance was born in Bristol, Philadelphia, and after returning from university in Germany he was employed in his uncle's canning factory. With a degree in science, Dorrance applied his knowledge to improving varieties of fruit and vegetables which were eventually developed into condensed soups. However, despite the success and ensuing fortune that Dorrance built, he was known as one of the stingiest men ever known, with his widow testifying that the doctor often objected to the size of electric light and gas bills in the household and told her to remove the bulbs from the servants' quarters because they burned too much light. Mrs. Dorrance also mentioned that her late husband would argue with her over food bills and was particularly enraged with a butler who went out to purchase food at what he deemed to be an expensive store.

For 'her soul's sake' a poor girl who later became a wealthy princess left £300,000 to a monastic order at Jerusalem. When the will became apparent upon her death in 1935, destitute relatives applied to court to have it set aside. At the age of 14, Karolina Prah ran away from her poverty-stricken home in the Slovenian Alps and became a waitress in Trieste. She was kidnapped by white-slave traders and taken to Cairo, where she met and married a poor Dalmatian worker named Ivan Tomitch. Ivan made a great fortune which passed to his wife on his death. Karolina set her mind to travelling and while visiting Greece she met young Prince Kokolanija, who proposed marriage. Later in life the princess retired to a convent where she decided to leave her fortune to the monks of Jerusalem. On hearing of Karolina's death, poor family members applied to the local Slovenian court to contest the will on the grounds that Karolina was 'never normal since she was fourteen.' The bequest to the monastery was upheld.

On New Year's Day in 1937 a curious old custom was followed at the Church of St. Magnus the Martyr, at the bottom of Fish Street Hill, Lower Thames Street, London, when the Master and Wardens of the Worshipful Company of Coopers attended the reading of the will of one of the benefactors of an ancient charity administered by the Guild. This was Henry Cloker, who had died almost four centuries before. His will was dated 10 March 1573, and in it he directed that the Master and Wardens of the Company 'shall upon New Year's Day, at afternoon yearly, for ever, provide some learned man to make a sermon, and he to have for his pains six shillings.'

'Ye sermon being ended…' it was Mr. Cloker's mind that his will beginning with the words, 'Now as touching my lands,' should be read by the parson, and that for his pains he should be paid twelve pence. The churchwardens, the beadle, and the Master and Wardens of the Company were also to be paid a few shillings. Under a decree of the Master of the Rolls, dated 23 January 1844, these sums were suitably increased, the fees of the Master and Wardens being handed over to the poor box.

A will to the value of £77,223 was proved in February 1939 and nods to a strong friendship during the First World War. Audrey Carden, the daughter of Sir John Carden, Army tank designer and aero engine specialist, who was killed in an airliner crash in 1935, left £15,000 to two friends who served with her. Remembering the day when all three used to drive Royal Mail vans, Audrey left £7,500 each to Ethel Southey and Kathleen Jennings, or £15,000 to the survivor. She also left all her personal effects to be divided equally between them. The trio served as drivers from March 1917 to April 1919, providing an essential communications service during wartime. A firm friendship sprang up between them and the women were inseparable during their time off. The residue of Miss Carden's property was bequeathed to the Professional Fire Brigade Association in Birkenhead and the Canadian Mounted Police.

The residue of over £180,000 was left for the repair and upkeep of St. George's Roman Catholic Cathedral in Southwark, London, after it was destroyed by fire in a bombing raid during the Second World War in 1941. The bequest was in the will of Agnes Esther Foley, of Fernwood Avenue, Streatham, daughter of the late Patrick Foley who was founder of the Pearl Assurance Company Limited.

Herbert C. Lott, aged 91 years, of Berkshire, England, died in July 1947, leaving his fortune of £266,000 to the Admiralty 'to encourage battle efficiency.' Lott, once a member of the Stock Exchange, lived in lodgings for many years, for which he paid an average of £3 a week, but he always insisted on staying in first-class hotels whenever he visited London. In one room he occupied in a small Sussex private hotel he refused to have a carpet as he believed floor coverings to be unhygienic. Herbert's last lodgings were in Berkshire and cost him 18/6 a week. Mr. Lott never chose material for a suit or overcoat without first applying the old test of holding a lighted match to the material. He said that this showed him if there was any cotton in the wool. In 1930, Lott anonymously founded a naval trust fund to make awards to Royal Navy servicemen and Royal Marines. His name as founder of the fund was revealed a year later and it was to this fund that he bequeathed his fortune. In the 1870s, while still a young stockbroker, Herbert Lott travelled to Australia by ship, and it was said that the excitement of the voyage gave him a love of the sea that always remained with him.

On 14 August 1950, a Russian born taxi driver made his will, leaving an undisclosed amount of money to be shared by any illegitimate children born in Queensland, Australia, on the day of his death. Jack Moskon, known as 'Russian Jack', was a native of Vladivostock who emigrated to Australia in 1903. Moskon forestalled any possible legal difficulties by obtaining a certificate testifying to his sanity from two Brisbane doctors before consulting his solicitor.

'I've seen young people illegitimate through no fault of their own kicked from pillar to post,' he was quoted as saying by the *Queensland Times*, 'Society for some reason looks down on them. Perhaps I'll help some of them to a better start.'

Jack Moskon, who refused to disclose his age, claimed to be the oldest taxi driver in Brisbane at the time of making his will. Ironically, he told reporters that he had left a wife and child behind in Vladivostock and hadn't heard from them in almost fifty years. Moskon was fluent in seven languages: Russian, Polish, Lithuanian, Estonian, Latvian, Mandarin and English, and had previously acted as a Supreme Court interpreter.

In 1954, lonely bachelor Robert Howard Shellenberger left an estate valued at $10,000 to a blonde waitress who had given him cheerful service in a restaurant. The 37-year-old from Marietta, Oklahoma, revised his will to give everything he possessed to Virginia Dell Michael and then committed suicide. Somewhat surprisingly, the Oklahoma court upheld the contents of the will.

In January 1961, Chelsea and England football player Jimmy Greaves was surprised to learn that a fan had left him £25 in his will. Apparently, Greaves was the idol of Frank Mills of Blythe Road, Hammersmith, London, although the bequest came out of the blue to the family. The 73-year-old builder was an avid football supporter but had never actually met his sporting hero in person.

Sadly, death duties and inheritance tax have for many years played a large part in reducing handsome bequests to a fraction of their initial size. One recent example occurred in 1972. A fortune of over £600,000 willed to the Spastics Society in order to help the mentally handicapped was whittled down through estate duties to a mere £130,000, it was announced by the *Herne Bay Press*. The money was left by one of its four founder members, Jean Garwood, who had devoted her life to the service of the mentally handicapped. Despite Miss Garwood leaving over half a million pounds to the Spastic Society, the Inland Revenue took a large portion. Had the money been exempt from duty, it would have enabled the foundation to build ten family support units throughout Britain. These homes would have helped parents caring for handicapped children at home to have a brief respite. Four units had already been built at the time of Miss Garwood's death, but plans for the others had to be shelved due to lack of funds. William Burn, Chairman of the Executive Council of the Spastics Society commented:

> The inroads made on this magnificent bequest are a terrible example of the essential unfairness of the law in its present form. Rates of estate duty in this country are probably the highest in the world, yet Britain appears to be the only developed country that does not grant any duty exemption on money willed to charity. It was Miss Garwood's wish to give this great fortune to improve the lot of the less fortunate in our society. The estate duty levied has tended to make a mockery of her wishes.

When wealthy American divorcee Santa Young Johnson made her will in 1984, she requested that her solicitor keep the news of her death a secret and scatter her ashes at sea. Howard McBrien complied with his client's wishes, boarding a cross-channel night ferry from Portsmouth to St. Malo in France and tipping the contents of the urn from the deck mid-voyage. However, Mrs. Johnson, who had been living in Maidenhead, also left her entire estate to the shocked solicitor, which amounted to £162,000. McBrien told *Evening Post* reporters that the testator was the landlady of his offices and that they had occasionally had drinks together, although he didn't know her very well. Mrs Johnson had no children and the reason for her wish to be scattered at sea remained a complete mystery.

Finally, in more recent years, a disabled Leicestershire businessman who died in 1992 left over £1.5 million to charity. Bruce Wake, aged 45, bequeathed the money to fund a charitable trust for disabled people throughout the UK with the fund being controlled and administered from his home county. Mr Wake was co-founder of the Market Harborough tour operator Travelsphere and suffered from motor-neurone disease for the final two years of his life. Bruce was described as an active and energetic man with a wide range of sporting interests, and despite his illness causing the businessman to become wheelchair-bound, he worked right up until five days before his death. The trustees of the charity included Wake's widow and was to be used to improve access for disabled people countrywide.

Chapter Ten

Convicts & Felons

In the days of capital punishment, it was a common occurrence for solicitors to be summoned to the cells of the condemned in order to legalise their Last Will and Testament, a document that was often witnessed by a prison guard or chaplain. It was the final tidying up of affairs for many convicted felons with their precious, but often meagre, belongings being bequeathed to their nearest and dearest.

Near to the site of the old Newgate Prison in London stands Saint Sepulchre's Church where, on 8 May 1705, Robert Dowe bequeathed 'fifty pounds to the vicar and churchwardens, to the end that through all futurity, they should cause a bell to be tolled and a serious exhortation to be made to condemned prisoners in Newgate during the night preceding their execution.'

For many years the custom was kept according to the will of the donor. At midnight a sexton came to the window of the condemned cell with a handbell, rang his toll, and delivered this address:

All you that in the condemned cell do lie,
Prepare you, for tomorrow you shall die.
Watch all and pray, the hour is drawing near,
That you before the Almighty must appear.
Examine well yourselves, in time repent,
That you may not to eternal flames be sent.
And when St. Sepulchre's bell tomorrow tolls,
The Lord above have mercy on your souls.

On the ensuing day, when the dismal procession, setting out for Tyburn, passed the gate of St. Sepulchre's Church, it paused for a brief moment while the clergy addressed a prayer on behalf of the prisoner, or prisoners, the bell continuing to toll all the time. Later the executions took place in front of Newgate and the clergyman's address was given up. Some years afterwards it was reported that the sexton was still accustomed to come and offer his midnight bell tolling, that the terms of Robert Dowe's will might be fulfilled, but the offer was always declined on the ground that all required services of the kind were thereafter performed by the chaplain of the prison.

In the seventeenth and eighteenth centuries it was a common event for kind-hearted testators to leave sums of money for the ransom of slaves – Englishmen captured by the Barbary pirates and held in prison until their friends, or the Government, could purchase their liberty. In 1713 Rebecca Hussey left £1,000 for the 'redemption of slaves, or the easement of their slavery,' with the condition that they were to be baptised as speedily as possible. The Barbary pirates and the merchants who purchased their captives were Muslim, and to secure better treatment many of their prisoners accepted the Islamic faith. Miss Hussey sought to provide for the salvation, as well as the liberty, of those persons who were rescued from slavery. However, for some reason the good lady's bequest was not utilised and, according to the *Pall Mall Gazette*, remained dormant for 172 years.

In 1865 the bequest had accumulated with compound interest to almost £20,000 and the Court of Chancery, the appointed trustees, having found no British slaves in the Riff, gave between £500 and £600 a year to missions and homes on the West Coast of Africa since that date. Some of the money went to the Anti-Slavery Committee, some to the Society of Friends at Pemba, some to the Lucy Memorial Freed Slaves Home, and some to the Onikha Industrial Mission, which instructed the children of field slaves in carpentry and farming.

In March 1886, a man who refused to give his name was charged in the Bow Street Police Court with being a lunatic wandering at large and not being under proper control. Police Constable Hall saw the man climb on to the parapet of Waterloo Bridge in London one night. He was about to throw himself into the river when the officer seized him. The man became very violent and was taken to the police station where Doctor Mills, the divisional surgeon, certified him to be insane. A letter was found on him addressed 'To whoever recovers my body' and read as follows: 'I, Thomas T.C....s, do hereby will my body found to the School of Anatomy for dissection. If not used in that way to be burned or cremated, if possible to be retained in the Museum of the University, Gower Street, Thos. T.C....s.' The prisoner was remanded.

Born in Darnall, Sheffield, in 1832, Charles Peace embarked on a life of crime after becoming permanently crippled in an accident at a steel-rolling mill as a boy. The youngest son of a shoemaker, Peace served two separate sentences for burglary before becoming obsessed with his neighbour's wife, Mrs Dyson, and subsequently being found guilty of her husband's murder. On the night before his execution, on 25 February 1879, a Leeds solicitor proceeded to Armley Gaol and drew up Charles Peace's last will and testament, which was attested by the prison's chaplain. It was understood that he equally divided his property, amounting to over £500, between his wife, Hannah Peace, his brother Daniel, his daughter and a friend named Willie Ward. For several days before his execution Peace was engaged in writing letters to members of his family and to his friends. By the Monday night, he had either written or dictated sixteen letters and handed them to the chaplain to post. They were all dated 25 February as Peace wished them to be considered as sent from the scaffold. The following is a letter to his wife:

> I have been a base man to thee for many years. Oh dear, if I had taken thy advice many years ago this would not have befallen me. I need not ask for thy forgiveness, for I know that thou hast already forgiven me for all I have done to thee, and my dear, I do not only forgive thee, but I forgive all persons, for I have not any ill-feeling against any living person. Oh, my dear wife, I do pray to Almighty God for thee, and I do hope that He will prosper thee in all thy doings, and bring thee to the Kingdom of Heaven at last, where I hope that thou wilt meet me at the last. So, oh my dear lass, do not forget that our next meeting-place, I hope, will be in heaven, so do not forget to prepare thyself to come.

He then wrote a copy of some verses he made in Woking Prison on the death of one of his children. Peace then continued:

> I think that this is a true view of how I stand in this world. In the first place my sentence was life, and with me, having been in penal servitude, I could not have got my freedom any more, so that I should have to die a miserable death in prison at the end. I might have lived two years or more, and have died in prison at the last. So, my dear wife, I do think that me and you and my children ought to think that it will be far the best if my blessed Lord and Saviour Jesus Christ will hear my prayers and forgive me my sins, and receive my poor soul into the Kingdom of Heaven. So think of this, and try to meet me there, all you, my dear friends. – I am, Husband and Father, CHARLES PEACE. God bless you all.

The letters to other members of the family were filled with good advice as to the life they should live. Peace also sent to his wife and children the cards and letters that had been sent to him since he had been sentenced. He also designed and sent to them a funeral card, upon which he had printed the following: 'In memory of Charles Peace, who was executed in Armley Prison, Tuesday Feb.25, 1879, aged 47, for that I done, but never intended.'

Born in 1865, Israel Lipski (born Lobulsk) was a convicted murderer of Polish-Jewish descent living in London's East End. Lipski was an umbrella stick salesman, employing Harry Schmuss and Henry Rosenbloom. On 28 June 1887, police were called to 16 Batty Street, where they found the body of a young woman who had been murdered. Forced to consume nitric acid, Miriam Angel was six months pregnant at the time. The constables didn't have far to look for the culprit, as 22-year-old Israel was found hiding underneath the woman's bed, with acid burns in his own mouth. Lipski was immediately arrested but blamed the murder on Schmuss and Rosenbloom. A jury took just eight minutes to find Lipski guilty and he was sentenced to hang on 22 August 1887. However, after his execution, a Mrs. Lyons, mother of a young woman who was engaged to Israel Lipski, applied to Mr. Lushington at the Thames Police Court for advice under the following circumstances: 'On Sunday last she received a letter from the condemned man, in which he left certain things for her. On going to the Inspector he said the case was out of his hands, and he could do nothing in the matter.'

Mr. Lushington said he had no power whatever to make any order about the things. If Lipski's belongings were not forfeited, and he had left no Will, they would go to his next-of-kin.

The following is the Will made by Doctor Thomas Neill Cream, convicted serial poisoner and long-time Jack the Ripper suspect prior to his visit to America early in 1892:

I, Thomas Neill Cream, on the 23rd day of December, in the year 1891, entered into an engagement of marriage with Miss Laura Sabatini, a daughter of Mrs. Ann Sabatini, of Berkhamstead, Hertford, England: and as this lady has, since I have had the pleasure of her acquaintance, brought happiness into my life I have never before known; therefore I appoint the said Laura Sabatini to be the sole executor and sole heir and legatee of this my last will as long as she shall remain true and faithful to our engagement and marriage. I give, devise, and bequeath all my estate and effects, real and personal, and all my earthly possessions, including all interest that I have in the estate of my father, the late William Cream, of the city of Quebec, in the province of Quebec, and the Dominion of Canada, which I may die possessed or entitled to, to my affianced wife, the aforesaid Laura Sabatini, and I by the document deprive myself of all right to make a later or any other will as long as the said Laura Sabatini shall remain true and faithful to our engagement and promise of marriage; and I hereby revoke all former wills and codicils, as witness my hand this 7th day of January, 1892, THOMAS NEILL CREAM.

However, after being arrested on murder charges later the same year, Cream made a second will by which the previous bequest was revoked. In the new document, Cream's solicitors benefitted substantially as compensation for the expenses incurred in defending him in court. The remainder of his estate then went to Rachel Cream, the convict's unmarried sister who spent time with him both during and after the trial, having made the journey over from Canada. So why the turnaround?

During Cream's trial and incarceration in London for the murder of three London prostitutes and the attempted poisoning of a fourth, Laura Sabatini failed to make a single visit to her fiancé's cell. In addition, to further dampen Cream's spirits, Laura gave evidence in court relating to a blackmail letter that the good doctor had asked her to write on his behalf, which was submitted as part of the damning prosecution against him. After a lengthy trial, Cream was convicted and hanged at Newgate on 16 November 1892.

A second Jack the Ripper suspect, Frederick Bailey Deeming, made a Will authorising that one-tenth of the proceeds from the sale of his biography and effects be given to Kate Rounsefell, a young woman whom he had duped into believing that his name was Baron Swanston. Unaware that her new beau was in fact a serial wife killer, Miss Rounsefell accepted the 'Baron's' rather hasty proposal, but it wasn't long afterwards that the body of Deeming's second wife, Emily Mather, was discovered. Months later whilst the murderer was in custody, the bodies of his first wife and children were dug up under the kitchen floor of Deeming's former home in Rainhill, Merseyside, England. It was reported in a telegram from Melbourne that Frederick Deeming's brain was to be examined and photographed, afterwards being frozen and sent to a European school for critical analysis. Authorities decided to have Deeming's brain extracted from the skull after his execution on 23 May 1892, and sent to England by one of the mail steamers for examination by medical experts there. The remainder of Deeming's possessions and literary profits were bequeathed to his solicitor, Mr Lyle, who was also appointed executor. It was also requested by the condemned man that his brain be given into the custody of three doctors who were not connected with his trial.

In November 1895, 26-year old labourer Edward O'Brien was sentenced to death at Liverpool Assizes for the murder of his sweetheart, Sarah Jenkinson, the previous July. O'Brien had previously been in the militia but was discharged after his training period. On the fateful day in question, Edward and Sarah spent the afternoon drinking in various public houses around Liverpool. Sarah, a domestic servant, went home at 10 o'clock and was followed by O'Brien who cut her throat with a razor. Death was almost immediate. There was practically no defence at the trial and sentence was passed by Justice Collins. The prisoner asked the judge to direct that his head might be handed over to the Liverpool doctors and a report of the examination published in the newspapers, although there is no evidence to show that this was permitted.

Joseph Kogler was suspected of having committed eight murders and robberies over a period of six years in North Bohemia, Germany, but proof of his guilt could not be unearthed. Eventually, after six days at trial in Reichenberg, justice was done when the gendarmerie obtained sufficient evidence to convict Kogler of the murder of George Rauchfuss, who was killed in the Bohemian Forest in 1894. The court was crowded with excited onlookers when the felon was taken before the judge, who asked Kogler why the death sentence should not be passed upon him.

Joseph Kogler replied cheerfully, 'Herr President, I will face the gallows. I have but one head to lose.' Then, stepping forward, he addressed the reporters as follows:

I have given you lots to write about, there is little more to add. I have now only to make my last will and testament. My umbrella, by means of which the police have been able to bring about my conviction, I bequeath to the court officer, my boots to the prison warder, and the rope with which I shall be hanged I leave to the police commissary of the village of Gablonz.

Joseph Kogler was duly sentenced to death by strangulation, which was received with much satisfaction by all present in court.

Whilst lying in a dying state in the Melbourne Hospital after being shot by his wife in November 1900, William Wright made his very thoughtful will, disposing of an estate valued at £2,875. As a sort of postscript, he added: 'I forgot to mention that I desire my wife, Nellie Wright, to receive £1 per week out of my estate when she is released from prison.'

Senior Police Constable Lanigan said that when he was called to the house by concerned neighbours, after Helene Wright, known as Nellie, was said to be under the influence of drink and had wounded her husband. She told him, 'My old man's shot,' and when the wound was discovered she added, 'Oh, he is hit. Good enough for him.' She then threw herself across the bed and said, 'Wright, I am going to be locked up for shooting you. Good enough for you. I told you if you hit me again I would shoot you.' Melbourne Court heard from the defence lawyer that it would be absurd to class the case as one of murder, as it lacked the element of malice. He commented on Wright's dying statement that he did not know whether Nellie fired the revolver or he caused it by pushing her arm. Nellie was subsequently sent for trial and found guilty of manslaughter.

However, a sensation was caused the following December when a sympathetic jury acquitted Helene Wright. It was proved that she had been under the influence of drink and had no premeditation to murder although, despite the not guilty verdict, there could be no denying that the shooting of William Wright and his death therefrom were caused by his irate spouse.

In 1902, a Mrs Stanton from New York bequeathed her brain to Cornell University. Her statement of reasons was published in November of that year and argued that 'It is important that the brains of educated and orderly persons should be available for study rather than those of the ignorant, the criminal and the insane.' In the same year, however, Woodward, the convicted American murderer, offered to sell his brain to defray the cost of an appeal.

An unusual case of a testator being unable to live on his generous bequest was that of a Connecticut man. In November 1874, George H. Mix was indicted for stealing $1,000 worth of fine lace from a store in New York and was brought up before the General Sessions for sentencing. The circumstances surrounding his arrest were quite unusual, in that Mix had respectable connections and was the son of a wealthy banker in Hartford. On his death, Mix Senior had bequeathed his son an estate estimated at $250,000, with the trustees allowing George $1,500 a year to live on, which is around $40,000 in today's money. However, this figure proved entirely inadequate to gratify George's extravagant lifestyle, forcing him to seek other means of funding his needs. Already having been arrested for swindling a year earlier, a matter in which his family intervened to save him from State Prison, Mix travelled to New York carrying forged letters of recommendation from a number of prominent businessmen, enabling him to secure a position as salesman in the lace department at Clatlin's Store.

On 9 November, George disappeared, and it was ascertained that a large quantity of valuable lace had been stolen at exactly the same time. Soon afterwards, Mix was arrested and informed detectives where he had secreted the stolen property. A search of his rooms uncovered the lace together with forged papers addressed to bankers in San Fransisco. On being taken to the bar George Mix wept bitterly and pleaded for mercy as he was told that he had brought disgrace upon his family and deserved no sympathy. Mix was sentenced to five years hard labour in the State Prison.

Edmund Hall, a 48-year-old labourer of Leeds, was executed at Armley Gaol in February 1905 for the murder of his father-in-law, John Dalby. There was an emotional scene on the scaffold as Hall addressed his last words to the county sheriff, Alderman W. Bentley. As executioner Billingham was about to draw the cap over his face, Hall turned and said, 'Please give my New Testament to my cousin. I hope he will be a good lad, not only as a soldier of the King, but of Jesus Christ, as I have been.' This Bible had been presented to Hall by the sheriff and was specially marked. The cap was then adjusted and the execution duly carried out.

Arthur Devereux was hanged at Pentonville Prison on 15 August 1905, by executioners Pierrepoint and Ellis, for the murders of his wife, Beatrice, and their twin sons Rowland and Evelyn. The case was reported in the press under the moniker 'The Tin Trunk' murders, referring to the large container in which the bodies had been placed. Arthur Devereux was, by all accounts, a respectable gentleman who worked at various chemist shops in and around Kilburn, North London, but having lost his position as manager in the January, the family finances were stretched to the limit. For some reason Arthur had not bonded with the twin boys, but was very close to his older son, Stanley, who was taken into care after his arrest by Ellen Gregory, Beatrice's mother. At the trial Devereux denied murder and claimed that Beatrice had killed the children and then herself in a fit of depression, but Home Office pathologist Sir Thomas Stevenson gave evidence that he had found morphine in all three bodies. It took the jury just ten minutes to find Arthur Devereux guilty of the crimes.

Arthur Devereux wrote a letter from his cell to his mother-in-law, Mrs. Gregory, asking that little Stanley be brought up in ignorance of his father's fate. It read:

I do not wish Stanley to come to see me, the sooner he forgets me the better, under the circumstances. All my belongings are to be disposed of for Stanley's benefit. I am very glad to hear that you have had some offers for his adoption. Tell him I have gone away on a big sea puffer again; then he will gradually forget me in time. He is a very brave little boy. Try to let Stanley think well of me always in the future as he has done in the past.

On the morning of 5 December 1905, William Yarnold was executed at Worcester for the murder of his wife, Annie, by stabbing her in the back. Yarnold was 50 at the time of his death and had served twenty-eight years in the army, serving for a long period in the Boer War. During her husband's stint in South Africa, Annie Yarnold secretly moved in with another man, which is where William tracked her down and stabbed her with a hop knife, severing the spinal cord. A petition was signed by numerous people for William's reprieve given his stressful domestic situation, but to no avail. Yarnold walked unassisted to the scaffold where executioner Pierpoint waited with his assistant, Ellis. A few days before the execution, William was confirmed by the Bishop of Worcester and was quite resigned to his fate. On the eve before his death, Yarnold made a will leaving £30 to Worcester Infirmary, where his wife had died from her injuries. Ironically, it was the exact amount for which Annie had insured William some time before.

On 1 August 1906, John Gillard, aged 39, was committed for trial by Bristol magistrates on a charge of attempting to murder his wife and then attempting his own suicide. John had allegedly badly wounded Florence Gillard and to escape further injury she pretended to be dead, later crawling out into the garden where police found her. Her husband was inside the home in a dazed condition. Although the couple lived apart, it was heard that they often met up and quarrelled with one another, with John having told a friend that he would murder his wife and cut her into pieces. On the night of the tragedy, John told his cousin, 'Go and kiss Flossie. It is the last time you will see her alive.' On a piece of paper found in the prisoner's possession after his arrest was written: 'I give and bequeath to my friend Florence Cuthbert Gillard the house I now live in, and don't forget it must be free of legacy duty.'

When removed from the dock, John Gillard threw kisses at his wife and shouted, 'Goodbye, my dear.'

In November of the same year, Harry Crick, a prisoner in Bathurst Gaol, New South Wales, Australia, who committed suicide, left 5s 6d to be invested in Tattersall's sweep for his wife's benefit.

In July 1908, a terrible crime was committed in Saxony, Germany, when Crete Beir, aged 22, killed her fiancé, Herr Pressler, and forged a will which left the victim's property to her. The daughter of a former Burgomaster of Braund, Beir also left documents at the house which were intended to suggest that Pressler had committed suicide. The young woman was tried and sentenced to death.

When Stanley Nazarko was executed on 14 October 1909, at the Luzerne County Jail in Wilkesbarre, Pennsylvania, for the murder of his common-law wife Mary Czeliowska in Pittson, he left a most unusual bequest. The condemned man made his will in the presence of Father Joseph Sargalski, and left $240 to the legally married wife he had deserted and his friend, Michael Mastoski, of Seranton. Nazarko said that he wanted his wife, whom he had cruelly wronged by leaving her, to be happy, and that he was doing all in his power to make amends by giving her and her prospective husband all that he had. Nazarko also requested permission for his wife and Mr Mastoski to view his execution, as a lesson of what may happen to an unfaithful husband, but this was denied.

Hawley Harvey Crippen, colloquially known as Dr. Crippen, was an American homeopath who was hanged in Pentonville Prison on 23 November 1910, aged 48, for the murder of his wife, Cora, a music hall singer who performed under the stage name Belle Elmore. Initially practising in New York, the couple moved to London in 1897 when Crippen was asked to manage fellow homeopathic doctor James Munyon's new branch office. However, two years later, Munyon fired Crippen and the American found alternative employment as manager for the Drouet Institute for the Deaf. It was there that he hired and fell in love with young typist Ethel Le Neve in 1900. After Cora openly had an affair with one of Crippen's lodgers, he took Ethel as his mistress in 1908. On the evening of 31 January 1910, the Crippens held a party at their Hilldrop Crescent home, after which Cora disappeared. Her husband claimed that she had died and been cremated in California, but rumours of foul play began circulating soon afterwards when Le Neve moved in with Crippen and began wearing his wife's clothes and jewellery. After an initial investigation, instigated by Cora's music hall friends, police searched the Crippen household but found nothing. Having aroused the suspicion of Chief Inspector Walter Dew, Crippen and Le Neve fled aboard the SS *Montrose*, bound for Canada. Meanwhile subsequent searches of the Hilldrop Crescent home revealed a human torso buried under the basement floor. After capture and a high-profile trial, Crippen was found guilty of Cora's murder and sentenced to death, while Ethel Le Neve was charged with being an accessory after the fact and acquitted.

The following April, in the Probate Division, Ethel Le Neve's rights were discussed before the President, Sir Samuel Evans. Mr W.O. Willis appeared for the relatives of Cora Crippen and Mr Grazebrook for Miss Le Neve. At previous hearings Willis applied that letters of administration should be granted in the estate of the late Mrs Crippen to her sister, Mrs Hunn, through her attorney, Mr. Seyd. Counsel contended that the executrix and sole legatee of Harvey Hawley Crippen's will, Ethel Le Neve, should be 'passed over' on the ground that a convicted felon had no right to receive any benefit from his own murderous acts. Cora Crippen left property which it was suggested formed the greater part of the estate that Dr. Crippen had bequeathed to his lover. On behalf of Miss Le Neve, Grazebrook argued that Dr. Crippen, having suffered the penalty of his crime, ceased to be a felon.

Sir Samuel said that the court had discretion in special circumstances to pass over a legatee. Harvey Hawley Crippen had been convicted of the murder of his wife, and the sentence carried out, therefore he would pass over Miss Le Neve and grant letters of administration to the solicitor of the sister, Mrs Hunn. An order was made accordingly in favour of Mrs Hunn.

In a bizarre twist of fate, probate was announced on the will of Lord George Sanger, the famous showman, who was murdered at his home in North London on 28 November 1911. Sanger's will was dated 17 August 1909 and contained a bequest of £50 to Herbert Cooper, the young man who killed him with an axe and afterwards committed suicide by throwing himself in front of a train. Lord George Sanger left an estate to the gross value of £29,348, with the bulk of his property bequeathed to his daughter and granddaughters.

On 27 May 1918 the Adelaide City Coroner, Dr Ramsay Smith, concluded the enquiry into the death of Frederick Johann Neumann who died in a police cell on 26 April. The deceased had been arrested at Loxton, South Australia, for having committed a breach of the War Precautions Act and was subsequently found with his throat cut, the wound having been inflicted with a piece of broken crockery. Lutheran pastor Reverend William Jansow produced Neumann's last will and testament which he said had been made at the prisoner's request as he lay dying from pneumonia in the Keswick Hospital. The coroner pointed out that he wished to know whether the dead man had made the will of his own accord and in those terms. The witness replied,

I said to him, you are about to die. Will you make over your property to your relatives? After a while, when I repeated the question, he said

'Yes', but later observed in German, 'I have made a mistake. I beg your pardon.' I asked, 'In respect to the money?' and he said, 'I want to make it over to the South Australian Government.' I asked, 'Why don't you want to make it over to your relatives?' and he replied, 'They all have a little money, but I want to make it over to the South Australian Government.' Sergeant Osborn wrote down the words and the deceased, after signing the document, remarked, 'May I go now?' which seemed peculiar to me. He then said, 'I wish to die in peace alone.' He was under the impression that he was in prison.

At the time of his death Neumann died in custody. He had been arrested and detained for having failed to comply with the conditions of his parole. He had twice tried to cut his own throat, and it was clearly regarded that the state of the man's mind was in turmoil.

Thomas Traynor was a member of the Irish Republican Army (IRA) who was hanged in Mountjoy Prison during the Irish War of Independence in 1921. A bootmaker by trade, he was married with ten children and was an experienced soldier. On 14 March 1921 Traynor was captured during an ambush on auxiliaries in Brunswick Street, Dublin, as he kept watch outside an IRA meeting. During the ensuing fight an IRA volunteer and two members of the Dublin Metropolitan Police were killed. Thomas Traynor was tried at City Hall on 5 April and sentenced to death for his part in the uprising. One of the witnesses to the condemned man's will was a policeman charged with keeping guard over the cell, and he commented that Traynor had left his cigarette case to a son whom he had once rebuked for smoking.

Perhaps wishing to save face on behalf of his family, convict J.C. Longenbaker left the following will when he was executed:

July 18, 1922

The West Side Building Loan Association, Dayton, Ohio

I am going to the hospital at Richmond, Indiana, today. In case I do not survive the operation, make all money I have deposited in your bank go to my brother, J.A. Longenbaker, Castine, Ohio.

It was signed and witnessed by two relatives.

Many wills have been changed, revoked or found nil and void over the centuries but when a convicted man bequeathed his treasured watch to his sweetheart after being found guilty of murder in November 1923, the bequest didn't quite go according to plan. Lance-Corporal Albert Dearnley, aged 20, was sentenced to death at Winchester Assizes for the murder of his friend, James Ellis, on 24 May at Aldershot. It was reported that Dearnley caused a shudder among those who listened to the concluding stages of the case when he described how he tied Ellis up as a punishment for insulting Dearnley's young lady. Both men were from Hull and enlisted in the 1st Leicester Regiment as drummer boys in 1918. On the evening of the murder they left the barracks together and Ellis was never again seen alive. His dead body, bound and gagged, was found four months later in a thicket within a mile of the army barracks.

Superintendent Davies, giving evidence in court, said that he had made inquiries about the prisoner's family, and had found that his brother was confined in a lunatic asylum and the mother had been in an asylum before she died. For the defence Dearnley went into the witness box. He claimed it was true that he and Ellis quarrelled occasionally but always became friends again. In January 1923 Dearnley became acquainted with a Miss Storey. Ellis did not seem to like the relationship and one day when the couple were going to a dance together Ellis went up and tried to get between them. Some nights later when in bed Ellis went into the room and said, 'I suppose you have been out with that _____ again?'

'I was very angry,' said Dearnley, 'and said, that girl is a respectable young lady. With that I struck him and took up his bayonet in its scabbard and hit him across the body saying, "Don't ever insult my young lady again."'

On the day of the murder, Albert Dearnley had discussed the question of deserting, and in the afternoon Ellis said he was going to desert with him. Later Dearnley bought two bottles of beer and shared them with his friend. They walked across the field and Ellis took off his coat. He also took his false teeth out, saying he seldom drank with them in, and with some rope pretended to lasso Dearnley, saying, 'You be a cowboy and I'll be an Indian.' He then lay down and said, 'Tie me up.' Dearnley then did as instructed, taking the rope and tying Ellis around the ankles and then hands.

In court Dearnley smiled as he recounted what happened next.

I thought I would try to give him that kind of punishment for insulting my young lady and said to him, 'I am going to leave you here til morning, and then make you promise never to insult her again.' I covered him with his overcoat and heard him say, 'Oh,oh.' I then said I would come and let him go the next morning. I covered his legs with some firs to protect him from catching cold.

Continuing, he said that next morning he did not get a chance to go and free Ellis. It never seemed to worry him or prick his conscience, as he never thought he was responsible for his friend's death.

In November 1932 an elderly white-faced, trembling man ran forward when the gates at Maidstone Prison opened at dawn, there to meet his son Albert Dearnley who was released by order of the Home Secretary. It had been nine long years since father and son had met. On that occasion two sheets of glass separated them and the meeting took place in the condemned cell the day before Albert Dearnley was due to be hanged. 'This is my Armistice Day, Dad,' Albert said on his release, before the pair drove off to have breakfast together.

The story of Dearnley's reprieve created a sensation in English newspapers. His appeal had been dismissed, a petition to the Home Secretary turned down, the scaffold had been erected and the grave in the prison yard dug. Albert had said goodbye to his father and had written his last letters, including the bequest to Miss Storey, when Home Secretary Lord Bridgeman stated that new information which he had received afforded grounds for remitting the death penalty. Two years after Dearnley had been reprieved his sweetheart, who had been to visit him in prison and was released by Albert from her engagement, was married.

A murderer's bequest of his corpse to science resulted in a strange dispute in December 1923. When Ferdinand Leclercq was sentenced to death, he invited proposals from research workers for utilising his body after death and finally accepted the offer of Monsieur Guedand, inventor of a pump with which he claimed to restore the blood circulation to a person immediately after death. Guedand arranged to take possession of the corpse directly after it had been guillotined and therefore hired a room overlooking the execution. However, the police said that the statute stated that a corpse must be taken formally to the cemetery before being handed to anatomists. Leclercq protested that he was willing to dispense with the ceremony and demanded that Guedand be allowed to carry out his experiments immediately after execution. Officers refused to acquiesce.

'I will now write the cheque called death. When it is cashed, my creditors will be paid in full. Thank the doctors and officials for all their kindness.'

This was the note left by George Jones, aged 78, whom a warder at Brixton Prison, England, found hanged from the window-frame in his cell. The noose was composed of a towel, a handkerchief and a bootlace. Jones should have appeared in court on the morning of his death on a charge of false pretences. The coroner's verdict was that the prisoner committed suicide while under mental distress.

'Give me a bunch of roses – red roses,' said Filipino prisoner Gavino Demiar as he waited to die in the electric chair at Sing Sing Prison for the murder of his employer in February 1932. The request was duly complied with and with the scent of fresh red roses pervading his cell, Demiar ate his last meal and died shortly afterwards. In June of the previous year Demiar, an ex-boxer and former butler, was convicted of first-degree murder for the killing of Doctor George Deely, a Brooklyn physician. It took the jury just seven minutes to deliberate. Demiar's defense before Justice Albert Conway was that he was so drunk on the night of the murder that he did not know what he was doing. He said he had gone to Dr Deely's home to borrow money, and the doctor had begun to fight him. He admitted he must have stabbed the doctor but claimed that he could not remember.

In January 1935 the dying confession of a conspirator in a plot to benefit in a will revealed one of the strangest hoaxes in modern criminal history. The confession resulted in the arrest of a former town barber in Riodades, Portugal, who, for two years, had lived a life of ease through a fortune left to him by a dear friend, Olinda Heitora, a rich old woman who had lived as a recluse for nearly half a century after the tragic death of her lover.

The friendship between the barber and the recluse had come as a great surprise to the villagers. The first they knew of it was when her will, leaving all she possessed to the barber, was published. The old woman had been an unusual citizen, and almost all her actions had been mysterious, sometimes secret. She had lived on a secluded estate, with only one ageing serving woman for company. The villagers had not even known she was ill, until the servant appeared one night at the home of the only lawyer in Riodades and requested that he hurry to the bedside of her mistress, who wished to make her will. Lawyer and servant sped to the house where the reclusive old lady, near death, dictated her will in a tremulous voice. 'I wish all my property, both real and personal, to go to my dear friend, Manuel Proenna, the village barber.'

The lawyer recorded the dying woman's words, and when he had finished his client took the pen in her trembling hand and signed the document. The lawyer then went to fetch a doctor but on their return the woman was dead. The will was attested and the court turned everything over to the barber, who adopted a mode of life more suitable to a wealthy man. Life had treated him well and continued to do so for a couple of years. The old serving woman continued to live on the estate but one day she was taken seriously ill. At that time Manuel Proenna was absent and another maid brought the doctor. What the medic heard next brought an abrupt end to the fortunes of the former village barber.

Realising that she was dying, the serving woman made a confession in which she alleged that Olinda Heitora was dead when the will was written. The recluse died very suddenly, and the servant had dashed to the village to spread the news when she bumped into Proenna. She declared that that the barber saw a chance for wealth in the woman's death and persuaded the servant to carry out his plans. The two hurried back to the deserted house and hid the recluse's body. The barber had stopped at his shop to secure a wig and, with grease paint, he made himself up to resemble the dead woman. In the flickering lamplight of the bedroom there was little chance that his deception would be discovered. He donned the nightgown that had been draped over the corpse and climbed into the dead woman's bed. The servant then went to fetch the lawyer and Manuel Proenna dictated the will that left a fortune to himself. When the lawyer left to get the doctor, the servant and the barber placed the nightgown on the corpse and put the body back into its bed. It was the dead woman that the doctor found when he arrived. This strange story might never have been uncovered had it not been for the servant's wish to clear her own conscience before she died.

In the course of his hearing by a military court in Paris, murderer Albert la Fosse interrupted proceedings to tell the presiding colonel, 'If I am condemned to death, I request that my body be given to the medical profession.'

The 38-year-old private in the French Army murdered a dressmaker's apprentice when he returned home to Paris on leave in February 1940. The body of the girl, 15-year-old Madeleine Lannoix, was found wrapped in a bloodstained sheet on a pavement in the city. In a statement made shortly after his arrest, la Fosse claimed that he had done it in a fit of temper after discovering that his wife had refused to meet with him.

Surgeons removed the corneas from the eyes of Andrew Sheridan immediately after he had been electrocuted in Sing Sing Prison in July 1949. Known as 'Squint', waterfront gangster Sheridan, aged 56, was executed for his part in the murder of stevedore boss Anthony Hinz, in January 1947. Sheridan once said that murder was as simple as ordering a cup of coffee, but his eyes were so weak that they betrayed him into murdering the wrong man. He willed his eyes to give sight to the blind. After they had removed his eyes, surgeons placed them in solution and handed them to the Red Cross eye-bank service.

A life-termer who died at Alabama's Atmore Prison in June 1950 left his life savings of $210 to help a crippled fellow prisoner. Officials reported that Warren Riggs, 63, asked them to give the money to Tyler Russell, aged 32, whose legs were paralysed and walked on padded knees. Warren Riggs had suffered from heart trouble and Bright's Disease and had been told by doctors that he didn't have long to live. Riggs was convicted of murder in 1937 and was described as having an unblemished prison record for his entire time behind bars. Russell had served two years of a five-year sentence for assault with intent to kill.

In January 1953, disgraced clergyman Reverend Arthur Milton Rumball, of St. Alban's Parish, Ventor, on the Isle of Wight, was jailed for three years for gross indecency and offences against boys. He died from natural causes in Maidstone Prison the following October after collapsing in his cell and left over half of his £159,000 fortune to the English Church, Windward Islands in the West Indies. Rumball had been appointed Priest-in-Charge of St. Alban's in April 1938. During the latter part of the First World War he served as a private in the Hampshire and Warwickshire Regiments and in 1942 he joined up as a naval chaplain at Devonport. Afterwards he returned to Ventnor and was a familiar figure in his bright-red open top 1927 vintage car. In 1950 he toured Norway, completing over 3,500 miles in three weeks, and the following year was a competitor in the Isle of Wight car rally. Rumball resigned from his position in the church in October 1952, shortly before his arrest.

In December 1953, the Will of an inmate of Britain's Broadmoor Prison for the criminally insane revealed that he had left £19,914 when he died the previous August. John William Elmore, an undertaker who had been incarcerated since December of the previous year when he was found unfit to plead to charges of having murdered his wife, left the whole estate to his son.

Tom Sisson, who was the oldest inmate in Arizona State Prison when he died in 1957 aged 86, left almost $10,000 which he willed to a fellow prisoner. Former Warden Alva Weaver, the executor of Sisson's estate, said that the money was saved by 'Old Tom' from a pension he earned as a US Army Indian scout in the 1880s. Sisson was sentenced to life imprisonment in 1918 for his part in the murder of three officers who attempted to arrest Tom and John Powers in a mountain hideaway for the First World War draft dodging. However, the beneficiary John Powers, would have had trouble in spending the unexpected inheritance, as he was also incarcerated on a life sentence!

Chapter Eleven

Unclaimed Estates

One of the most intriguing mysteries relating to unclaimed estates spanned almost two years and was recorded in detail by Professor Oliphant, lecturer in Elizabethan Literature in the University of Melbourne, Australia, in 1935. Attempting to solve a centuries-old mystery, his article reads:

In the year 1706 Arthur, Lord Altham, a poor Irish peer, was married to an illegitimate daughter of the Duke of Buckingham. The couple separated in 1716. My Lord died in 1727, and my lady two years later. The deceased peer's brother Richard (who later became Earl of Anglesey) succeeded to the title, no exception being taken from any quarter.

In 1739, a youth of about twenty-four appeared in the fleet of Admiral Vernon (which was then off Porto Bello), and claimed to be James Annesley, son of the late Lord Altham. His story was that he had been acknowledged as his lordship's son and heir until he was nine or ten years of age, that, after his father's death, he had been kidnapped and sold to slavery in America, and that, after nearly thirteen years as a slave, he escaped. The story of his adventures was very romantic and not easily credible. He came to England with his story and was soon engaged in a shooting accident which resulted fatally for his companion. There is not the slightest reason to doubt that this was purely an accident, but the Earl of Anglesey had him charged with murder and declared that he would give £10,000 to see him hanged. The trial resulted in James Annesley's acquittal and there can be little doubt that the Earl's infamous conduct in the matter prejudiced the jury against James in the subsequent proceedings instituted by the young man for the recovery of his father's estate. The hearing lasted fifteen days and there were almost a hundred witnesses. No suggestion of imposture on his part was ever made. It was virtually admitted that if Lord Altham had a son and heir, this was he. The question was, did his lordship have a legitimate son?

Major Richard Fitzgerald testified that he had been shown the child a day after birth. John Turner, seneschal (steward) to the former Earl of Anglesey, swore to having seen the child and held him in his arms when Lord Altham kissed him and called him 'Jimmy.' This witness had subsequently, after the separation of the parents, seen the child with Lord Altham, who told him in 1722 that he might become seneschal to the youngster when he succeeded to the Anglesey title.

Those who were declared to have been sponsors for the child at his baptism were all dead; but there were many servants to depose to the christening and all the festivities attendant upon it. Not only was there evidence of the bonfires and banquets on this occasion. Some witnesses even swore they had been present at the birth. No attempt was made to question the credit of any of these witnesses or to break down their evidence and no inconsistencies were perceptible. Could any evidence seem stronger or more explicit?

Yet, we have Mary Heath, Lady Altham's woman, who had attended her for sixteen years till her death (with only one absence of a week) swearing that no such child ever existed, though another woman swore that Heath had been present with her at the birth. The man Palliser, on whom Lord Altham based his excuse for separating from his wife, gave evidence that his lordship had expressed to him his intention to be rid of her because of her barrenness. He never saw any child in the house, yet a woman named Laffan said that she was present at the time, with the child, who had been in her care for eighteen months. After the separation, Lord Altham moved to County Kildare. It was admitted that in the household there was a child who was treated as a member of the family, but it was contended by the defence that this was the illegitimate son of one Joan Landy, brought to the house after Lady Altham had been got rid of. The claimant, said the defence, was this boy. Later Lord Altham met another woman, who seems to have persuaded him to cast off the unfortunate boy, who went to Dublin, where he lived in dire poverty. Soon after the death of the peer his successor had the boy kidnapped and shipped off to Philadelphia. There can be no doubt of this, since the agents he employed made no bones about admitting it.

The outcome of the trial was scarcely less remarkable than the trial itself. A verdict was, not unreasonably, found for the claimant, James Annesley. Mary Heath was then charged with perjury, but when tried was found not guilty. Despite the verdict in his favour, James seems to have taken no steps to obtain possession of the title and estates which had been judged to be his. He died in January 1760, leaving a son who died in infancy, and a daughter who married and bore children but died young.

This case is a complete mystery. If James was the legitimate heir, why didn't Lady Altham claim the succession for him? Why wasn't Joan Landy called to give evidence that James was not her child? Was James bought off in some way? On the other hand, why should the Earl of Anglesey have had the boy kidnapped and sold into slavery if James was only an illegitimate son? The natural explanation is that there was heavy perjury on one side or the other, but on which? There was no clear sign of false witness on either side, so the case must go on record as a seemingly unsolvable mystery.

Under the title of 'Windfalls Of A Year' in 1893, Sidney Preston, editor of the London paper 'Unclaimed Money' wrote as follows:

During the eventful year just closed some thousands of advertisements have appeared in the agony columns of the leading newspapers, at home and abroad, seeking missing relatives, heirs-at-law, legatees and others. Many of these notices are of an extraordinary and romantic nature, and often, though very valuable from a monetary point of view, fail to be seen by the persons sought, by reason of their having emigrated, etc.

The heirs of a lieutenant and his wife, who were killed during the Indian Mutiny of 1857, and of a surveyor who died in London in 1827, are missing; 300,000 marks await the unknown heirs of a colonel who died abroad; and information is urgently wanted as to a doctor who was entrusted with a scientific mission on the coast of Tunis, and who strangely disappeared from his vessel. A ship's engineer, supposed to be living in Hull, is requested to communicate with his relations in Germany 'on account of Inheritance Regulations' and the grandchild of William Barrett, a pig-jobber of Norfolk, who died in 1830, is entitled to funds.

In the days before modern communication methods, it was a fact of life that many people disappeared and were often not heard of again. Many emigrated and were long afterwards advertised for by trustees or solicitors to claim inheritances or legacies of considerable value, the various legal documents and letters taking weeks to arrive at their destinations. Several instances of this nature occurred in the 1920s including the searches for Frank Warmsley of Lancashire, who was last heard of somewhere in Philadelphia, William Bowen, of Llandudno, who disappeared in 1893, and Edward Parry, who left England for America in 1886 and lost all contact with the family he left behind.

A classic example of the struggles in searching for missing heirs is the case of William Charles Pierce, who died at Bendigo, Australia, in October 1904. The deceased left a fortune of £30,000 to relatives back in England. Having emigrated to Australia to seek a better future some fifty years prior to his death, Pierce became rich and settled in his adopted country. It was therefore left to William's widow to trace the missing legatees, which she tried to do by writing to a cousin, Mr. Andrews, in Hove and asking him to trace her late husband's cousins whom she believed to live in the region of King Street in London. Despite the letter coming as a great surprise to Mr. Andrews, an optician, who had not heard from his cousin for over twelve years, he made inquiries at the address given but could find none of the missing heirs.

Sidney Preston, of Lonsdale Chambers, Chancery Lane, London, who issued an annual list of missing heirs to property, sent the following summary of notices which appeared in the 'Agony' columns in 1917 to *The People* newspaper:

The widow of Donald Morrison, whose body was washed ashore at Trevon, France, is entitled to property. The heirs of Robert Mailer, who was discharged from the Army in 1822, are entitled to £12,000, and Andres Messer, of Midlothian, who died in Canada in 1871, has left £40,000 for his unknown kindred. Richard Taylor, of Liverpool, at one time a waiter in a New York hotel, and W.S. Walton, known by the name of 'Swifter', last heard of as travelling with a circus, are missing, also the children of William Halnan, a messenger in the War Office twenty years ago. William Cormack, of Chelmsford, is wanted for something 'greatly'

to his advantage; also Henry M. Harvey, who left for Cape Colony sixty
years ago. Among other missing beneficiaries are George Green, who left
his wife in 1853; William Williamson, of the Shetland Islands, missing
since 1844; and Mary Turner, daughter of Patrick Turner, last heard of
in New York.

A report published in the *Washington Sunday Star* on 5 March 1922, claimed
that in Great Britain alone there was the equivalent of $27,500,000 waiting to
be claimed by legatees who could not be traced. One example given was that
of Jane Eales who was born in Wales in 1835 and left an estate worth $300,000.

Due to the number of Americans who could trace their ancestry back to
Britain, the British authorities became inundated with letters from expectant
would-be heirs trying to find their inheritances from deceased relatives. One
London Sunday newspaper claimed to have found over 600 missing heirs and
each week printed an updated list of heirs who were being searched for. One
case involved a woman from Bristol who had emigrated to Australia forty years
before her death. She married, survived her husband, and left a fortune in her
will to her sister and her nephews and nieces.

Perhaps the most remarkable instance of an unclaimed estate was that of a
Parisian woman who left $40,000 to 'whomsoever would watch by her tomb day
and night for twelve months and hold no communication with anyone except
the person who served the watcher with meals.' One man sat in vigil for nine
months, enduring cold and silence but eventually lost his reason. The money
remains unclaimed.

One case that sat unsettled for a long period was that of Mrs Mangini
Brown who died intestate in London in 1871, at the age of 93. Mrs. Brown had
survived all her children and known relations, and left personal property to the
value of £200,000, which in today's money would be worth over £29 million.
However, unclaimed inheritance is a sure way for the most unlikely of heirs to
climb out of the woodwork, and it wasn't long before several interested parties
appeared to claim their kinship to the old woman. After a laborious and detailed
investigation, in 1876 it was judged that five members of a Genoese family
named Freccia had successfully proven their blood ties to Mrs. Brown's father.
It wasn't long before a default claim was brought forward by the Crovetto
family, also from Genoa, stating that Mrs. Brown had in fact been illegitimate.

According to records, Mrs Mangini Brown was the daughter of Antonio
Mangini, from St. Ilario, who anglicised his name to Anthony Mangin when

he settled in England around 1771. The parentage is clear on the paternal side as she was acknowledged as his daughter, educated at Mangini's expense and married an American named Aguila Brown in 1792 with her father's consent. For ten years, Mrs. Brown lived with her husband in Baltimore, United States, and when her father died in 1803, she lost no time in claiming his property. Having established Mrs. Brown's genealogy, the Crovetto claim was set aside.

However, in an unexpected twist, it was found that there were actually two Antonio Manginis born near Genoa within two years of one another, both registered with a father named John Baptiste! On reviewing this evidence, the Vice-Chancellor came to the conclusion that Anthony Mangin was indeed the Antonio Mangini born at St. Ilario and therefore the Freccia family, as his surviving next of kin, must be the rightful heirs to his daughter's property. The whole story is both curious and remarkable, in that half a dozen hopeful Italian heirs should be disputing the parentage of a Genoese native in an English court three-quarters of a century after his death!

On occasion a remarkable amount of time can pass before inheritors become aware of their good fortune, such was the case with the heirs of one Timothy Clark from Akron, Ohio, who died in 1874. His relatives all lived in the far west of the United States and didn't hear about Clark's death until January 1899. In the intervening years, the money had been turned over to the county and placed in the unclaimed inheritance fund. Appearing in court to establish their rightful claim, the family were successfully paid their dues.

An interesting article was published in Australia on 22 May 1896, purporting to the many unclaimed estates and fraudulent agents seeking their share. It was written by Mr. H. Sydney Everett and reads:

One of the most hopeless delusions prevalent in the United States, and not confined to the illiterate classes, is the belief that there are in Europe estates innumerable and of unlimited value, awaiting rightful heirs and claimants. In the meantime, these estates are supposed to be locked up in probate or chancery courts, in the Bank of England, and similar institutions, or in the occupancy of fraudulent or wrongful, if innocent tenants.

Most of the claimants of these estates are probably ignorant how well founded their claims may be, the idea of their having any claim having been first suggested to them by the advertisements, catalogues, or circulars of fraudulent and unscrupulous claim-agents. The latter sometimes compile a list of names purporting to be those of persons who have been advertised for in proceedings of the Court of Chancery, and otherwise, to claim money and property, also the names of testators in cases in which heirs are not known, and of persons advertised for in respect to unclaimed dividends.

The agents also state that on the receipt of one guinea they will search records and documents relating to any name in the list, which in one publication extends over 228 pages, containing four columns of 67 names each, making a grand total of 60,000 names, after allowing for over 1,000 repetitions, which seem to be numerous.

It gives one example as:

The Townley estate, which is situated in the counties of Lancashire and Yorkshire, England, has been for many years in the possession of its rightful owners, and there are no unknown heirs in America or anywhere else to any portion of it, yet American claimants of this estate were advertised for and encouraged by a person calling himself Colonel James F. Jacques, with a confederate named Howell Thomas. These two swindlers were finally stopped in their career by the London police. Thomas was convicted of swindling Jacques and sentenced to five years' penal servitude. Jacques was tried later for conspiring with Thomas to obtain money under false pretences, was convicted, and sentenced at the Old Bailey, November 29, 1894, to twenty months' imprisonment with hard labour. Colonel Jacques, at the preliminary hearing in the police court in July 1894, confessed that he had received from his dupes in America about £10,000 between 1876 and 1885 and that between 1885 and 1894 he had received at least £22,000.

A peculiar intestate estate case was dealt with in London Chambers before the Chief Justice in May 1897. Joseph Parker and his wife Matilda were found dead in bed the previous January, the woman with a gunshot wound, the husband evidently from natural causes. Parker died intestate, leaving some property. The question was, which one of them had died first. A badly written but decipherable letter was discovered, presumed to be written by the wife, in which she said she had found old Joe dead, and so decided to commit suicide. The Solicitor General claimed that the husband died first and therefore the whole estate should revert to the Crown. The Chief Justice thought otherwise and ruled that Matilda Parker's relations were entitled to half the estate.

When Richard Walters died in Auckland, New Zealand, in 1912, it was revealed that he was the long missing heir to a $15 million estate in Chancery. Walters, a gardener, apparently knew that he was the heir to a great fortune, and his employer had urged him to claim his inheritance, but the old man said that he was satisfied with his station in life and sent word that he regarded the fortune as not worth the trouble.

Vast sums of unclaimed inheritance money were turned over to County Treasurer Joseph Kilduff by retiring officer George Reynolds in Ottawa in 1922. The money, held by the trust while they awaited claimants to show up, was said to have been there for many years and related to 561 different estates. One of the best-known estates being held in the area was that of the late Jeffrey O'Connell, who served in the Canadian army during the First World War and died of influenza in 1919. After funeral expenses were taken care of, a balance of $143.14 was left to his rightful heirs, but none could be located. A Chicago man appeared at Mr. Kilduff's office in December 1922, claiming a legacy of $1,000 which had been held for him since 1916. The man claimed that he knew his brother-in-law had intended to bequeath him something but hadn't bothered to inquire whether his relative had passed away!

In the same year, the case of a very mysterious inheritance was reported from Paris. An inquiry into the case of Madame Leotardi, who claimed that a mysterious American woman named Lilian Fair Heller made her heiress to $85 million, was being pursued with mainly negative results. Madame Leotardi stated that in 1920 Mrs Fair Heller made out a warrant authorising her to buy houses to the value of thirty million Francs. Trace was found of the two witnesses who signed the agreement, one of them being abroad at the time of the inquiry. The other stated that he was asked to act as witness by a friend who had made the acquaintance of the rich American on a railway journey, but that he did not actually know the woman introduced to him as Mrs Fair Heller.

In the warrant, Lilian Fair Heller was described as having been born at Bolivar, Venezuela, in 1876. Her address was given as Boston Steel Works, United States. However, the American Consul at Marseilles stated that this company was not known to him. A Police Commissioner in charge of the inquiry used this information to try to prove the existence of Lilian's sister,

Madame Cattani, the wife of a Cairo banker, but all inquiries proved to be fruitless. In the course of a search made in the apartment of Monsieur and Madame Leotardi, a receipt was found for 38,000 Francs, which had been paid into a Paris bank in early December 1922. As the Frenchwoman could give no explanation as to the origin of the money it was retained pending inquiries.

According to the Paris Press, Maitre Malauzat, Notary at Marseilles, recalled a well-dressed woman visiting him two years earlier. He said that she represented herself as having great wealth and planned to buy 20 million Francs worth of property in the South of France. She asked the notary to make out a warrant for that exact sum. Some months later she wrote, saying that she was very ill, and had drawn up a will that she wished to place in his care. This was duly received, together with an attached note stating that in the case of death Madame Leotardi, whose Paris address was given, was to be informed.

A few months before the investigation, Madame Leotardi called upon Maitre Malauzat and stated that Mrs Fair Heller had died on 21 July, 1922, on board her yacht, *Old Chap*. The notary refused to open the will as Madame Leotardi had brought no death certificate with her. She then asked for an advance of 15,000 Francs, but the request was not granted. In the course of subsequent inquiries, Malauzat could find no trace of a yacht named *Old Chap* and ascertained from the French Consul in Boston that the steel works from which Lilian Fair Heller was supposed to draw her immense revenue were not known there under the name given. Did Lilian Fair Heller really exist? Or was Madame Leotardi creating a scam? The mystery remains unresolved.

Antiquarians in Grasse, France, discovered that their knowledge of English literature was lacking considerably in 1927. At the settlement of an estate of an Englishwoman living on the Riviera, a case of seventy books was offered up for sale. A French collector successfully bid on the lot, but on discovering that they were all written in English he sold them on to a book-buyer for the equivalent of ten dollars. The English dealer discovered that the collection included many first editions by Dickens, Keats, Shelley, Lamb, Goldsmith, Smollett and Fielding, and were valued at thousands!

In July 1928, a grey-haired lady of 63 sat placidly knitting a jumper on the porch of a house overlooking the harbour in Sydney, Australia. A few months later she became a millionairess. Such is the story of Mrs. J. Douglas-Jennings, who was part heir to £52 million which had been lying in Chancery since 1798. There were forty-four other heirs, all descendants of two nephews of William Jennings, bachelor and miser, who died at Acton Hall, Long Metford, Sussex, in 1798, leaving an unsigned and invalid will. The claim of his 45 descendants was proved, with three in Australia and the others in America.

William Jennings, in addition to big holdings in the East India Company, owned very extensive factory sites in the city of Birmingham. Jennings left a will, but as it was invalid, a search began for relatives. The only people who could be traced with direct connections were two nephews. One, Henry, had gone to English colonies in America, and the other, James John Jennings, had deserted from the British Navy in Sydney. Like most searches of the kind at that time, the quest was carried out in a half-hearted manner, and the miser's fortune was held in Chancery by the Crown, while Acton Hall passed into the possession of Lord Horne, in whose family it remained ever since.

It is the history of the deserter, James John Jennings, that provides the romance to the story. Originally intended for the church, young James preferred the Navy and, after the death of his miserly uncle and his own poor parents, found himself a position as sub-lieutenant on a ship bound for the convict settlement at Sydney, under the command of the notorious bully Captain Natchbull, who was subsequently hanged on a gibbet in Sydney for the brutal murder of an old apple seller. So harsh was Natchbull's treatment of his officers and men that young Jennings and a dozen of his comrades deserted when the vessel reached Port Jackson, and from there took to the bush. After many struggles the naval men arrived in Adelaide and made a fresh life on the land. As the years went on Jennings heard on several occasions from friends in England who urged him to return and claim the fortune that awaited him. This he resolutely refused to do, fearing the strict punishment meted out to deserters. He died in Adelaide, and at the end urged his family to spare no effort in laying claim to the famous 'Jennings' millions.'

In fact, James John Jennings left a will, which came to be in the possession of his granddaughter, Mrs. Douglas-Jennings, in which he set out that, failing male heirs, the claim was to be prosecuted by the eldest female issue of his eldest son, who must, if married, retain the name of Jennings. Mrs Douglas-Jennings complied with that condition and her claim was duly proved. The other nephew, Henry Jennings, went to America and fought in the revolution under Washington, and then settled in Cleveland, Ohio. His 42 descendants also proved their claims.

An estate amounting to £43,000 fell to the Crown in August of 1909, a sum which represented the value of the property left by Frederick Blake of Broadfield Lodge, Crawley, and Seghill, Northumberland. Late officer of the 2nd Queen's

Royal Regiment, who died on 6 May 1909, intestate, a bachelor and without any known relatives. Under the circumstances, letters of administration were granted to the solicitor to the Treasury. The death of Frederick Blake recalled a romantic story of a previous windfall left to the Crown by a member of the same family.

In 1876 Helen Blake of Earl's Terrace, Kensington, died intestate, without known heirs, leaving real and personal estate valued at nearly £300,000. She was the wife of General R.D. Blake. Helen's maiden name was Sheridan, and she was born in Ireland of humble County Mayo parents. It was her beauty which attracted the officer, who had Helen privately educated, and became her husband when he was serving in Dublin, and the couple eloped, soon after sailing for America and settling in Ohio. Subsequently General Blake was disowned by his family, but he and his wife established a large millinery business in the United States, from which they derived a considerable income. While on a visit to England the General, who was a son of second baronet Sir Francis Blake, died and left his fortune to his wife, who afterwards moved to England and set up home in Kensington. Helen Blake was a strikingly beautiful woman and was courted by many men, but she remained faithful to her late husband's memory and refused to remarry. When Helen Blake died the Treasury Officials took possession of the personal estate, valued at £140,000, and advertised for heirs in *The Times* newspaper, inviting any next of kin to apply. Needless to say, there were many claimants, but not one succeeded in establishing their eligibility to the satisfaction of the Chancery Court. One 70-year-old man from America applied, believing himself to be Helen Blake's long-lost cousin. Although being well cared for during his visit, the man spent so much money in his efforts to establish his claim to the inheritance that he ended his days in a poorhouse in Lambeth. Another man, Patrick Sheridan from Liverpool, had an even worse experience.

A local solicitor convinced Patrick that he was the rightful heir to the Blake fortune and showed him some persuasive evidence. The 'exhibits' included a silver watch inscribed 'From Helen Blake to her dear nephew, Patrick Sheridan, 1866.' The other was an old family Bible, the fly leaf of which recorded the family of Martin Sheridan, Helen Blake's father, and referred to the marriage of his daughter. Sadly, for Patrick, a jeweller to whom the solicitor had given the silver watch to inscribe became suspicious when the customer started shouting at the man having made a very natural mistake of engraving 1896 instead of 1866. The jeweller dutifully altered the inscription as desired but afterwards reported the incident to local police, which resulted in the solicitor being arrested for forgery and conspiracy. On searching the legal representative's office, they made another startling discovery; it was a regular factory for faked Bible records! Sensation followed sensation, for in Ireland it was discerned that the solicitor had actually ordered some old gravestones to be inscribed and placed in the appropriate Sheridan family graveyards. That ended Patrick's quest for inheritance, and he was forced to console himself with the fact that he had been a victim of cruel deception.

That, however, was not the end of the 'Blake Inheritance' story. It transpired, that among the deceased woman's papers were documents indicating her intentions as to the disposal of some of her property, including land in British Colombia, and a few of these were paid out by the Treasury, to a total of £19,000, including an 'intended legacy' of £1,000 to the late Prime Minister, William Gladstone. The residue of the estate remained in the possession of the Crown, for no claimant was able to produce proof of Helen Blake's birth or indeed the legal marriage of her parents. General Blake's brother, third baronet Sir Francis, died without legitimate issue, but he bequeathed a considerable sum to Frederick Blake, who was also at one time an officer in the 2nd Queen's Royal Regiment. It was the personal estate of this gentleman which lately passed to the Treasury.

Judgment was delivered in November 1910 in the Probate, Divorce and Admiralty Division of the Supreme Court in London, in the case of Charles Phillips, an upholsterer, formerly of Australia and New Zealand. The previous February Phillips had died at Rowton House, Vauxhall, one of the cheap lodging-houses which was founded by the late Lord Rowton in various parts of London. Phillips had lived there for many years on six shillings a week. It was afterwards discovered that he had a bank balance of £3,000 and property worth around £7,000 in the colonies. No will was discovered, and the court declared the estate intestate.

There have been occasions where persons have acted upon impulse and consequently been charged with forging a will. One such case was brought before the court in Melbourne, Australia, in April 1924. Edward Haire, Jabez Lees and William Robinson were all charged with having forged a will to defraud the Government of a portion of the estate left by Margaret Haire in 1920, after she died intestate. Haire was further charged with 'uttering', a term used to describe putting forged money into circulation. According to the Crown, after his wife's death Edward Haire told Robinson that, as she had left no will, he would lose out on £4,885, which the Government would take. It was alleged that

Haire suggested to Robinson that he should forge a will. Robinson told the court that he did so, carefully tracing the dead woman's signature from the fly leaf of a Bible. It was agreed between the men that Robinson would get a share of the estate. Probate was granted on the will, but it was not until Haire and Robinson had returned from a trip to England that Robinson is alleged to have made a confession to the police on account of Haire not paying his full share. Lees, it was alleged, participated in the engineering of the scheme. In the defence of Haire it was stated that Robinson had conceived a brilliant scam for putting one over on Haire. He had told Haire that he had found his wife's will, and everything went alright until Robinson threatened to proclaim it a forgery. He tried to blackmail him, and demanded £1,000 from Haire, who was described as 'a poor doddering old man, and half blind with one foot in the grave.' The trial extended over three days, after which both Edward Haire and William Robinson were found guilty with a recommendation for mercy. Both men were sentenced to imprisonment. Lees was acquitted by direction of the Judge.

In the search for missing heirs, there is often much disappointment for those hoping to reap the rewards of fortune by hearing of a newly deceased long-lost relative, and such was the case in 1936 when Canadian telegram operators made a grave spelling mistake. When attorneys contacted offices in Scotland asking for information regarding relatives of a Mr. Blackadder, the message read 'Blackburn' and wasn't corrected for several weeks, causing great excitement amongst Blackburn families until a second telegram rectified the issue.

A unique case was heard in the Western Australian Full Court in August 1937, when Edith Frearson, aged 11, the child of an adopted child, was declared to be entitled to the whole intestate estate of Mary Ann James to the exclusion of the deceased's brother and five sisters. Mrs. James, a widow, died in January 1937 and had adopted the child's mother in 1907. Sadly, the adopted daughter died first, leaving only her daughter, Edith, for whom it was claimed that she was Mrs. James' lawful granddaughter and therefore entitled to the estate. The court found that an adopted child was deemed to be a child born in wedlock of an adopting parent as regards all rights and consequences of natural relation of parent and child. The adopted daughter would have been entitled to the whole of the estate had she survived, as she didn't Edith Frearson stood in her mother's shoes and became sole heiress.

Chapter Twelve

Laws & Disputes

Inheritance law goes back thousands of years, with Roman Law being one of the strictest and most complex in terms of who could inherit and how. It was governed by civil law, with inheritance law taking up eleven of the fifty volumes concerned with Roman Law, and almost 70 per cent of Roman litigation was connected to inheritance. Although male and female children were treated equally in terms of heirdom, wills had to follow a specific structure, naming an heir, and stating the identity of legal guardians if the children were underage. However, widows were usually excluded from inheriting their husband's property, as they would be assumed to take a part of their father's estate, rather than the husband's. Wills usually took the form of three wooden writing tablets. One surface of each was covered with wax and a copy of the will was written on two of the tablets. They were then tied together, so that one copy was visible and the other hidden. Seals of the witnesses were placed over the cord, so that officials could ensure that the document hadn't been tampered with.

Nowadays, an individual can decide exactly who they wish to benefit from their estate by making a legally drawn up will, but it hasn't always been that way, with blood heirs taking precedence. Different cultures and countries also have their own laws on who can inherit, and the United States regulations have varied greatly from state to state over the past two centuries. One golden rule that encompasses all wills, however, is that the testator be of sound mind, with the presumption that there be a will at all. Many have passed over intestate, in other words without a written document portraying their wishes, and this is where disputes, long probate sessions and family rifts have caused no end of strife.

One of the ablest lawyers of his generation was Lord St. Leonards, Lord Chancellor, who famously said, 'I could, without difficulty, run over the names of many judges and lawyers of note, whose wills, made by themselves, have been set aside or construed so as to defeat every intention they ever had.' Lord St. Leonards himself drew up a will that he never tired of reading to his friends and visitors as a model testament, and he always impressed upon them the importance of making one's will, of entrusting the drawing up thereof to one's solicitor, and of keeping it in a safe place. The last of these precautions Lord St. Leonards observed with so much care that when he died no one was able to find his will, and finally it was 'probated from memory' by his daughter, who had learned it by heart, having heard it repeated hundreds of times.

Rightful inheritance has been disputed for centuries, with cultural and religious differences making headline news all over the world. One such point of law regarding Indian Inheritance came before Civil Judge Lucknow in 1876. Begum Muntaz Mahal was born a Hindu but converted to Islam after her marriage to King Nasirud din Haidar. Upon her death a Hindu brother of the deceased came forward to claim property, but an adopted daughter of the deceased woman disputed the claim. The question put before court was whether a Hindu brother could inherit the property of a Muslim sister.

Disinheritance was also a bone of contention in India when a shocking story of mass murder unfolded in 1922 concerning a villager who lived just outside Bombay. It appears that the man had eight sons, two of whom he disinherited in his will, with the result that litigation ensued, the Privy Council finally upholding the will. As a result, supporters of the two disinherited sons armed themselves with axes and entered the houses of the other six brothers and murdered everyone they found, men, women, and children, after which they cut off the women's limbs in order to gain possession of their jewellery. The raiders also seized a quantity of cash and ornaments valued at several thousand rupees. The Sessions judge sentenced thirteen of the accused men to death and two to transportation for life.

One of the oddest law cases on record rose out of the will of the Dowager Lady Rashleigh, the centenarian widow of Sir John Colman Rashleigh, whose son became the Second Baronet of Prideaux in Cornwall. Lady Rashleigh had a rooted hatred of lawyers which she carried to the extent of drawing up her own will. This was found, after her death in 1880, to have been torn in two and stitched together. The point of the law case was whether the first piece, in which a nephew of the old lady was made residuary legatee, was written at the time the will was signed. The case excited great public interest, not only on account of the novelty of the facts, but because a sum of £30,000 was at stake. Eventually the will was upheld and the nephew inherited.

Another curious legal question of inheritance arose in July 1880 following a railway accident in Florimont, France, known in Germany as Blumenberg, which resulted in the death of several passengers. Among the victims were two gentlemen from Breslau, Herr Koechel and Herr Callinich, who had been close friends for many years. In fact, the pair were so strongly attached to one another that, some months prior to the fateful journey, they had bequeathed their entire property to one another, the sole survivor in effect getting the whole estate of the other. However as both parties to this heritage agreement, or *Erbvertrag*, perished in the accident, the question arose as to which of them died last. The bodies of both men were found among the ruins of a second-class carriage in which they had been travelling together, yet it was impossible to distinguish which had died first. The heirs-at-law to Herrs Koechel and Callinich were advised to apply to the Breslau Court of Equity regarding this complicated problem, where Prussian legal circles were left to distribute both estates as they saw fit.

A strange marriage law pertaining to inheritance was reported from the island of Haiti in 1883, causing uproar amongst French settlers who had married natives. A Haitian woman married to a foreigner thus became a foreigner, and a child born of a marriage between such parents was not allowed to inherit property in Haiti. On the death of the parents there was an immediate compulsory conversion of the property into money. The net proceeds of the sale were then handed to the heir, but the immediate conversion into cash usually involved a heavy loss of funds.

Sometimes it can take years to settle inheritance disputes and in one case, reported from Berlin in 1889, over a decade. Around 1874 two brothers named August and Fritz Plocke, shoemakers by trade, moved from their native town of Reppen, near Frankfurt to Berlin with their sister. At the beginning of the nineteenth century their grandfather had emigrated to England and then later to the Cape, South Africa, where he succeeded in business and acquired a fortune of several hundred thousand thalers (German silver coins). After his death in 1835, his heirs were advertised for in the newspapers and the Plockes' submitted their claims. The Cape Government, however, disputed the documents and, by the time conclusive documentation was sent over, declared that they were superannuated, and that the inheritance had therefore fallen to the English Crown. At length, however, the Cape Government acknowledged the Plockes' claims and the capital, amounting to nearly a million German marks, was paid to them at the beginning of 1890.

Inheritance law the world over is often brought into question when an heir attempts to claim the riches which they presume to have been passed down to them, and it is not only English laws covering this matter that have caused turmoil through the centuries. In January 1893, the *Loftus Advertiser* printed the following interesting article concerning the singular law of inheritance which prevailed amongst the Bantu tribe in South Africa:

A chief's wives have each their own rank and station assigned to them by law and custom. Frequently the youngest is the chief wife, and for this reason: as a man advances in life his influence and power grow, and he can then make more favourable alliances than at an earlier period when his chances are doubtful; and so it happens that an old chief of sixty often marries the daughter of a powerful neighbour, and promotes her to the position of chief wife, whose son is his heir. Of the others, one is what is called 'the right-hand wife.' Her son has, as soon as he becomes of age, a considerable portion of the government assigned to him by immemorial custom, and this he retains while the heir is a minor. This elder brother has many opportunities of increasing his influence and becoming a powerful or even dangerous rival to his younger brother, so it happens that there are numberless legends, chiefly of the marvellous order, but partly true no doubt, of the perfidy of the right-hand wife's son, and the sufferings and ultimate triumph of the true heir.

Furthermore, an even earlier article, published in 1885, refers to inheritance law in part of the Congo where children were considered to be the property of the wife's relations, giving their natural father little or no control over them. The right of inheritance was from uncle to nephew, thus a man's property and slaves would go to the eldest son of his brother or sister, or the next of kin on such lines. A wise nephew would therefore leave his father's house and go to live with his uncle, whom he hoped to succeed. An uncle, knowing that the nephew would be his rightful heir, while his own children belonged to his wife's clan, would naturally care more for his nephew than his own offspring.

Chinese laws regarding inheritance have often been vague and complex, but in 1893 the Governor of the Straits Settlements succeeded in obtaining a translation of the laws of the Qing Dynasty (1644–1912) on family inheritance among the Chinese. A section of it is included here:

When a division of a family estate takes place between the sons of the wife and of the concubines – except where there are official honours inherited, when preference must be given to the eldest son of the wife and his eldest son – each son is to have an equal share, no matter whether he is a son by the wife, or by a concubine, or by a maid. A son by adultery shall be given one-half of a share received by the sons.

When a person has no sons, he is allowed to choose as his heir a young relative (nephew) of the same stock and of the proper generation (i.e. the man in question must choose a son of a brother). Preference must be given to the descendants of his father, then to those of the relations who have to wear mourning for his death for nine months, then to those who have to wear mourning for five months, then to those who have to wear mourning for three months. If there are none of these relations, he is allowed to choose and appoint an heir from a distant branch of the clan or select a person bearing the same surname. But if after an heir is appointed a son is born to him, then the family property must be equally divided between the son and the appointed heir.

A widow, having no son and not marrying, shall remain in possession of her deceased husband's property, and shall, through the elders of the clan, choose a person descended from the same ancestors as her husband (that is, a son of the husband's brother) to be heir. As to a widow who remarries, the property of her deceased husband and her original dowry shall be disposed of as his family likes.

Perhaps it is little wonder that the wives often chose not to remarry!

A report detailing the laws concerning inheritance in Holland, France and Germany, and the procedure that should be adopted by claimants was published in 1896 after it was found that several hundred courts were holding estates in trust. Since 1879, the American legation at The Hague had been responsible for notifying claimants, either directly or through the State Department, as the Netherlands had no probate courts and wills were deposited with the notary or solicitor who drafted them. A duplicate copy would have been made, a registration number assigned to the document and then this was examined and verified by a registrar once a month. However, in many cases names, addresses and relationship information was often lacking, making it necessary to settle estates by expensive advertising, which after one or two generations in a time when it was common for people to frequently move, was no easy feat. In 1852 the Dutch parliament established a state commission for the settlement of claims on the estates of deceased persons. This board gave notice that all claims to property in their hands must be brought before them within five years and six months, after which such estates would revert to the government.

The greatest inheritance sought after in Holland was that of General Metzgar who died at the end of the seventeenth century, leaving the equivalent of around $12 million. One minister at The Hague noted 200 years later, that if ordinary interest were added to the principal sum of the estate, all the European governments together would be unable to pay the heirs should they appear.

At the time of the 1896 report, the American Embassy in Paris were unwilling to give the names of any claimants of estates in Europe but said that the number of enquiries was large. Under French law the liquidation of estates was ordinarily in the hands of the notary, with the usual method for searching for heirs being to address a circular letter to every notary in the area which they suspect the relations to be, giving the name and date of death of the original estate owner. If nobody came forward to claim the estate, the government were to take it in trust for a period of thirty years, after which all claims were barred.

Inheritance law favouring male heirs was fairly common across the globe until the twentieth century and a curious case, which excited interest among the Polish nobility was tried in court at Posen in June 1901. The Count and Countess Zbigniev Wesierski-Kwilecki, both of aristocratic Polish descent, were blessed only with daughters. Consequently, another branch of the family looked forward to inheriting their vast estates on the death of the Count. In 1897, however, after an interval of sixteen years, the Countess presented her husband with another child, this time a son. The disappointed side of the family decided to believe that a fraud was being perpetrated and appealed to the law courts for redress. Their case was that after such a long period of time a lady of 50 years old could not possibly have another child, that she feigned accouchement and substituted someone else's child for her own in order to ensure the inheritance stayed within that side of the family. The *Morning Leader* reported that a most animated aristocratic crowd watched the proceedings in court, which lasted for eleven hours. Fifteen witnesses and physicians gave evidence that the Countess had really been *enceinte*, and had born a son, and the little 4-year-old boy was also perched on a table for inspection by the court. The plaintiffs, the expectant inheritors, demanded an adjournment in order that they might obtain fresh evidence. This the court refused, and they left the building. The presiding Judge then quietly settled the matter by giving a verdict against the plaintiffs in absentia, compelling them to acknowledge the little boy as rightful heir to the estates, and to pay all the costs of the proceedings.

When one thinks of inheritance, we ordinarily assume that it comes in the form of some monetary bonus or gift, but the frequency of child murders in India in the early twentieth century had deep-rooted connections to Hindu laws of inheritance, with the motivation of these attacks being robbery. It wasn't uncommon in the Punjab, for example, to see sparsely dressed little boys glittering with silver bangles and necklaces, and the girls even more lavishly laden. At the time a Hindu could not attribute any portion of his property, either by will or gift, to his wife or other female family members. However, in turn the male heirs were precluded by law from claiming any jewellery or ornaments given by a father to his female relatives. These would always remain the property of the women, and it accounted for many cases of hoarding in India.

In 1914 Sundara Iyer, a Madras economist, said that with the spread of Western ideas Hindus felt it their duty to make better provision for their wives, daughters and other female relatives. The result was an enormous increase in the melting of sovereigns to make gold ornaments. In a middle-class family, for example, by the time a girl reached the age of 12, between 50 and 100 sovereigns would have been collected for her dowry and then converted into ornaments. These ornaments or jewellery could not be attached by any legal process or reclaimed by the giver. A Hindu wife was expected to cease wearing her jewellery when her husband died but could sell the pieces and live on the proceeds. Gold ornaments were not, however, made only as a provision for the women. They were a convenient method of guarding against a rainy day and were particularly popular with prospective bankrupts. Mr Iyer quoted the case of a merchant who failed in business, and who handed over all his assets to the Official Receiver. It was afterwards found that he had given his wife jewellery and ornaments to the value of £600,000, but under the law the creditors could not seize a single one of those articles.

Under a strange law in Nairobi, East Africa, in 1922, a boy of fifteen inherited his dead brother's wife, aged 36, and her three children. It was noted in a newspaper that the wife was valued at £70. However, the youth from Nairobi was not allowed to enjoy possession of his new 'property' until he had undergone the native manhood ceremonies.

An interesting article regarding Russian inheritance law was published in the *Daily Mirror* on 20 May 1924. It reads:

One of the most fateful meetings in the history of the Anglo-Russian negotiations will be held in London today, when M. Rakovsky, the Soviet Minister in London and President of the Russian delegation, will reply to certain proposals regarding British claims to property which has been nationalised or confiscated in Russia since the revolution.

The British Government proposed that the Soviets should undertake 'to give fair compensation' in regard to these claims. The question, however, is complicated owing to the difference of the British and Soviet social systems.

'All wealth in Russia,' Rakovsky declared, 'ultimately reverts to the State, in whom all power is vested. As regards private property, a plot of land granted to a peasant according to Soviet law cannot be redistributed for a period of twelve years, and only then in the event of the population of the village increasing.'

Rakovsky added that there was no law of inheritance. At death, he said, all real property reverts to the State. A Russian subject may leave his heirs only £1,000 and his private effects. His widow and children have, however, the first right to continue his business. The penalty for the evasion of all laws relating to the ownership of property is confiscation by the State. Gifts before death would be considered evasion of the law.

'As far as foreigners are concerned,' he said, 'it can be arranged that the rights of inheritance follow the laws of their own country provided that property of Soviet citizens who die in their territory is subject to Soviet legislation.'

Rakovsky emphasised, 'The best safeguard for foreign capitalists, provided they comply with our laws, is our desire to attract foreign capital. Every worker and peasant understands that foreign capital in Russia would be to the mutual interests of both parties.'

It is interesting to note that whilst some western countries were strictly adhering to outdated laws concerning inheritance at the turn of the twentieth century, smaller states were embracing change. In August 1925, the *Christian Science Monitor* reported that the Jugoslav National Women's Federation were taking energetic action for the equalization of the rights of male and female heirs under civil law, demanding that Parliament should give equal rights to both. A circular was sent to all social and humanitarian institutions appealing for support. The Federation also asked its branches to collect signatures from the whole Jugoslav kingdom, with the intention of sending it to Parliament. A number of lectures were also given on the subject, with Dr. Arandjelovitch, professor of law at Belgrade University, delivering an address which was printed as a pamphlet and distributed throughout the country.

It should be explained that an old civil law existed in Serbia by which boys and girls did not have the same rights of inheritance. A male heir had the right to a greater part of an inheritance, while a female heir only had the right to a decent marriage settlement, i.e. to a dowry, which was not fixed, but depended on the amount distributed by the male heir. Such a vague legal provision often entailed great loss to daughters. It is apparent that the government long felt that the law ought to be changed for one based on fairer and more modern lines, but nothing was done until Yugoslavian women took the matter in hand.

Legal authorities in the United States ruled that a nun may inherit property despite the fact that she had taken a vow of poverty requiring her to turn over any property she may acquire to her community. In April 1928, the case of Sister Imelda, of the Sisters of Mercy, was decided in the Supreme Court of Mississippi, affecting the rights of Sisters to inherit property under the laws of the State. The Sister, whose previous name was Emma Wood, fell heir as the next of kin to a valuable estate consisting largely of real estate in Natchez, Mississippi. Shortly afterwards, Sister Imelda transferred the inheritance to Bishop Gerow and his successors in office, as trustee, to be held and disposed of in trust for the benefit of the Sisters of Mercy.

The State then filed a Bill contending that the Sisters of Mercy were holding the property in violation of the law, and that it should fall to the ownership of the State. At the same time, a group of relatives, more distant from the testator than Sister Imelda, filed a cross bill contending that they were entitled to the property. Both parties appealed to the State Supreme Court. The other relatives insisted that they should receive the property because, by her vows to hold for the benefit of the community all property she might receive, Sister Imelda had surrendered any right to inherit and had become 'dead in law'. However, the

Supreme Court dealt firstly with the State's claim, then dismissed that of the relatives, saying that the decision with regard to the State also threw out the relatives' contention. In effect, the decision established that a Sister may inherit property despite the fact that she has taken a vow of poverty requiring her to turn over to her community any estate she may acquire.

In 1931 a Parliamentary Committee was appointed to consider the Will and Intestacies Bill, which sought to provide against the total disinheriting of a testator's children, widow, or widower, but reported that legislation on the lines proposed would not be justified. The report, issued on 3 July, expressed the view that children or a spouse left without means of support owing to the terms of the will of the deceased should be able to obtain such means by application to the court. It was recommended that the amount be measured by the value of the estate and the circumstances in which the family had been living.

Inheritance law connected to religious buildings can be a grey area at best, but one very odd inheritance was brought to the attention of the press when a Miss Garner became the sole heir of Rectory Farm, near Melton Mowbray, England, in April 1931. With it she inherited the unusual title of lay rector of Melton, with a special seat in the chancel of the church. There were also obligations attached for the lay rector to maintain and keep in repair the chancel to the parish church. This old law caused both surprise and concern in its time, for many an old house with these type of conditions attached had been purchased by people who knew nothing about the situation enforced upon them. A few years before Miss Garner's inheritance, for example, the new tenant of a rectory was imprisoned for not complying with the law.

Described as the most important change in German law since the freeing of the peasants after the Napoleonic wars, a Nazi law was approved by the Prussian Ministry of Justice in 1933. It altered the law of inheritance to prevent the splitting of peasants' holdings. Going forward these lands or properties would only be able to pass to the eldest son. Other children in the family would only be entitled to education, clothes and food from the estate. Holdings became saleable only with the permission of a special court. However, it was also stated that peasants must be of German blood and the marriage of a peasant with anyone of Jewish or coloured ancestry would automatically disqualify the offspring from inheritance.

A very interesting article on the topic of inheritance appeared in the *Daily Independent* on 6 November 1937 and reads:

It is difficult to legislate for hard cases. This was amply demonstrated in the debate in Parliament yesterday on the Bill to prevent the disinheritance of wives (or husbands) and children in wills. To begin with, it is human for a person to wish to dispose of his own money in his own way, and no interference with that right will be readily tolerated.

It is quite true that some people use their wills to show disapproval or vent spleen or impose punishment. On the other hand, there are sons and daughters not fit to inherit money. It would only help to ruin them. Many cases are known where the inheritance of money has spoiled life for those who have come into possession of it. They do not know how to handle it. They waste it. They squander it.

While we are all anxious to stop such hard cases as that of the good and devoted wife who on the death of her husband was left penniless because of 'some new love for some fluffy bit of stuff when he was an old man', we are also eager to prevent money going to a worthless son. A letter was read in the House of Commons from the head of a big business, who said that his son had for years spoilt the life of his father and mother, and that he (the father) would get rid of his money rather than bequeath it to his son.

On balance things are likely to work out more equitably if there is no interference, for hard cases are comparatively rare and make bad law. It is difficult by legislation to prevent human desire to get one's own back.

Members of Parliament had been attempting to get English Inheritance Laws brought in line with those of Scotland for years and in September 1937 a petition signed by 250 MPs was presented to the Prime Minister, asking the Government to give the necessary time for the passing into law this session of the Inheritance Bill. On this subject, Eleanor Rathbone MP said:

The Inheritance Bill does not, as does the law of Scotland, entitle the surviving spouse or children to a definite share in the estate without regard to their own financial position or past conduct. All it does is to provide that where a will is patently unjust and cruel an appeal to the Courts may, if they think fit after reviewing the circumstances, allot a reasonable proportion of the estate to the plaintiff. The English law in this matter is not only behind that of nearly all other civilised countries but is inconsistent. During life a man is bound by law to support his wife according to his position in life, and his wife if she has a private fortune and he becomes chargeable to the rates is legally bound to support him. Both parents are bound by law to support their dependent children. But at death this liability is removed, and the family income can be handed at will to a cat's home, while the surviving spouse and young children may be left destitute. The class whose income is small enough to bring them under the Insurance Acts are compelled by law to insure for a pension for their widows and children. Is there any reason in justice or humanity why people with larger incomes should be allowed to put the responsibility for their families on relations or the State?

At the end of 1937, members of the House of Commons addressed themselves to the task of remedying wrongs done by the way in which some people disposed of their property. Complaint was frequently being made of hardships inflicted upon the surviving wife and children who, on the death of the husband and father, found themselves disinherited. Several attempts had already been made to establish in law the right of the dispossessed to share property which would seem naturally to belong to them rather than to outsiders. A few years before, a committee of both Houses recommended that when such cases occurred the courts should, upon application, be empowered to make reasonable provision for the neglected family. The Bill in 1937, sponsored by Stanley Holmes, sought to carry out that recommendation.

However, the subject was not without difficulties. Admittedly Holmes did overcome an objection from the previous year by making its provisions cover cases of vindictive wives, as well as vindictive husbands. But the question still remained of whether there was an inherent right in the survivor of a marriage to share the fortune. It does not always follow that the exclusion of a person from a will is an act of injustice. In enabling the courts to exercise discretion a less objectionable course was considered, quite at odds with Scottish law under which a third of a man's property must go to his wife and another third to his children.

A legacy of less than £100 was received by a woman whose mythical inheritance of more than a million Francs forty years before created the worst inheritance scandal of her time. The woman was Therese Humbert, or La Grande Therese, as she was then known, when she basked in luxury and renown. In 1939, at the age of 80, she lived in a little hotel on the outskirts of Paris, with the small legacy left to her by her brother, Louis, saving her from absolute poverty. The marriage of Therese Daurignac and Frederic Humbert was a wonderful event, with Humbert coming from one of the most respected families of the French bourgeoisie. Therese's contribution was the famous 'million francs' which she claimed to have inherited from two American brothers named Crawford. Two nephews of the phantom Crawford brothers were supposed to have contested the will. Litigation dragged on for quarter of a century, all the time Madame Humbert stating that the million francs remained untouched in her safe awaiting the Court's decision. No one thought of doubting the word of 'La Grande Therese' and neither did anyone hesitate to lend thousands to the couple. Then one day the safe was opened and the bubble burst. There was nothing but a few pieces of paper and cheap jewellery inside. Throughout the years of his sister living the high-life, Louis Daurignac lived a humdrum life selling thermometers and barometers, dying a bachelor with no surviving relatives but Therese.

In the 1930s and 40s thousands of needy children in Sweden were cared for under the provision of a novel inheritance law. The statute provided that if a person died intestate his property would revert to the state in the absence of near relatives, and more remote family being excluded from inheriting. This brought the 'General Inheritance Fund' more than 8 million Kroner in a ten-year period, the equivalent to £412,000 at the time. The law stipulated that the money must be used entirely for child and infant welfare. Fifty-seven 'summer colonies' for sick children and those from poor families were established with contributions from the fund and another fifty received additional support. The fund also contributed to the establishment of thirty permanent children's homes and financial support to sixty others. Some were set up for tuberculosis sufferers, others for psychopathic or 'difficult' children. Baby welfare, institutions, creches and kindergartens also received help. It also provided grants and scholarships to many other organisations, such as the scouts and YMCA. Of the money inherited by the state, one-third was added to the capital of the fund while the rest, together with the interest, was distributed. It was reported that the General Inheritance Fund grew much faster than expected, as many testators bequeathed money to it from their estates.

In December 1970 Italy's Supreme Court abolished a law which limited the wealth an illegitimate child could inherit from their mother or father. The decision was a key move towards providing equal rights for illegitimate children, a particularly important problem in Italy where, up until that point, divorce was not legal. Apparently, hundreds of thousands of children were born each year to technically adulterous couples who were unable to divorce and remarry. The law invalidated by the court stated that an illegitimate child could receive an inheritance of only a half of the wealth bequeathed to the least favoured of the heir's legitimate children, and in any one case no more than a third of the total inheritance. The court ruled that this violated the post-war Italian Constitution that guaranteed 'equality of all citizens before the law, without distinctions of personal or social conditions.'

In April 1977 an inheritance case in Mount Isa, Australia, exposed the repressive Queensland Aborigines Act when Aborigine Annie Hansen was robbed of her $12,000 inheritance left to her by an uncle named Little Paddy. Ruth Kaplan, who handled the Hansen case, had been working on it for several years before it finally went to court. The judge demanded proof 'on sworn evidence' that Annie Hansen was Little Paddy's lawful niece but, as Kaplan explained, the Queensland Aborigines Act didn't provide for the issue of birth or death certificates. She offered evidence from a family who had helped rear Miss Hansen and a letter from the Palm Island Superintendent, but the judge remarked that the latter 'didn't prove a thing.' Ms Kaplan complained that Aborigines were placed under the jurisdiction of an Act which did not issue them with a birth certificate but expected them to attend to the preparation of a will. Justice Mathews said Miss Hansen's case would be determined by the 1939 Queensland Act because Little Paddy had died in 1961. He dismissed the case but did not order any costs against Annie Hansen. The Hansen case is similar to hundreds and possibly thousands of other inheritance cases over the years. From 1972 to 1973, $59,299 was transferred from the 'Assisted Persons Estates Trust Account' to the Aborigines Welfare Trust Fund. This was used to pay the expenses of the Department of Aboriginal Affairs, but very little else.

It is important to remember that inheritance laws are not universal, changing from country, religion and tribe. Intestate laws are also subject to various legalities dependent upon country. For example, if an individual in Nepal dies without having made a will, their property is divided equally among their offspring. However, if one of the children has died before their parent but has children of their own, that share will be divided amongst the grandchildren instead of being shared between the surviving children of the deceased.

There are countries whose inheritance laws have restrictions on the distribution of estates. For example, in Sweden there is a *'maintenance portion'* law which ensures that, even if a person has written a legal will, a certain portion of their assets will go to the surviving spouse and children. In France there is a forced heirship, which means that the deceased's children are entitled to between half and three-quarters of the estate. In Singapore the law is quite different. The estate will be shared equally between the surviving spouse and the deceased's parents, should they outlive their child. Wills continue to be disputed around the world on an almost daily basis, with sibling rivalry, charitable bequests and persons dying intestate being some of the most common causes.

When singer Michael Jackson died in June 2009, so began an ongoing legal and financial dispute over his estate, after it was discovered that the King of Pop's siblings had been left out of the will. They claimed the will was fake and that the named executors of Jackson's fortune were taking advantage, eventually signing a petition which failed after brother Jermaine retracted his signature. Guardianship of Jackson's three children, Prince, Paris and Blanket also came under scrutiny when Katherine, their grandmother, allegedly went missing for a short period but she was reinstated shortly after 20 per cent of the total estate was bequeathed to charities.

Similarly, when South African President Nelson Mandela died, in December 2013, he left money to his children and grandchildren, personal staff and the African National Congress, but nothing to his first wife, Winnie or his three daughters by her. The estate was estimated to be worth 46 million Rand (£2.52 million) a seemingly small sum given Mandela's prominent position, but trust funds were said to contain more wealth. According to a forty-page summary of the will, three of Mandela's daughters and one granddaughter had all received $300,000 loans in his lifetime and a clause stated that if the money had not been repaid at the time of his death, they were all to be excluded from receiving a portion of the will. Nelson Mandela's third wife, Graca Machel, who kept vigil by his bedside, waived her right to inherit the family home but accepted four properties in Mozambique, as well as several cars and expensive jewellery.

Courts in Pakistan have claimed to be upholding the rights of women to inherit property, but in actual fact very few cases have actually been brought before the justice system. In Balochistan, a mountainous region in the west of Pakistan, in particular, if there are male offspring in the family the women are not entitled to inherit anything at all. When women have tried to enforce their legal right to bequests or estates, there have been incidents of male relatives committing murder in order to stop them. Many of the Pakistani women in this region simply give up when faced with such opposition, but one such case that did go to court took over twenty-five years to resolve. A family dispute began in 1991, after a father died, leaving a house, four shops and agricultural lands in Swat. Apparently, the property had been bequeathed to his three sons, Islamuddin, Rehmanuddin and Shahabuddin two years previously. The man's daughter, Noor Jahan, contested the division of her father's estate, but sadly it dragged on through court without resolution until long after Jahan's death. In its final order in the Supreme Court in 2016, the Justices on the bench observed: 'A sister, to claim her rightful inheritance, was compelled to go to court and suffered long years of agony. However, before she could get what was rightfully hers, she too departed from this world. A quarter of a century has elapsed since the death of Haji Sahraney (the deceased father). Such a state of affairs, to say the least, is most unfortunate.'

Sometimes it is not just the Last Will and Testament of the deceased that causes concern to the heirs, as a supplement in the form of a codicil, which can revoke or modify part of the original document or put restrictions in place.

When Sir Hugh Percy Lane, of Lindsay House, Chelsea, one of the most successful art dealers in the early twentieth century, went down with the sinking of the *Lusitania* on 7 May 1915, it was a codicil found by his aunt that caused ruffled feathers. In a letter to the *Dublin Daily Express* Lady Gregory stated that the document was discovered at the Dublin National Gallery, but although written and signed in her nephew's own hand, it had not been witnessed and was therefore invalid. The codicil, dated 3 February 1915, states:

> This is a codicil to my last will, to the effect that the group of pictures now at the National Gallery (London), which I had bequeathed to that institution, I now bequeath to the City of Dublin, providing that a suitable building is provided for them within five years of my death. The group of pictures I have lent to Belfast I give to the Modern Gallery in Harcourt Street. If a building is provided within five years, the whole collection will be housed together. The sole trustee in this question is to be my aunt, Lady Gregory. She is to appoint any additional trustees she may think fit. I also wish that the pictures now on loan at this (National Gallery of Ireland) remain as my gift.

(Signed) HUGH LANE

I would like my friend Tom Bodkin to be asked to help in the obtaining of this new gallery of modern art for Dublin. If within five years a gallery is not forthcoming, then the group of pictures at the N.G., London, to be sold and the proceeds go to fulfil the purpose of my will.

(Signed) HUGH LANE

Lady Gregory added that she was glad that the codicil had been found, as it showed that the natural irritation caused by the mistaking of Hugh's motives and the underrating of his gift had passed away. She was glad to believe there was hope through a friendly arrangement between all concerned the provisions of the codicil would be carried out.

When Lady Caillard died in 1935, it was revealed that she was not as wealthy as family and friends had supposed, but the ensuing codicils really twisted the knife with regards to her children. The general belief was that Lady Caillard was worth a large fortune, her two husbands having left her £150,000 between them, but her final estate was valued at no more than £15,000. Under her will, drawn up in July 1934, her daughter, Mrs Arthur Hulme, was left £200, but this was cancelled in a codicil added the following August and she received nothing from the estate. To her son, Commander Guy Maund, Lady Caillard left a signet ring which had belonged to his father. This gift was also cancelled by the same codicil and he also received nothing. Annuities of £150, £100 and £52 respectively, were left to a personal maid, a companion help and the housekeeper of Little Brook Place, Lady Caillard's house at Leatherhead. Olivette Rees, an adopted daughter living in Canada, received three-quarters of the residuary estate, with the remainder going to Guy Maund's ex-wife, who was also his cousin. In a second codicil, added in November 1934, trinkets and various pieces of furniture which had been left to various friends under the will were cancelled.

Commander Maund was reported as saying, 'I decided to withdraw my opposition to the will when I learned that my first wife was left part of the estate. The whole affair has been distressing enough without entering into litigation with members of my own family. I only feel very sorry for my sister. She has nothing except the pittance she earns in a small secretarial post.'

We close by looking at some of the restrictions put upon legatees by those who named them in their wills. The following article was written by Stephanie

Thompson in the *Sunday People*, 2 March 1975, entitled 'A Legacy To Live In Sin':

> Wealthy widow Shelagh Tennant inherited a fortune when her husband died – and lost the right to be a wife. Her legacy was to live in sin. For if she ever remarries, 32-year-old Shelagh stands to lose her £30,000 villa in Mijas, Spain, and a guaranteed income from a £40,000 fortune. The marriage vow 'till death us do part' wasn't enough for the Honourable David Tennant, who died seven years ago. And his widow says she is forced to live in sin with the man she loves, Reginald Conrad, a 44-year-old restaurant owner. It means the baby they are expecting next month will be born out of wedlock. Mrs Tennant, whose husband was forty years older than her is now taking legal advice to see if the conditions of the will can be reversed.

The article goes on to give another example of post-mortem will stipulations:

> Few go as far as miser Hans Muller to settle old scores. His grudge against his family went far beyond the grave. After his funeral, the relatives he had come to despise dutifully followed his last wish and filed into an upstairs room to hear his will. No more than half a dozen sentences had been read out when the floor collapsed killing several 'beneficiaries.' Hans' last will and testament had left nothing to chance. Before he died, he had sawn through the beams of the house where the will would be read in Munich, West Germany.

Another case of bitter-sweet revenge was that of businessman Samuel Bratt, whose wife had never allowed him to smoke at home. When he died Samuel left her £330,000 on the condition that she smoked at least five cigars a day!

Occasionally the last laugh can turn sour, as it did with Wilfred Mee. The report says: 'He expressed a wish in his will that first option on the sale of his home at Mountsorrel, Lincolnshire, should go to an Indian or Pakistani – a move which his neighbours claimed was designed to upset them. Neighbour Jim O'Neill, 80, said, 'Because of the Race Relations Act he wasn't allowed to do it.'

Glossary

Bequest – A gift left in a will
Chattels – Any item of personal property that can be moved
Codicil – An addition to a will that explains, modifies or revokes it
Disbursement – A payment made to a third party
Executor – A person or persons appointed in a will to administer the estate
Intestate – A person who has died and not left a legally valid will
Legator – Someone who has left a legacy in their will
Liabilities – Financial obligations that need to be settled after death
Litigation – The process of taking legal action
Probate – The official proving of a will
Residuary Gift – Share of an estate after all other payments have been made
Residue – Everything left after liabilities, tax and legacies have been paid
Testator – A person who has made a will or given a legacy

Bibliography

Abilene Weekly Reflector – 28 June 1888

The Advertiser (Adelaide) – 13 January 1914

Advocate – 15 January 1924

The Afro-American Advance – 28 July 1900

The Age (Melbourne) – 23 March 1931, 25 April 1952

The Age Herald – 24 July 1910, 14 June 1914

Airdrie & Coatbridge Advertiser – 2 December 1911

The Alaska Daily Empire – 19 September 1922

The Albury Banner – 7 August 1914

The Argus – 10 June 1932

Arizona Daily Citizen – 18 June 1901

The Armidale Express – 23 May 1911, 27 August 1937

The Ashbourne Telegraph – 8 December 1905

The Atherton News – 15 October 1915

The Australian Star – 1 August 1903, 9 February 1905

Avon Argus – 17 January 1952

Barrier Miner (NSW) – 17 January 1949, 30 March 1949, 14 August 1950, 21 December 1953

The Bathurst Times – 14 July 1913

Beauties of England & Wales – 1801

The Bee, Omaha – 24 April 1912

Belfast Telegraph – 23 August 1929, 9 September 1937, 9 March 1940

Bellshill Speaker – 15 October 1915

Bill Barlow's Budget – 19 May 1897

Birmingham Daily Mail – 3 June 1881

Birmingham Mail – 23 September 1875, 1 September 1888

Bismarck Daily Tribune – 28 September 1906, 26 February 1912

The Black Hills Union – 22 April 1898, 11 March 1904

Blyth News – 12 January 1931

Border Watch – 18 February 1903, 25 July 1933

The Bourbon News – 6 July 1917

Bradford Daily Telegraph – 14 August 1903

Bradford Observer – 22 January 1936

The Braidwood Review – 7 January 1930
Bridgeton Pioneer – 11 February 1915
Brighton Gazette – 28 January 1905
The Bromyard News – 14 November 1889
The Brownsville Herald – 30 June 1930
Buckingham Advertiser – 10 September 1887
Buckinghamshire Examiner – 29 January 1897
The Bundaberg Mail – 7 January 1911
Cairns Post – 6 January 1939
The Canberra Times – 27 April 1931, 27 October 1931, 11 March 1967, 24 August 1977
The Central Queensland Herald – 19 May 1955
Central Somerset Gazette – 3 May 1884, 2 July 1904, 30 September 1910
Chicago Herald – 29 July 1915
The Citizen – 6 September 1912
The Civil & Military Gazette – 20 January 1927, 19 March 1951
The Coalville Times – 1 December 1911
The Colac Herald – 2 December 1912
Connecticut Western News – 24 August 1911
Coolgardie Pioneer (WA) – 24 November 1900
Cordova Daily Times – 10 January 1923
Coventry Evening Telegraph – 30 December 1959
Crewe Guardian – 25 May 1910
The Crittenden Record-Press – 6 June 1912
Crossville Chronicle – 6 June 1917
The Daily Alaska Empire – 18 August 1927
Daily Capital Journal – 23 September 1909
Daily Chronicle (London) – 20 September 1929
Daily Examiner – 15 July 1925
Daily Express – 20 May 1924
Daily Gazette – 15 April 1887
Daily Herald – 27 April 1921
Daily Independent (Nevada) – 19 November 1891
The Daily Independent – 6 November 1937
Daily Kennebec Journal – 12 July 1920
The Daily Mail – 19 April 1922
Daily Mercury – 2 September 1927, 12 September 1930, 27 November 1930
Daily Mirror – 15 June 1921, 19 December 1928, 6 March 1934, 31 October 1941,
    27 March 1950, 11 July 1950, 14 May 1951, 21 September 1951, 30 November 1954
Daily Mirror (Sydney) – 28 August 1948
Daily News – 26 December 1929
Daily News (London) – 2 May 1936
Daily News (Perth) – 30 May 1929
The Daily Record – 15 July 1896, 1 February 1955

The Daily Sentinel – 4 November 1904
Daily Standard – 19 October 1935
The Daily Star-Mirror (Idaho) – 1 February 1912
Daily Telegraph – 25 June 1872, 4 November 1880, 16 February 1927, 27 May 1933
Daily Telegraph (Tasmania) – 31 December 1907
The Daily Tribune – 17 June 1904
The Dalkeith Advertiser – 19 December 1935
Darling Downs Gazette – 5 April 1929
The Dawson News – 8 February 1911, 4 August 1925
Derby Daily Telegraph – 4 October 1929
The Derry Journal – 28 January 1969
Detroit Evening Times – 12 July 1942, 5 October 1942, 4 April 1943, 13 August 1944, 4 January 1945, 26 August 1945
Dublin Evening Mail – 2 April 1947, 17 May 1949
Dundee Courier – 18 September 1909
Dundee Courier & Argus – 29 June 1886
Dundee Evening Post – 4 November 1901
Dundee Evening Telegraph – 26 September 1936, 9 May 1939
Eastbourne Gazette – 25 February 1863
East Oregonian – 20 February 1914
Eastern Post – 12 September 1931
Edinburgh Evening News – 19 August 1876, 18 March 1880, 12 February 1932
Emmons County Record – 19 May 1886
The Emporia Weekly News – 10 September 1885
The Evening Advocate – 6 November 1947, 1 September 1954
The Evening News – 8 October 1935, 7 January 1961
Evening News (Sydney) – 4 March 1886
Evening Post – 3 October 1984
Evening Star – 18 September 1922
Evening Star (Washington DC) – 5 March 1922, 1 May 1923, 17 November 1927, 7 November 1930, 22 December 1930, 28 February 1932, 11 November 1932, 7 March 1934, 3 August 1934, 6 February 1942, 19 September 1942, 21 June 1950, 9 May 1953, 19 November 1958
The Evening Statesman – 2 November 1905
Evening Telegraph – 17 April 1882, 12 January 1910, 13 September 1926
The Evening Times (Grand Forks) – 14 February 1911
Evening Tribune – 27 July 1889, 21 December 1889, 23 July 1897
The Evening World – 23 June 1893, 14 August 1894, 19 July 1919
Examiner (Tasmania) – 18 February 1908
The Examiner – 16 July 1927, 1 November 1928
The Exmouth Journal – 24 September 1910
The Express & Telegraph – 27 July 1907, 7 June 1913
The Fargo Forum – 4 November 1909

The Fife Free Press – 28 July 1928
The Florence Daily Tribune – 27 February 1902
The Forest Republican – 2 August 1905
The Forfar Herald – 30 May 1902
Framlingham Weekly News – 6 April 1929
Geelong Advertiser – 17 April 1879
The Gentleman's Magazine – 1788
Gilpin Observer – 1 August 1912
Glasgow Evening Post – 5 December 1895
Glen Innes Examiner – 8 January 1935
Globe, London – 10 January 1900
Gloucester Journal – 22 July 1922, 4 July 1931
Goulburn Evening Penny Post – 21 February 1929, 5 February 1931
The Grenada Sentinel – 4 November 1882
The Guardian – 31 December 1909
Halifax Evening Courier – 5 December 1905
Hamilton Spectator – 21 March 1911
Harrisburg Telegraph – 25 January 1919
Hartlepool Northern Daily Mail – 14 October 1892
The Hattiesburg News – 6 November 1909
The Hawaiian Star – 13 May 1904
Helena Weekly Herald – 26 November 1874
The Herald (Los Angeles) – 1 December 1895
The Herald – 25 November 1910, 7 January 1924, 23 November 1953
The Hereford Times – 26 August 1882
Herne Bay Press – 4 February 1972
Herts Advertiser – 24 February 1900
The Hope Pioneer – 9 August 1917
The Hull Packet – 20 January 1871
The Indianapolis Times – 7 June 1935
Irish Independent – 18 February 1997
Innisfail News – 15 January 1935
The Inverell Times – 10 November 1916
The Irish Times – 1 May 1911
Iron County News – 31 January 1891
Kalgoorlie Miner – 2 January 1924, 6 June 1939, 15 December 1953
The Kenosha Telegraph – 15 July 1875
Kyabram Free Press – 24 November 1893
Lancashire Daily Post – 29 August 1930
Lancashire Evening Post – 27 July 1896
Larne Reporter – 6 July 1872
Leamington Spa Courier – 10 February 1967, 28 August 1987
The Leavenworth Echo – 22 December 1922

Leicester Evening Mail – 24 January 1917

Leicester Mercury – 27 August 1992

The Lexington Advertiser – 4 January 1906

Liverpool Echo – 29 November 1910, 11 November 1935, 30 December 1936

Livingstone Enterprise – 9 July 1892

Loftus Advertiser – 28 January 1893

London Daily Chronicle – 8 November 1926

The London Magazine – 18 December 1737

London Telegraph – 15 November 1892

The Lynn News – 4 January 1938

Macleay Argus – 22 May 1897

The Madison Daily Leader – 26 September 1912

The Mail – 12 January 1924

The Mail (Adelaide) – 3 May 1930

The Maitland Daily Mercury – 8 June 1910

Maitland Mercury – 8 February 1952

The Manitowoc Pilot – 16 April 1903

The Marietta Daily Leader – 14 January 1899

Marlborough Times – 15 August 1891

Matin, Paris – 23 July 1915

The Mercury – 13 April 1921, 18 May 1937

The Mercury (Hobart) – 2 August 1937, 13 July 1939

Miami Times – 22 September 1951

Midland Catholic News – 7 April 1928

Midland Counties Tribune – 8 December 1905

The Midland Journal – 12 July 1912

Milford Chronicle – 5 October 1951

The Million – 19 August 1893, 10 February 1894

The Miners Daily News – 29 May 1897

Morgan County Democrat – 13 October 1905

Morning Bulletin – 27 March 1928, 18 February 1939, 17 August 1945

The Morning Call – 22 July 1894

Morning Journal – 16 September 1882

The Morning Leader (London) – 22 August 1906

The Morning Tulsa Daily World – 24 February 1922

Motherwell Times – 21 February 1936

Mudgee Guardian – 30 January 1913

The Nagambie Times – 22 May 1896

National Advocate – 28 December 1948, 6 November 1951

Newark Evening Star – 11 October 1912, 31 March 1913

New Britain Daily Herald – 20 November 1928, 21 January 1920

Newcastle Chronicle – 8 August 1885

Newcastle Daily Chronicle – 6 October 1928

The Newcastle Daily Journal – 21 March 1872
Newcastle Evening Chronicle – 13 August 1889
The Newcastle Sun (NSW) – 30 November 1946
New Haven Daily Morning Journal & Courier – 28 January 1888
The Newmarket Journal – 22 August 1925
News Chronicle – 1 March 1934
New York Daily Tribune – 1 August 1909
New York Herald – 14 May 1921, 5 November 1921
New York Tribune – 1 October 1905
The Nome Nugget – 16 July 1921, 1 February 1957
Norfolk News – 19 August 1905
The Norfolk Weekly News – 22 September 1911
The Norfolk Virginian – 23 October 1895
The Northern Champion – 22 July 1925
Northern Daily Mail – 31 March 1941, 28 November 1956
Northern Daily Telegraph – 26 December 1911
Northern Star – 28 August 1922, 14 April 1924
Northern Weekly Gazette – 2 January 1915, 20 February 1926
The North Western Advocate – 3 July 1908
The Northern Whig – 30 July 1931
The Nottingham Daily Express – 8 December 1903
Nottingham Evening Post – 7 December 1900
Nottingham Journal – 1 October 1909, 8 January 1933, 23 March 1937, 5 May 1937
Oakleigh Leader – 11 February 1893
The Odd Fellow – 19 January 1839
Omaha Daily Bee – 6 November 1884, 12 October 1902
The Omaha Morning Bee – 29 July 1923
Ottawa Fair Dealer – 4 December 1922
The Pacific Commercial Advertiser – 9 August 1904
Pall Mall Gazette – 28 July 1893
Passaic City Record – 23 June 1900
The People – 30 December 1917, 16 November 1947, 8 May 1960
Philadelphia Record – 19 July 1901
The Pioneer Express – 18 November 1904
Picturegoer – 5 December 1936
Portsmouth Evening News – 13 April 1883, 22 April 1938
Preston Herald – 28 June 1905
Queanbeyan Age (NSW) – 2 October 1936
Queensland Times – 15 August 1950
Reading Weekend Post – 10 May 1996
The Register – 14 December 1909
The Register (Adelaide) – 28 May 1918
The Reporter – 13 April 1907

The Republican – 20 March 1906
Republican News – 30 August 1912
Reveille – 1 November 1953
Reynolds Newspaper – 8 August 1909, 13 July 1913
Richmond Dispatch – 25 May 1902
The Richmond River Express – 27 July 1928
The Salt Lake Herald – 8 January 1890
San Antonio Daily Light – 12 September 1884, 25 April 1896, 28 July 1894
San Antonio Light – 17 March 1923, 2 August 1925
The San Francisco Call – 30 September 1911, 1 April 1912, 5 September 1913
The Savannah Morning News – 20 November 1884, 3 March 1901
The Scotsman – 9 December 1961, 30 December 1970, 13 April 1977, 8 September 1990
The Sheffield Daily Independent – 24 January 1925, 27 July 1931
The Sheffield Daily Telegraph – 16 May 1892
Sheffield Evening Telegraph – 5 April 1901
Sheffield Independent – 19 January 1931
Shipping Gazette – 15 June 1912
The Sidmouth Observer – 10 April 1889
Singleton Argus (NSW) – 24 June 1913
Singleton Argus – 11 July 1949
The Smyrna Times – 24 November 1909
The Socialist Press – 20 March 1915
The Somerset Guardian – 31 December 1909, 27 February 1920, 17 October 1930
Southern Times – 6 June 1896
South Wales Echo – 17 October 1885
The Standard – 29 January 1914
The Statesman (Denver, Colorado) – 21 April 1905
St. Croix Avis – 20 March 1912
St. James Gazette – 10 July 1884, 22 August 1895
St. Johnsbury Caledonian – 27 May 1886
The St. Mary Banner – 18 November 1911
The Sun – 24 December 1939
The Sun (Sydney, NSW) – 4 February 1925, 22 June 1933
The Sun News (Melbourne) – 3 July 1953
The Sunday Herald – 21 January 1951
Sunday Mirror – 25 December 1921, 25 February 1940
Sunday People – 2 March 1975
Sunday Times (Sydney) – 24 September 1911
Sunday Times (Perth) – 27 June 1937
The Sydney Morning Herald – 19 December 1946
Tamworth Herald – 28 June 1884
The Tarrangower Times – 7 August 1872
Tasmanian Weekly News – 20 March 1858

Taunton Courier – 7 July 1962

The Tavistock Gazette – 4 September 1885

The Telegraph (Brisbane) – 25 September 1924, 27 October 1925

The Telegraph – 25 June 1927, 12 May 1933, 8 May 1936

The Tewkesbury Register – 28 April 1906

Time – 12 May 2014

The Topeka State Journal – 25 January 1907

Toronto Globe – 27 August 1869

The Torquay Times – 21 June 1927

Totnes Weekly Times – 30 April 1898

Townsville Daily Bulletin – 18 May 1953

The Tribune – 1 March 1890

The Tribune (Sydney) – 27 April 1977

The True Democrat – 20 February 1897

Truth (Salt Lake City) – 28 July 1906

Tweed Daily – 23 January 1939

Ulster Echo – 26 January 1883

Ulverston Mirror – 27 January 1883

The Virginia Enterprise – 29 May 1903

The Vote – 21 August 1925

Wagga Wagga Advertiser – 17 September 1910

Wagga Wagga Express – 3 November 1906

Warwick Daily News – 6 December 1938, 12 September 1945

Warwick Examiner – 22 September 1894

The Washburn Times – 19 September 1907

The Washington Times – 3 December 1930, 8 March 1935, 3 September 1937

Waterbury Evening Democrat – 16 December 1932

The Watertown News – 20 September 1918

Watertown Republican – 13 August 1879

Weekly Dispatch (London) – 10 November 1957

Weekly Telegraph – 19 November 1932

Weekly Times – 25 July 1936

Wells Journal – 30 May 1907

The West Australian – 28 September 1935

Western Morning News – 27 March 1922, 22 January 1926, 6 November 1937

Western Star – 6 February 1926, 15 September 1926

The Western Times – 14 August 1903, 27 May 1927

The West Somerset Free Press – 21 February 1880

The Willimantic Journal – 18 May 1888

Windham County Reformer – 18 December 1903

Wolverhampton Express & Star – 7 December 1970, 30 July 1976

Woodford Times – 10 July 1880

The World (Hobart) – 25 May 1923

The World's News (Sydney) – 31 May 1924
The World's News – 21 May 1927
Worthing Herald – 24 June 1994
The Yackandandah Times – 29 June 1900
The Yarragon News – 31 May 1917
Yorkshire Evening Post – 6 December 1923
The Yorkshire Factory Times – 6 August 1914
The Yorkshire Observer – 17 December 1937
The Yorkshire Post – 28 December 1922, 6 March 1925, 10 March 1928, 4 September
    1928
Young Witness (NSW) – 26 June 1917
The Ypsilanti Daily Press – 23 November 1945
Zeehan & Dundas Herald – 7 June 1920